THE COLD CASE FILES
ON THE TRAIL OF IRELAND'S UNDETECTED KILLERS

The Author
Barry Cummins is a journalist with RTÉ and the author of four previous bestsellers:

- *Missing*
- *Lifers*
- *Unsolved*
- *Without Trace*

For updates on the work of Barry Cummins please visit
www.facebook.com/barrycummins

THE COLD CASE FILES

ON THE TRAIL OF IRELAND'S UNDETECTED KILLERS

BARRY CUMMINS

Gill & Macmillan

Gill & Macmillan
Hume Avenue, Park West, Dublin 12
with associated companies throughout the world
www.gillmacmillan.ie

© Barry Cummins 2012
978 07171 4802 8

Typography design by Make Communication
Print origination by Síofra Murphy
Printed in the UK by CPI Cox & Wyman, Reading

This book is typeset in Minion 11/14 pt.

The paper used in this book comes from the wood pulp of
managed forests. For every tree felled, at least one tree is
planted, thereby renewing natural resources.

A CIP catalogue record for this book is available from the
British Library.

5 4 3 2 1

For every murder victim still awaiting justice

For further information visit www.barrycummins.com
You may reach me in confidence at unsolved@barrycummins.com

If you have any information about any of the cases featured in this book, or indeed any unsolved cases, you can contact:

Garda Serious Crime Review Team	(01) 6663444
Garda Confidential Line	1800 666 111
Police Service of Northern Ireland	0845 600 8000
Crimestoppers (Republic of Ireland)	1800 25 00 25
Crimestoppers (Northern Ireland)	0800 555 111

CONTENTS

FOREWORD

By retired Garda Commissioner Noel Conroy

A Sunday night in October 1981, and an impromptu engagement party is being held in Dublin. As family and friends celebrate with the happy couple, two armed and masked raiders suddenly burst in, shooting the newly engaged man dead. In a matter of seconds a robbery had gone wrong, and an innocent life was taken. I was the Detective Inspector in the District. The phone in my home rang at 11.50 p.m. that night and I remember going out immediately to The Anglers Rest pub in Knockmaroon, the home of the murdered man, Lorcan O'Byrne. Along with a team of detectives, I met with Lorcan's shock-stricken and devastated family and friends. The scene was preserved immediately. Amid their grief, Lorcan's loved ones found the strength to answer all our questions, giving important witness statements. Two men wearing balaclavas, one of whom was armed with a shotgun, had burst in the door of the O'Byrne home, which was above their family-run pub. The raiders were looking for the pub takings, but just moments after entering the O'Byrne home the two-man gang had fled empty-handed, having fired one shotgun blast, fatally wounding Lorcan. The gunman had entered a room where close to twenty people were celebrating the engagement of Lorcan and his fiancée Olive. Witnesses described the gunman and his accomplice, and also their distinctive getaway car. In the following hours and days back at Cabra Garda station myself and fellow officers held many case conferences. Descriptions of the suspects were circulated and the suspect transport described—a green Hillman Hunter.

Information gleaned from enquiries suggested the suspects were originally from Dublin West.

Within the next few days the sawn-off shotgun used in the murder was recovered. It had been hidden in undergrowth approximately five miles from the scene of the crime. The burnt-out shell of the Hillman Hunter was recovered on the banks of the canal near Monasterevin and the engine found in the canal. One of the culprits was soon charged, and later served a sentence for Lorcan's killing. However, the man who actually fired the shotgun was not brought to justice, despite our very best efforts. Thirty years later he is the reason that this particular cold case has now been re-opened.

Barry Cummins has researched this case and many other cases of homicide and abduction spanning the past five decades, which he recounts in great detail in this superb book. He brings to the fore the suffering and pain of those left behind, the pain of parents, of siblings, of partners, children and friends of the victims. He highlights that cold-case reviews can bear fruit, particularly where readers of this book may have fragments of information and might now be willing to divulge this information to the right people.

He begins the book with the case of Brian McGrath, aged 43, who disappeared from his home in Westmeath in 1987. After six and a half years a body was found in the garden of his home. Because of the limits of forensics at the time, the body was not identifiable then as that of Brian McGrath, but subsequently in 2008 this body was exhumed and a DNA profile of the body identified it to be that of the missing man. Charges of murder followed and justice was finally brought to bear. Through his description of this harrowing case, Barry Cummins shows us that cold cases re-visited can, and do, bring closure.

Similarly, we remember the case of Kildare woman Phyllis Murphy, who disappeared in Newbridge in December

1979. Her body was found 23 days later in the Wicklow Mountains. Many suspects were interviewed then, including the person eventually charged in 1999 and who was finally convicted in 2002 of Phyllis's murder. Again Barry shows a cold case revisited with success due to DNA profiling, which was not available in 1979. I personally believe a DNA database for our country to support investigations of this kind would be of enormous benefit.

Barry Cummins includes in this book many unsolved murder cases in Northern Ireland. One chapter examines how a full DNA profile found at the scene of the murder of German student Inga-Maria Hauser is now available to police, which was not the case in 1988 when she was murdered. The PSNI is constantly encouraging anyone with any snippet of information regarding the case to phone, even with what may appear to the caller to be irrelevant information. A phone call could solve this case.

Barry sensitively shows us in this book some of the cases solved and the many others unsolved north and south of the border. One solved case is that of the murder of Lily Smith, strangled in her apartment in Belfast in 1988. It was 23 years later that the culprit was identified due to DNA from bloodstains which had been retained from the time of the murder. Barry outlines the value of re-opening murder cases because of modern forensic science developments.

Barry draws to our attention in this well-researched book the sadness encountered when children are murdered and when children are missing and not found or their bodies are not recovered.

He remembers the missing and murdered in all of Ireland, north and south of the border, during the years of the Troubles. He includes detail of the murders of Gardaí, RUC, Prison and Army personnel in the book.

Barry Cummins undertook an onerous task when he began the immense research which has resulted in this work. The aim of the book is to highlight the plight of many suffering people and also to highlight these heinous crimes. Among the cases which are profiled in detail, the victims include a man looking forward to being married, an elderly widow, a teenage backpacker, a mother of two, a father of four and a 12-year-old boy. Each unsolved murder has left a grieving family still seeking justice. Barry's work may prompt people who have knowledge that could solve or help to solve these cases to come forward or it may indeed prick the consciences of those responsible to come forward. Some of these criminals are older and possibly wiser now, and may be ridden with guilt. This book may stir them to at least help families and the authorities get answers. Barry outlines the several ways in which this can be done.

The recently revisited cold cases which Barry delves into disturb us. These cases whet our appetites for further information and he renews our interest in new developments. Barry shakes us. He stirs us. He believes that the dead, their living relatives, and the murderers, must not be forgotten. He ensures that these people and the cases connected with them will not be forgotten until their cases are solved. He shows us that nowadays, with new resources for investigation, there is hope that these cold cases will finally be put to rest.

My congratulations and best wishes to Barry Cummins for this important work.

Noel Conroy was a member of An Garda Síochána for 44 years, from 1963 until 2007. He was Garda Commissioner from 2003 until November 2007. One of his last acts as Commissioner was to oversee the establishment of the Garda Serious Crime Review Team, more commonly known as the Cold Case Unit.

ACKNOWLEDGMENTS

First and foremost I wish to thank the families of murder victims who spoke to me during my research for this book. In particular I say thank you to the families of Lorcan O'Byrne, Nancy Smyth, Inga-Maria Hauser, Brooke Pickard, Grace Livingstone and Stephen Hughes Connors. The grief these families experience is compounded by the fact that their loved ones' murders remain unsolved. These families gave generously of their time and often of their hospitality and I am grateful for their time and trust. Thank you to Niall and Gerard O'Byrne for speaking on behalf of the O'Byrne family about their memories of the night Lorcan was shot dead by armed robbers in 1981. One of the two-man armed gang was later caught and convicted but the man who pulled the trigger was never brought to justice. Thank you to Des Murphy in Kilkenny for speaking with me on his family's behalf about his aunt Nancy Smyth, who was murdered in Kilkenny in 1987. In Germany, I say a special thank you to Almut Hauser whose youngest daughter Inga-Maria was murdered in Northern Ireland in 1988. Thank you Almut for your hospitality and for sharing your memories of Inga-Maria. Thank you to Penny Pickard whose husband Brooke vanished in Co. Kerry in 1991. A group of men from Northern Ireland are suspected of abducting the father of four. Penny and her family continue to hope that answers will be forthcoming about the case. Thank you to Jimmy Livingstone for speaking with me on many occasions about his ongoing campaign for his wife's killer or killers to be brought to justice. Jimmy's wife Grace was murdered in her home in Malahide in 1992 and, as a result of

Jimmy's persistence, the Cold Case Unit are now investigating the case. Thank you to Stephen Hughes Connors's parents Liz and Billy for welcoming me into their home and sharing memories of their eldest child. The killing of Stephen in September 2001 is one of the few child killings in Ireland which remains unsolved. Thank you to each of you for your trust and I sincerely hope you get answers, and see your loved one's killer or killers caught and convicted.

During my research I received invaluable assistance from An Garda Síochána. Thank you especially to former Commissioner Noel Conroy for penning the Foreword for this book. Noel was Commissioner when the force established its Cold Case Unit in 2007. Thank you also to the members of the Serious Crime Review Team, otherwise known as the Cold Case Unit. In particular thank you to Detective Superintendent Christy Mangan for his interview about the ongoing and increasing work of the Unit. Thank you also to Detective Sergeant Noel Mooney for his briefing on the work of the Violent Crimes Linkage Analysis System (VICLAS), which is utilised by the Cold Case Unit. Thank you also to Detective Sergeant Alan Bailey for his pointers on the process of reviewing unsolved murders. Both Noel and Alan retired from the Cold Case Unit in 2011 after decades of service.

Thank you to Superintendent John Gilligan, Inspector John Ferris and all Gardaí at the Garda Press Office, and thank you to Director of Communications Sinéad McSweeney.

There are many Gardaí, both serving and retired, who provided crucial assistance with historical research. *Go raibh maith agaibh go léir.* Thank you especially to former Assistant Commissioner Tony Hickey and former Detective Superintendent Michael Byrne. Thanks again to Inspector Syl Hipwell and thank you to retired Garda Paul Downey.

I also received invaluable assistance from the Police Service of Northern Ireland in relation to my research into the murder of Inga-Maria Hauser in Co. Antrim in 1988. In particular thank you to Detective Superintendent Raymond Murray and Detective Inspector Tom McClure. Thank you also once again to Ken Devlin at the PSNI Press Office.

Thank you also to British cold-case expert, retired Detective Superintendent Mick Burdis, who works with Jimmy Livingstone to uncover the truth about the murder of Jimmy's wife Grace.

Thank you to Eamonn Balmer and to Mick and Breda O'Byrne for recounting their memories of the night Lorcan O'Byrne was murdered in his home above The Anglers Rest pub in 1981.

In Germany I thank Nele Obermueller who worked as my translator during my interview with Almut Hauser, Inga-Maria's mother. In Switzerland thank you also to Nele's fellow victim support worker, Susanne Nielen, who put me in touch with Nele.

In Westmeath I thank funeral director Michael Cassidy for his poignant memories both of the occasion in May 2008 when the body of murder victim Brian McGrath was exhumed as part of a cold-case review, and also the occasion when Brian's body was finally laid to rest for ever more in late 2010.

Thank you to Kilkenny Coroner Tim Kiely, Westmeath Coroner Dr Wilfred Hoover, Clare Coroner Isobel O'Dea, Offaly Coroner Brian Mahon, Kildare Coroner Dr Denis Cusack and also to Bríd McCormack in the Kildare Coroner's Office. Thank you to Dublin City Coroner Dr Brian Farrell and to Jerry Ryan and all the staff in the Dublin City Coroner's Office. Thank you to Dublin County Coroner Dr Kieran Geraghty and to Ciara Geraghty and Eileen Tobin in the Dublin County Coroner's Office. Thank you to Kildare County Registrar Eithne Coughlan.

Thank you to the staff of the Births, Deaths and Marriages Offices and also to the staff of the National Archives. Thank you to Amanda Dully of the Dublin Fire Service Communications Department.

Thank you to all at KCLR, especially Sue Nunn and John Purcell. Thank you to journalist Seán Keane of the *Kilkenny People* and to Padraig Hoare and Ann Murphy of the *Evening Echo*. Thank you to Alex Hatton of 4FM. Thank you to David Harvey and Genevieve Brennan of City Channel for arranging a copy of *Crimeline* programmes from years gone by. At Coco Television, thanks to Stuart Switzer, Linda Cullen and to Ceoladh Sheahan for arranging copies of *Crimecall* programmes from more recent years.

There are many others who by the nature of their assistance must remain anonymous. *Go raibh maith agaibh* one and all.

At Gill & Macmillan, I say thank you to Publishing Director Fergal Tobin, and also to Peter Thew, Deirdre Rennison Kunz, Teresa Daly, Ciara O'Connor, Jen Patton, Nicki Howard and Antoinette Doddy.

Thank you to all my colleagues in the RTÉ Newsroom, especially Crime Correspondent Paul Reynolds and Midlands Correspondent Ciarán Mullooly. Thank you also to Neil Burke, Ross Byrne, Billy Hanrahan and all in the RTÉ News Library and also to Carolyn Fisher and Anne Gill in the RTÉ News Press Office. And a very special thank you to both Ray Purser and Marguerite Sheridan for crucial technical support.

Thank you to my former colleagues in Today FM, and thank you as always to my former boss in Midlands Radio 3, Barry Flynn. Thank you to the staff of my two former schools— St Mark's Primary and St Mark's Secondary in Tallaght.

Thank you to my parents Patricia O'Neill and Barry Cummins for their constant support and interest. Thank you also to my brother Mark for his ongoing interest and encouragement.

Finally, thank you to my wife Grace, our daughter Ruby and son Conor for their constant and wonderful support, ideas, motivation, guidance and encouragement, and without whom I could not have written this book.

PROLOGUE

The exhumation began at first light. Members of the Garda Cold Case Unit and local detectives from Westmeath stood silently as Brian McGrath's body was removed from Whitehall Cemetery. It was just after 6 a.m. on Monday 19 May 2008. A small digger began the task of removing topsoil from the plot, which was sited close to a wall. When the digger finished its work, Gardaí completed the task of removing the coffin from the ground. The exhumation was done in dignified silence; it was a momentous moment in terms of a fresh murder investigation, but it was also a time for reflection on what Brian McGrath had suffered all those years before. Those present knew that it couldn't yet be said beyond all mathematical certainty that the body was indeed the father of four last seen alive 21 years ago. That was the whole point of the exhumation—to establish once and for all the identity of the man whose bones had been found hidden beneath the soil near Brian McGrath's home at Coole in 1993. People might have long believed the body was Brian's, but now as part of a cold-case investigation it had to be proven beyond all doubt that the body was Brian's. The evidence had to stand up in court.

By the time they came to stand at the graveside in Whitehall that morning, cold-case detectives had worked for months re-investigating the suspected murder of 42-year-old Brian McGrath. They had built up a picture of how it was believed Brian had been beaten to death, secretly buried, dug up and burned, and then secretly buried again. It was a most distressing crime, but one which seemed very solvable to the newly established Garda Serious Crime Review Team, or Cold Case Unit as it would become known.

When Gardaí had initially found Brian's remains near his home in 1993 the body had been secretly resting there since 1987. Forensic science in the early 1990s was nowhere near as advanced as it is today, and the bones recovered in 1993 could not be identified as Brian's to a mathematical certainty. Gardaí in 1993 had a great deal of information to go on, in what was a major murder enquiry. They only found the body because they were specifically looking for Brian and believed he had been murdered and buried on his land. They had arrested the two suspects, but in the absence of an absolute identification of the human remains, the DPP would not permit charges to be brought. The suspects were released and the body was later buried in 1993 without being formally identified. It was a most complicated, bizarre and violent murder which seemed destined to remain unsolved. Over time the case began to gather dust. And then in late 2007 the Garda Cold Case Unit was formed.

It was a retired detective who alerted cold-case detectives to the unsolved murder of Brian McGrath. John Maunsell had been a detective in the Dublin suburb of Tallaght, and in 1993 had received crucial information about the murder in Westmeath. Maunsell had been involved in a separate successful investigation into the murder of a woman in Dublin, and it was through publicity surrounding his role in that case which led someone to contact him about the murder of Brian McGrath. John Maunsell agreed to meet the person in a pub in Dublin, and they outlined how Brian McGrath had been missing from Westmeath since 1987, and that Brian's daughter Veronica was very distressed and wanted to tell what she knew.

Veronica met with John Maunsell and his colleague Kevin Tunney and outlined how she had seen her then fiancé

Colin Pinder and her own mother beat her father to death. She had seen her mother Vera goad her future son-in-law into attacking Brian without warning sometime in March or April 1987. Veronica had seen her father being beaten with various implements and had seen him being struck by both Colin Pinder and Vera McGrath. Veronica had witnessed the subsequent secret burial of her father in the back garden, she had also seen the body being subsequently placed on a large fire after it had been dug up, and she knew her father's body had been reburied on land just beside the family home. Detectives Maunsell and Tunney spoke with Gardaí in Westmeath, who carried out a search of the McGrath land and they soon found a body where Veronica said it would be. Colin Pinder had by now returned to his native Liverpool while Veronica's mother Vera still lived at the family home in Westmeath. Both were interviewed by detectives and a file was sent to the DPP, but word eventually came back that it was impossible to positively identify the body and in those circumstances the DPP was unwilling to press charges.

John Maunsell never forgot the case. While the murder hadn't happened in his district, he was the Garda who had first received the crucial information, he was the person Veronica McGrath had trusted enough to come forward and make a statement to. Maunsell had been greatly frustrated when no charges had later been brought, and he often thought about Veronica and her late father, who had been denied justice. When he heard about the formation of the Garda Cold Case Unit he quickly picked up the phone and rang one of his former colleagues, Maurice Downey, who was one of the members of the newly formed cold case squad. Maunsell and Downey had known each other from their days in the Central Detective Unit, and Downey listened carefully as Maunsell outlined the history of the unsolved murder which was on his mind.

John Maunsell was convinced that with the right amount of time and resources this was a case which could still be cracked. Soon after speaking with the retired detective, Maurice Downey went and got the full murder file from the Garda archives in Santry. He studied it thoroughly and spoke with his colleagues, including the head of the Cold Case Unit, Detective Superintendent Christy Mangan. They all agreed with John Maunsell's belief that this was a case that was indeed 'solvable'. There were prime suspects, there was a crucial witness, a body had been recovered, and advances in forensics might now prove the unlocking of the mystery. The unsolved murder of Brian McGrath became one of the top priorities for the Cold Case Unit. First and foremost they would have to see that the body in Whitehall Cemetery was formally identified.

As plans were made for the exhumation, members of the Cold Case Unit met with Brian McGrath's three sons, Brian Jnr, Andrew and Edward. In January 2008 the three men permitted Gardaí to take swabs known as buccal swabs from the inside of their mouths. Those swabs gave full DNA profiles of all three men and would allow for a direct comparison with the body at Whitehall Cemetery. It was only the DNA of Brian Snr's children which would be able to be compared to the as yet unidentified body. Brian had been brought up in State care after being abandoned as a newborn baby in Monaghan in 1944. He never knew his birth parents or whether he had any brothers or sisters.

Now Brian's own three sons were to provide the DNA which would help to identify their father. The three men had been young children when their father had mysteriously vanished in 1987. In early 2008 they were told that their father's disappearance and suspected murder was being looked at anew and a major re-investigation was underway.

Detectives knew that once the exhumation began on 19 May the media would soon find out and the whole country would know about the cold-case review. Sometimes Gardaí choose to publicise cases they are re-investigating and other times they like to work away quietly. In Brian McGrath's case, Gardaí were working behind the scenes on the case for a number of months before it hit the headlines on 19 May.

On 8 May 2008 Inspector Brendan Burke and Sergeant Michael Buckley of the Cold Case Unit met Forensic Anthropologist Laureen Buckley and State Pathologist Marie Cassidy to discuss the plans for the exhumation at the cemetery in Westmeath, and also for a major fresh search of the McGrath family home at Coole nearby. Arrangements were made for a company called Earthsound Associates to carry out a geophysical survey of the field beside the McGrath home to detect any evidence of soil disturbance. The following day Detective Inspector Martin Cadden from Athlone requested an order for the exhumation of the bones of a man from Whitehall Cemetery which had been discovered at Coole in 1993. The request was granted and preparations were made for the operation to begin at first light on Monday 19 May. Within two hours of the exhumation taking place, news of the operation broke on the 8 a.m. RTÉ radio news. Gardaí issued a lengthy press release confirming that detectives were indeed re-investigating the disappearance of Brian McGrath, who was last seen alive in early 1987.

Dr Stephen Clifford of the Forensic Science Laboratory and Dr Marie Cassidy provided crucial work in what would be the first major success for the Garda Cold Case Unit. It was Dr Clifford who positively identified the exhumed bones as being those of Brian McGrath. In order to make a positive match he had first ground down some bone material from the remains to allow DNA to be extracted and captured with a special DNA kit. He had then compared the profile he generated with the samples from the three sons of Brian McGrath. His result was as clear as could be—the probability of the bones being those of Brian McGrath was greater than 99.5%. It was a phenomenal success—DNA technology had advanced to such a degree that bones which had been burned and buried in a field for six years before being buried in a coffin for fifteen years had still been successfully analysed to give a clear match. Forensic science was unveiling the truth about this cold case. Brian McGrath's wife had consistently claimed he had gone off and abandoned the family and was living in another country. And all that time he was actually lying buried in the field beside his home.

Dr Marie Cassidy studied Brian McGrath's lower jaw, or mandible. Despite the extensive degradation which Brian's body had suffered at the hands of his killers, the lower jaw was still almost complete. Dr Cassidy found evidence of a fracture between two right teeth, which separated the bone into two parts. The right half of the jaw bone was unburned and it was clear to the State Pathologist that the fracture to the jaw had happened before the body had been put on a fire by the killers. Marie Cassidy said such significant blunt force to the jaw was consistent with a blow from a blunt object. Such violent trauma could cause death from blood inhalation as a result of a mouth injury, or bleeding into the skull cavity, or a brain injury. Ultimately it would prove impossible to establish what exact form of death Brian McGrath had suffered, but the exhumation allowed not only for his identity to be established, but also for the post-mortem examination to be carried out, which found clear evidence of violence. It all tied in with the account given by his daughter Veronica, who said she had seen her father being beaten to death in a sustained attack. This was no longer an investigation into the discovery of an unidentified male body. This was now very much an investigation into the murder of Brian McGrath.

As they had stood at Whitehall Cemetery, and watched Brian McGrath's coffin being taken from the ground, detectives knew they had the elements to potentially solve this cold case. They had the forensic and pathology experts who in time would give evidence of identity and cause of death. But they also had that most important element—a witness to the murder, a witness who was prepared to stand up in court and give evidence. Veronica McGrath had first come forward in 1993, seven years after she had witnessed her father's murder. It would take another sixteen years before she saw her mother jailed for life for murder, and her own former husband jailed for nine years for manslaughter. But Veronica was a determined woman, determined to get justice for her father, determined to see his killers brought to justice.

The other important factor in the Brian McGrath case was that the suspects were still alive. Cold-case detectives knew well that sometimes time catches up with a suspect before Gardaí had a chance to knock on their door. While the Brian McGrath case was the first successful prosecution for the Cold Case Unit, another case might have got in ahead of it if circumstances had been different.

Soon after being set up in late 2007 the Unit began working on the unsolved murder of a woman who was strangled to death with a man's necktie in the 1980s. The woman's body lay undiscovered in her home for over two and a half months. A man quickly emerged as the prime suspect—he had fled the country and gone to the United States. It was believed he had later gone to Mexico, Portugal and then to England but had never returned to Ireland. On 7 November 2007 the Cold Case Unit under Detective Superintendent Christy Mangan was commissioned by an Assistant Commissioner to review this case and they began an international search for the man. Detective Garda David O'Brien was appointed the Family Liaison Officer, and Detective Garda Padraig Hanly was appointed Exhibits Officer for the fresh review of this unsolved murder. Within a short time the Cold Case Unit had found their man; they learned he had been living in England under his real name for many years. Now that they had an address for the man they began making plans to travel and speak with him, and they liaised with the local English constabulary. However, the initial excitement at finding the suspect's address was short-lived when it was confirmed by English authorities that the man had actually died of natural causes on 16 September 2007, shortly before the Cold Case Unit was set up.

By July 2010, when a jury found Vera McGrath guilty of murder and Colin Pinder guilty of manslaughter, there was much public interest in the work of the Garda Cold Case Unit. The murder trial had put the spotlight on the work of a dozen detectives based at Harcourt Square. While their work involved close co-operation with regional detectives, it was the cold-case team which was catching the public's imagination, the idea that a group of Gardaí spent their entire working day trying to solve murders going back as far as the 1980s. The Unit welcomed some publicity, seeing the media as a means to publicise their work, and to make appeals for people with information about unsolved murders to come forward and ease their consciences. The cold-case investigation into the murder of Brian McGrath put the Cold Case Unit firmly on the map. It led to the successful prosecution of two killers and it brought some solace to Brian's grieving daughter and his three sons. There was huge potential for solving historic murders if the right elements were in place.

When the Cold Case Unit was launched in October 2007, many observers remembered the successful cold-case investigation in the late 1990s which had led to the capture of

John Crerar, who had abducted and murdered a young woman, Phyllis Murphy, in Co. Kildare in December 1979. Phyllis vanished in Droichead Nua as she walked towards a bus-stop; her body was later found hidden in the Wicklow Gap. For 23 years John Crerar had evaded justice, and it was only when Detective Inspector Brendan McArdle of the Garda Technical Bureau organised for blood samples that had been taken back at the time of the murder to be re-analysed that a full DNA profile of Crerar was matched to the semen found on Phyllis's body. Two Gardaí, Christy Sheridan and Finbarr McPaul, had safely maintained the blood samples in their lockers from 1979 until Detective McArdle began his work in 1998. When a jury later found John Crerar guilty of murder in November 2002, this successfully solved 'cold case' became a perfect example of how advances in forensic science could unmask the identity of a killer many decades after the crime. It had also shown that when confronted by Gardaí in 1999, the man who had given Crerar a false alibi twenty years previously had immediately told the truth. The man had never suspected he had given a false alibi for a murderer, he had merely thought he had been covering for a work colleague by telling a 'white lie' to say the man had arrived at work on time on an evening in 1979. The detail of the Phyllis Murphy case was clear evidence that people carry secrets, and sometimes don't even realise the significance of those secrets. By the time the Garda Cold Case Unit was established five years after John Crerar was convicted, detectives had long known that when the dynamics were right, historic murders were very solvable.

As they prepared to begin examining over 200 unsolved murders which had occurred since 1980, the Garda Serious Crime Review Team met with cold-case detectives from other jurisdictions. They studied the workings of American police forces, and cold-case police officers from Scotland, England

and Wales, among others. They also began to liaise closely with the Police Service of Northern Ireland. Authorities in the North had been to the fore in proactively re-investigating unsolved murders from the 1960s, 70s, 80s and 90s. Central to the work of rebuilding Northern Ireland in more peaceful times has been the Historical Inquiries Team, which is tasked with investigating 3,269 deaths attributable to 'the Troubles' between 1968 and 1998. A number of retired police officers from other jurisdictions are involved in this work too. The PSNI is also actively re-investigating cold-case murders which are not linked to the Troubles. In more peaceful times and with cross-community confidence in the police service, detectives have made significant breakthroughs in a number of unsolved murders in Northern Ireland, and hope to have more successes. One of the most troubling unsolved murders was that of 18-year-old German backpacker Inga-Maria Hauser, who was murdered in Co. Antrim shortly after she got off a ferry from Scotland in 1988. The case had stalled and eventually hit a brick wall, and then in 2005 a full DNA profile from the crime scene was established and the search is now very much on for that man.

In the Republic, among the many cases the Garda Cold Case Unit would eventually take on were the murder of 56-year-old Grace Livingstone, who was shot dead in her home in Malahide in north Co. Dublin in 1992; the sinister disappearance of Englishman Brooke Pickard in Co. Kerry in 1991; the murder of Nancy Smyth, whose killer tried to hide his crime by setting a fire in Nancy's home in Kilkenny in 1987; and the shooting dead of Lorcan O'Byrne, who was celebrating his engagement when armed robbers burst into his family home in Dublin in 1981.

The Garda Cold Case Unit established a liaison with Dr Martina McBride at the State's Forensic Science Laboratory in the Phoenix Park. Much of the work of the Unit would be the tracing of original crime scene materials for forensic re-examination. They also arranged to avail of various profilers and crime scene interpreters who might study original crime photographs or visit a crime scene and give insights into what might have been going through a killer's mind. Poring over the original case files would be crucial to establishing which witnesses might still be alive and available. A number of families of murder victims were by now actively seeking out the Cold Case Unit. Some people were calling directly to their offices at Harcourt Square in Dublin. Gardaí knew they had to manage the expectations of people; there were certainly some cases which they might be able to progress, but there would be many that despite their best efforts would probably remain unsolved.

When it was launched in October 2007, the Cold Case Unit said it was initially going to examine 207 unsolved murders which had occurred since 1980. The year 1980 was chosen simply because they had to start somewhere. The Brian McGrath case was the first success for the Cold Case Unit, so it might have been thought this would reduce the number of unsolved murders to 206. But such figures are only ever a guide to a situation which is impossible to accurately quantify. For example, what about the cases of missing people where it was quite possible the person had been murdered and their body hidden? What about murders which had never been recognised as such—unexplained deaths where no crime was ever detected but where one couldn't be ruled out? What about more recent murders which have occurred since 2007 and which have not been solved, and which in time will come under the remit of the Cold Case Unit? The only certainty is that there are hundreds of unsolved murders, hundreds of families seeking justice, hundreds of killers who have quite literally got away with murder. Every killer has a family, has friends, has a social network, perhaps has work colleagues. The more you look at the scale of Irish cold cases, the more you realise there are potentially thousands of people on this island who have direct information or strong suspicions about the identity of killers who have evaded justice for far too long.

01 | THE UNSOLVED MURDER OF LORCAN O'BYRNE

Lorcan O'Byrne and his fiancée were celebrating their engagement with Lorcan's family and friends when he was fatally shot by an armed raider who burst into the O'Byrne family home at around 11.30 p.m. on Sunday 11 October 1981. The O'Byrne home was directly above the pub they ran—The Anglers Rest—at Knockmaroon, close to Dublin's Phoenix Park. The two raiders who forced their way into the building were after the pub takings. It's quite likely they didn't expect to find over twenty people in the O'Byrne home when they broke in. As well as Lorcan and his fiancée Olive, Lorcan's parents and two brothers and two sisters were there, and some friends and fellow workers. Lorcan was 25 years old and was a bar manager at the family pub. His parents were planning to retire and let their eldest child take over the business. Lorcan and Olive had been going out for around three years and had only that evening announced that they were getting married. Everyone was absolutely thrilled. Olive was from the country and had been living and working in Dublin for a few years. She was already part of the family. When the couple announced their engagement that Sunday evening, an impromptu party was organised for later that night. Lorcan's mother made sandwiches and once they got the pub closed early, the family and a number of friends all adjourned upstairs to the sitting room at the back of the building. Lorcan and Olive were sitting on a couch and people were sitting and standing around the room. Lorcan's brother Ger was down at the stereo on the ground and was acting as the DJ. Everyone was chatting and toasting the bride and groom to be. Lorcan's parents Bernie and Lar were there, and his sister Anne and his youngest sister Dorothy, who was just 15 years old. There was a wonderful happy and excited atmosphere in the packed room. The chat was all about Lorcan and Olive getting married. And then, from nowhere, a masked man suddenly burst through the sitting room door brandishing a shotgun.

Meeting Lorcan's brothers Ger and Niall three decades on, it is the first time they have spoken with a journalist, and the loss of their brother is clear. What is particularly upsetting about Lorcan's brutal killing is that his fiancée Olive and his parents and two sisters all saw it happen. Niall O'Byrne didn't see his brother being fatally wounded because he himself was being attacked elsewhere in the house by the second raider, who had forced his way in the front door. But Ger was in the sitting room. He saw it all. "I was down on my hands and knees at the stereo changing an album," he recalls vividly.

> Lorcan was sitting on the right-hand side as you come in the door, and Olive was sitting beside him. There were between fifteen and twenty people in the room. There was music on, not too loud. It happened so fast. My back was to the door and I heard shouting and roaring and I looked up and I saw someone with a balaclava on and holding a shotgun and roaring at us. I couldn't make out what they were saying.

Lorcan stood up to see what was going on. He had his back to the door and as he turned around the shotgun went off and there was a big flash and a cloud of smoke everywhere and Lorcan fell to the ground. Then I could see blood everywhere.

The attack seemed so surreal, so unreal, that for a split-second some people thought it was some type of prank. But once they saw Lorcan on the ground the horror hit home. Just moments earlier everyone had been celebrating, chatting, laughing. Now Lorcan was lying on the ground having taken the full blast of the shotgun in the chest. Olive was by his side. Everyone started screaming. Ger and one or two others were the first to react and they grappled with the barrel of the gun as the masked man started to back out of the room.

We were trying to get the shotgun from him. He was very fit and very strong. I clearly remember he was pulling backwards trying to get out of the room. Once the shot went off he was trying to get out of the room as quickly as possible. We were pulling the barrel of the shotgun and we didn't know if he had a second cartridge in it. Someone tried to catch him in the door but he got out the door, but the shotgun was caught in the jamb of the door. I still remember pulling the barrel as the gun went up and down in the jamb of the doorframe. And then he was gone. And Lorcan was lying there.

What is particularly galling for the O'Byrne family is that, although the gunman's accomplice was later caught and jailed for six years, the man who fired the shotgun, the man who took one life and tore so many other lives apart, is still free. While the accomplice confessed to his part in the attempted robbery and killing, the man who brought a loaded shotgun to the scene, and who fired it directly at Lorcan, never owned up. The fact that one other person had been brought to justice meant very little to the O'Byrne family. That person wasn't the person who fired point-blank at Lorcan, he wasn't the person who took away the life of a son, brother, and fiancé. When the Garda Cold Case Unit was set up in late 2007, the O'Byrne family contacted the Garda Commissioner and asked that Lorcan's case be re-investigated. The family believed there was enough evidence to warrant a full review of the case. The Cold Case Unit examines historic murder files, looking for angles that might benefit from a fresh analysis. This includes considering advances in forensic science which can link a killer to a crime scene, and revisiting witnesses who may be able to shed new light. There might also be witnesses who hadn't come forward before. The murder of Lorcan O'Byrne seemed like a case of an attempted robbery which had spiralled rapidly into murder. Detectives believed it was very likely the killing had been spoken about at length in the criminal world. The more it was spoken about, the more new witnesses might come forward. And there was already a lot to go on. Cold-case detectives read in the file that the murder weapon had been located, the getaway car had been found, and one of the two members of the gang had been successfully prosecuted back in the early 80s. Gardaí took time to study the file in detail and then came back to the O'Byrnes saying yes, they would indeed carry out a full cold-case review to try and catch the man who shot Lorcan O'Byrne.

The other member of the two-man gang which broke into The Anglers Rest that night in October 1981 was John Meredith, a 32-year-old criminal from Ballyfermot who at the time was living at Sillogue Road in Ballymun. Meredith's role that night was very violent, but he didn't carry the loaded shotgun; instead he used his hands to drag Niall O'Byrne by the hair through a number of rooms apparently in a search for the pub's cash box. Meanwhile Meredith's accomplice, who had entered the front door first, had gone on ahead to the sitting room where he shot Lorcan. The two raiders fled the scene empty-handed but the massive Garda investigation which followed saw John Meredith being identified as a suspect within days. Less than two weeks after the murder of Lorcan O'Byrne, Meredith was charged with the crime. In February 1982, just four months after the killing, Meredith pleaded guilty to manslaughter and this plea was accepted by the State. He was jailed for six years, and in later life he wrote to the O'Byrne family seeking forgiveness for his part in the killing. The O'Byrne family did not respond to his letters; they wanted nothing to do with him. In late 2007 John Meredith took his own life.

From the admissions of John Meredith about his own part in the raid, and the recovery of the murder weapon and the getaway vehicle, Gardaí had a good deal of information from very early on in the case. It would seem that while the attempted robbery had been ill-thought-out on the night in question, some degree of planning had gone into targeting the pub's takings. Meredith and his accomplice had been watching the O'Byrnes. It's most likely both men had been in the pub in previous weeks under the guise of being customers, but were secretly watching the movement of cash, and watching the movement of Bernie and Lar O'Byrne and the bar staff. Certainly Meredith would later tell Gardaí that he had watched Bernie O'Byrne bring cash to a bank in Ballyfermot and he knew that she drove a Renault. He and his accomplice had discussed trying to snatch the cash another time that Bernie might be walking from the pub to her car to make the journey to the bank.

Monday was normally the day that Bernie and Lar would go to the bank with the pub takings. They usually went to the

Bank of Ireland on Camden Street, but would also sometimes go to the Ulster Bank in Walkinstown, and to a bank in Ballyfermot. Meredith and his partner may have originally intended to hold up the O'Byrnes on the Monday as they went to the bank, but for some reason decided to break into the O'Byrne home instead the night before. When later arrested, Meredith claimed that he and the gunman had hatched a plot about two weeks before the attack to rob the takings of The Anglers Rest. For some reason they decided to strike that Sunday night, but they apparently failed to carry out any surveillance of the pub and living quarters that evening, because until they had actually broken in, they seemed oblivious to the fact that there were around twenty people still inside. And this is despite the fact that there would have been some cars parked outside the premises.

The two gangsters drove to The Anglers Rest in Meredith's own green Hillman Hunter car. He had bought the car for £400 from someone on Dublin's southside. Using his own car as the getaway vehicle was not a smart move. When Meredith and his accomplice fled the scene in the Hillman Hunter they drove to Finglas, en route to abandoning the car at Dublin Airport. As they drove in a panic along River Road near Finglas, a Garda attending the scene of a traffic accident saw the car and saw Meredith driving it, and the Garda could clearly see another man in the passenger seat. The officer got a good look at both men. Meredith drove on past the accident scene, but for some reason the Garda fortuitously made a mental note of the car. The shotgun used to murder Lorcan O'Byrne would later be found hidden in a field just a few hundred yards from where the Garda spotted Meredith's car in Finglas.

Before that terrible night, life at The Anglers Rest had been idyllic for the O'Byrne family. They had been living at and running the premises for over twenty years. Lorcan had been a toddler when the family had bought the pub and moved in. His Dad Lar was in the pub business all his life. Originally from Aughrim in Co. Wicklow, Lar had come to work in Dublin in the 1930s and had worked in many pubs in the city centre.

Lorcan's mother Bernie was from Dublin's Liberties. Bernie and Lar had a dream of owning and running their own pub, and in late 1959, early 1960, they set their sights on The Anglers Rest. The couple by now had two children—Lorcan and Anne—and were living near the Navan Road in north Dublin. The Anglers Rest was up for sale and soon after the O'Byrnes viewed it, they bought it. Ger, Niall and Dorothy were all born in the early to mid-1960s, as the family began a long process of turning the pub into a major attraction. "The first couple of years were very tough," Niall tells me.

Both Mam and Dad were working long hours in the pub, doing it up, and it needed a lot of work. It had a little small bar when they bought it. Upstairs there were about 14 rooms, it was a big rambling house, because it had been a hotel in its early days. Underneath the living area there was a lot of storage space and sheds. Dad gutted all that and ended up with a lounge that held between 250 to 300 people. In the 1960s and into the 70s music was becoming a major part of the pub scene with cabarets and singalongs. Mam and Dad built up a reputation that 'The Anglers' had a bar and a big lounge with music and a singalong.

The premises itself was close to 200 years old and had once been a coach stop and hotel. In decades gone by, people heading between Dublin and the West by horse would stop at 'The Anglers' for a break. The pub was in a quiet location close to the top of Knockmaroon Hill, near the western wall of the Phoenix Park. The pub was just a few miles north of

Ballyfermot, Palmerston and Chapelizod. The O'Byrne family turned 'The Anglers' into a major success. Its exterior was characterised by whitewashed walls and neat window boxes. With just a few cottages along the quiet road which overlooked greenery many hundred feet below, 'The Anglers' was a little piece of the countryside on the outskirts of Dublin city. "People came from Ballyfermot and beyond, Finglas and Cabra, to drink at 'The Anglers', it was a little oasis for them," explains Ger O'Byrne. "It was set out on its own, and 'The Anglers' became a place where whole families came, your Granny came with you and the kids came with you. You knew everybody and they all had their favourite seats."

For the O'Byrne children, there was no better place to grow up. "The whole area at the time, the best way to describe it is like the Dublin version of Walton's Mountain," says Niall. "It was like you went back in time, it was the place that time forgot. From aged four or five we were all running around the bar. We grew up with most of the people in the pub, they knew us. From about the age of ten we were sorting bottles in the morning and hoovering the lounge at weekends."

When I interviewed Niall and Ger thirty years after their brother's murder, we visited The Anglers Rest together. They showed me the door through which the two attackers had burst into what was then their home. The O'Byrne family left in 1984, just three years after Lorcan's murder. They simply couldn't stay where their son, their brother, had been shot down in such a random and callous manner before their very eyes. Newspapers at the time of the murder referred to the crime as having taken place in the pub itself. While the two raiders were indeed after the pub takings, they never entered the pub premises; they violated the O'Byrne home upstairs. Eventually the family couldn't bear to stay. The Anglers Rest was sold and the family left the pub trade altogether.

John Meredith and his armed colleague wore balaclavas as they approached The Anglers Rest. It was around 11.30 p.m. on Sunday 11 October 1981. They had spent the earlier part of the evening at a pub on Dublin's southside. They had been in the company of a couple and another man, but sometime around 10.30 p.m. Meredith and his fellow criminal left the other three and drove from the Dublin 4 area to Finglas, where they got a shotgun which was hidden in a hedge on River Road. They then drove to The Anglers Rest by going around the Phoenix Park via the North Circular Road, Conyngham Road and Chapelizod and then driving up Knockmaroon Hill.

They parked Meredith's car close to the pub and walked up the concrete steps at the side of the premises to enter the upstairs living quarters. The criminals had prepared balaclavas by tearing off the arms of a jumper which they took from the backseat, and they used a pen knife to make slits for their eyes. Meredith later told detectives that soon after parking the car outside The Anglers Rest, a yard light had come on which lit up the car park and two people walked by and he had quickly pulled off the balaclava. By the time he was putting it back on and getting out of the car his accomplice was already out of the car and, armed with the shotgun, heading for the concrete stairs at the side of the premises.

They walked quickly across the veranda to the front door at the side of the building. The two-man gang knew they were entering a home, they knew the pub was the downstairs part of the building, and the upstairs was a private dwelling. Perhaps they had been watching the patrons leaving the pub. Maybe they had seen the front door of the pub itself being shut. Perhaps they thought they would just find the O'Byrne family still inside the building upstairs. As the two attackers approached the front door of the O'Byrne family home, Meredith's accomplice was in front, carrying a loaded double-barrel shotgun.

Even today, Niall O'Byrne's recollection of that night is chilling. He relives it often. Niall was on the inside of that front door when Meredith and the gunman burst in. He was only 17 when his brother was murdered.

Lorcan had taken that night off, and we didn't know what he was at, but he had obviously planned on going to ask Olive's parents for permission to marry her. He came back into the pub that night with Olive and we all heard the news. Lorcan rang some of his friends and Mam and Dad and everyone was so excited. It was the first time I was allowed have a drink. Lorcan gave me a pint of Heineken which I couldn't even drink. We couldn't wait to close the bar and have a party.

During the evening Lorcan, Olive, Ger and some friends headed out to another pub for a few hours. They wanted to come back to 'The Anglers' when it was quiet to have a bigger party. When they later got back home to 'The Anglers' Lorcan's mother had made sandwiches and they all headed upstairs to the sitting room for a party. Some friends were there, and some of the bar staff who were good friends went up too. It was going to be a long night's celebrating.

As it approached 11.30 p.m. Niall was standing at the front door with two of his friends, Eamonn and Roger. They were all just 17 years old. Eamonn and Roger were in the same school as Niall and they did some part-time work in the pub. The three teenagers were some distance away from the party itself. The sitting room was at the back of the house. The three friends were sitting on a large table and chatting away. By 11.30 p.m. it was time for Roger to head home. He said goodbye to his friends and Niall went to open the big hall door to let his friend out. He heard footsteps on the outside, they seemed to be coming closer and were very quick. And then the whole front door came in on top of Niall and his friends.

At the back of the house, in the sitting room, no-one heard the sound of the raiders breaking through the front door. No-one in the sitting room heard the raiders attacking the three boys at the front door. Roger jumped across a table, Eamonn turned and ran back into the house. Niall had been closest to the door and so was closest to the raiders as they entered. The gunman hit Niall in the face with the shotgun and then moved quickly on into the premises. The other raider, who Niall now knows was John Meredith, then subjected Niall to a ferocious attack. "I remember seeing the balaclavas and being pushed backwards," he tells me.

I remember seeing the shotgun and being hit on the face with the butt of the shotgun. I was being forced backwards all the time. The armed raider passed me. I had long hair at the time and Meredith grabbed me by the hair and dragged me along the ground, and my head was killing me. I was dragged backwards, I was out of it. I was dragged in through the kitchen, I remember being on the floor of the kitchen and being kicked. I remember hearing a lot of shouting. I was between the kitchen and the sitting room door, against a wall. I was trying to point out the money box, I was trying to say 'there's the money box, take the money box.' I was pointing at it. It was a big metal box with cash in it. I remember getting up and seeing them run out the door.

The raiders never picked up the cash box; they fled empty-handed. When Niall saw the raiders flee the house, he still didn't know that one of them had just shot Lorcan at point-blank range. He had heard a bang but didn't know his brother was fatally injured. Niall had run after the raiders, making it to the front door where he saw the raiders drive off. Over thirty years later he has a clear memory of those moments. The two raiders got into Meredith's car and couldn't get it started at first. Niall had an interest in cars, and would later be able to give a very good description to Gardaí. Meredith and the gunman fled in a green Hillman Hunter, a special edition Sunbeam model, it had double headlights with a vinyl roof. It was olive green, and had alloy wheels.

Niall went back into the house and it was then that he discovered his brother had been shot. "A friend of Lorcan's who was in the sitting room was a nurse and she was trying to help Lorcan. We were all put out of the room. Then I saw him being carried out. That's when I lost the plot." Garda records show that the alarm was raised by a 999 call made from The Anglers Rest at 11.36 p.m. that Sunday night. The raiders had entered the building around six minutes earlier. They had been inside the premises just two or three minutes.

Lorcan O'Byrne took the full blast of the shotgun in the left side of his chest. The State Pathologist Dr John Harbison would later determine that Lorcan had been standing about two yards from the weapon when it was fired. Dr Harbison concluded that the shot was fired either from straight in front of Lorcan or very slightly from his left.

Lorcan lived for just over two hours after he was shot. He was rushed to St Laurence's Hospital in north Dublin, where the Dublin Metropolitan Court is now located at North Brunswick Street. Doctors did all they could, but Lorcan's wound was too severe. His heart couldn't take it and he passed away from shock and blood-loss at around 2 a.m. At 3.10 a.m. Lorcan's brother Ger was brought into the mortuary and in the presence of Sergeant Sean Ferriter and Garda Joseph McKeown, Ger formally identified the body of his 25-year-old brother.

When Meredith and his accomplice drove away from the scene they drove up the hill towards the junction of Knockmaroon Hill and Tower Road. Meredith later told Gardaí that they then drove the same route back to Finglas as they had earlier taken—driving into Chapelizod and then along Conyngham Road, Infirmary Road, North Circular Road and into Cabra before arriving eventually at River Road in Finglas. Even today, part of River Road is an isolated unmarked country road. It seemed like a perfect place to hide a weapon. Meredith and the gunman put the shotgun into a plastic bag and hid it in a dense hedge. It was subsequently found by Detective Garda John Lyons during a planned search following Meredith's arrest. Gardaí later did a test drive from The Anglers Rest to River Road, nine and half miles away. It took them twelve and a half minutes.

John Meredith would later tell Gardaí that, having hidden the weapon near Finglas, he dropped his accomplice off at a location and then drove his Hillman Hunter on to Summerhill where he threw the two balaclavas out the window. He went home to Ballymun but couldn't sleep. He heard on the 6.30 a.m. radio news about Lorcan's death. His met his accomplice an hour or two later and they drove in convoy to Dublin Airport where Meredith effectively abandoned his car. The gunman then dropped Meredith at a pub in Ballyfermot. But as he continued drinking during the day Meredith became worried that the Airport Police might come across the Hillman Hunter. The next morning, he and his accomplice went and retrieved the car from the airport. They bought petrol, which they placed in a container, and they drove to an isolated field near Monasterevin in Co. Kildare. Having removed the engine of the car in an effort to hide the identity of the vehicle they then set the car alight. The men then dumped the engine in the Grand Canal.

In the early hours of the morning of Sunday 12 October word came back to The Anglers Rest from St Laurence's Hospital that Lorcan had not survived. As Gardaí began the crucial work of sealing off the premises and taking witness statements, Lorcan's family were absolutely distraught. The memories of that night have not dimmed with the passage of time. The Gardaí who were there didn't know what to say to the family. As one officer broke the news to the O'Byrnes, a number of Gardaí stood with the family and said a decade of the rosary. And then they began the methodical and necessary process of taking witness statements.

Detective Garda John Fitzpatrick of the Garda Technical Bureau studied the sitting room door where the gunman had burst in. The marks were clearly visible where the gunman had used the weapon to force open the door. When the shotgun was later recovered from near River Road in Finglas, the detective found paint from the O'Byrnes' door on the barrel of the shotgun. The weapon itself was an over and under shotgun—one barrel directly under the other. When officers examined the weapon they found that a degree of force was necessary to fire it.

Within days of Lorcan's murder, officers began building up a profile of the two-man gang. Intelligence led them to John Meredith, a criminal from Ballyfermot with twelve previous convictions. His first conviction was in 1973 when he was caught for housebreaking. He also had convictions for obstructing Gardaí and for road traffic offences. He was married with a young child, and had previously worked as a labourer and a busker. Gardaí were on the lookout for John Meredith. They knew he was originally from Ballyfermot and they carried out enquiries in this area and in other parts of Dublin. Just before 3 p.m. on Thursday 22 October, Detectives Jerry Nolan and Brian Sherry stopped a brown Rover car at Ballyfermot Road. Meredith was driving the car and he was immediately arrested. The front seat passenger, a 32-year-old man, was also arrested. He was questioned by detectives investigating Lorcan's murder and was later released.

When he was taken into custody John Meredith soon made a lengthy statement outlining his involvement in the attempted raid on The Anglers Rest. He told detectives that he and his accomplice hoped to get about £10,000 from the raid. "On the night of October 11 we decided to rob the pub," he told Gardaí. "We went to a field in Cabra where we had a gun hidden and tore up a jumper which was in the car to make hoods." On Friday 23 October 1981, less than two weeks after the killing, John Meredith was charged at Kilmainham District Court with the murder of Lorcan O'Byrne. As part of a two-man gang to break into the premises, Meredith was part of a 'common design', and although he did not carry the shotgun or fire the weapon, it was argued that he was partly responsible for the consequences. On 2 February 1982 Meredith pleaded guilty to manslaughter, and this was accepted by the State. Meredith could have got a maximum sentence of life imprisonment, or a minimum of a suspended sentence. He got six years.

There was no such thing as counselling when Lorcan O'Byrne was murdered. There was no recognition of the trauma and stress that the O'Byrnes and Lorcan's fiancée must have endured. One moment, a vibrant happy man with so much expectation was celebrating his engagement to the love of his life. The next moment he was gone. And the man who shot Lorcan dead was still walking the streets.

"Only for Mam we all would have gone off the rails," remembers Niall. "Dad never spoke about what happened to Lorcan." Ger O'Byrne agrees, adding, "Dad took it really bad, he wouldn't talk. Lorcan and Dad had been planning a major renovation of the pub, and in 1981 Dad would have been thinking Lorcan might take over the pub. We stayed on in the pub until 1984 but the heart had gone out of it and we really didn't want to be there anymore."

Bernie and Lar O'Byrne had also owned a site close to 'The Anglers'. It was a beautiful spot up on the hill behind the pub. Before Lorcan was murdered, his parents had a plan that they would build a house on the site and retire, letting Lorcan take over the pub. After Lorcan was shot dead, his parents never built the house and the planning permission lapsed. Both Ger and Niall said they did not want to be involved in the pub anymore, so the family sold up and moved out.

Niall and Ger show me some wonderful photos of Lorcan. With his red hair, moustache and ever-present smile he is very distinctive. In one image, he is pictured with his mother behind the bar in 'The Anglers'. Lorcan and his two sisters and two brothers were very close. Anne was 23 when her brother was murdered, Ger was 19, Niall was 17, and Dorothy was 15. The family's memories of their big brother are a mixture of sadness and anger at the circumstances of his violent death, and happy treasured memories. "Lorcan had a Renault 12," recalls Ger. "He called it 'the Lady' and I stuck a CB radio in it and we would keep in touch that way when he would be driving." "He was a qualified pilot as well," says Niall. "I was up with him once or twice. He was close to getting a commercial licence."

In the first few nights after Lorcan was murdered, Niall O'Byrne was brought out by two Gardaí to try and spot the car used by the raiders. The officers trawled around different areas of Dublin with Niall in the back seat of the patrol car but they didn't spot the Hillman Hunter. However, soon it was found burnt out in a field in Monasterevin.

Lar O'Byrne died in 1990, aged 74. He had spent his whole working life in the pub trade and had a huge circle of friends who were barmen or publicans. He and his wife also knew many Gardaí. From the early 60s right through to the early 80s, generations of young Gardaí assigned to Dublin stations had socialised at The Anglers Rest.

Sometime after Lorcan's murder Lar O'Byrne got a gild painter to make a gold sign which read 'Lorcan's Lounge' and he placed it on the wall of the pub. But Lar never spoke to his family or to anyone else about what they all had witnessed that awful night. He simply couldn't. When the family left 'The Anglers' in 1984 Lar would still go back to the new owner and make suggestions about what they should do to keep customers or attract new ones. Lar and Bernie had built up a vibrant music scene at the pub, both Irish traditional music and cabaret. By October 1981 business was thriving. And then their eldest son was murdered in front of their eyes.

In 2009, Bernie O'Byrne passed away, aged 85. By the time of her death she knew that the Garda Cold Case Unit was re-investigating her son's murder. She took comfort from that fact. Niall tells me that his Mam welcomed the new publicity being given to the case. "Mam's whole attitude was that at the end of the day, if the armed raider was sitting in a pub somewhere watching the news and had beads of sweat running down his face looking up at a picture of Lorcan, that would be something. At the very least to feel uncomfortable and for him to be looking over his shoulder for the rest of his life, for the Gardaí to come knocking. She'd be happy with that. There would be some satisfaction to see him worry for the rest of his life. If he went to jail it would be like winning the lottery."

When I visited The Anglers Rest with Niall and Ger thirty years after their brother's murder, we went upstairs. Where once there were 14 rooms in what was the O'Byrne family home, now there is one large function room which runs the length of the building. 'The Anglers' is no longer a home as well as a pub, it is now purely a licensed premises. The current owners have done a good job on transforming the upstairs to cater for large gatherings, and they have recognised that good food as well as drink is a key to success. Thirty years ago, the O'Byrnes had spotted the trend of the time that good music as well as drink was the order of the day—different times and different business plans to ensure 'The Anglers' keeps on top of the game. Niall and Ger point to one particular corner and then another. The sitting room where Lorcan was fatally shot is gone, as is the hallway where Niall was standing with his two friends when the two attackers burst in that Sunday night in October 1981. What was once the front door to the O'Byrne home is now a fire escape.

Some years ago John Meredith was interviewed on radio. He was talking about a group he had helped to set up in Ballyfermot for ex-prisoners. It was mentioned during the interview that Meredith had served a sentence for 'a shooting in the Strawberry Beds'. It wasn't specified that Meredith was one of the two-man gang which had caused the death of a young man celebrating his engagement.

As well as Lorcan's family witnessing the murder, friends and work colleagues were also in the room when the gunman entered. Each of those people would keep harrowing memories of that night with them. Mick Byrne was a barman at 'The Anglers' and he and his wife Breda were among those helping Lorcan and Olive celebrate their engagement that night. "I remember Lorcan standing up and the next thing he took the full blast of the shotgun," says Mick. "When the gun was fired it blew Lorcan backwards. My brother Paddy was also in the room and he was hit on the face with the gun during the attack. I remember people grappling with the gunman trying to get the gun and then he was gone." Breda tells me how she was eight months pregnant at the time. "I remember people trying to calm me down, I was in shock, we were all in shock. Lorcan was a very nice young man. Myself and Mick were very fond of him, of all the O'Byrnes." The month after Lorcan was shot dead, Breda gave birth to a baby boy. Herself and Mick decided to call the baby Lorcan.

Niall O'Byrne's friend Eamonn Balmer was one of the first to see the gunman that night. He was standing in the hallway near the front door along with Niall and another friend Roger. Eamonn was only 17 years old at the time, and thirty years on his memory of that night is vivid.

Niall and I had done our Leaving Cert that year. We had got to know each other at school at Moyle Park in Clondalkin and I did a bit of work in 'The Anglers' too. That night we were just inside the front door as we were waiting for my parents to call and collect me. I remember the door was open and suddenly a masked man appeared in the doorway. I remember the mask more than the weapon but I knew he had a weapon of some sort. He was a big guy, stocky build. He said nothing, there was absolute silence, but the sense of terror was immediate. We all turned in different directions. I ran to raise the alarm. I remember being pushed to the ground in the sitting room. I think I was pushed by the raider. I heard the shot. As I got up, I saw Lorcan on the ground and could see the seriousness of his injury.

The lead detective involved in the original investigation into Lorcan's murder was Detective Inspector Noel Conroy, who later became Garda Commissioner. He retired from the force in November 2007, shortly after he oversaw the establishment of the Garda Cold Case Unit, which is now re-investigating Lorcan's murder. "A substantial team of investigators worked on the original case", Noel tells me. "We received good descriptions of the culprits and their mode of transport. Information gleaned from Lorcan's family under the most trying and harrowing of circumstances was of great benefit in establishing the make, model and description of the getaway car which in turn led us to suspects. I am conscious one person was convicted before the courts but the other person to commit this crime was not prosecuted. It would bring a lot of peace to the family of Lorcan O'Byrne if the person responsible for this shooting was finally brought to justice."

Throughout the 1980s and into the 90s the murder of Lorcan was rarely spoken about in the O'Byrne home. They spoke about Lorcan and their happy memories of him, but they couldn't speak about the night he was murdered. Each member of the family had memories of that night, memories that never faded. As Lorcan's brothers and sisters grew older they began to ask questions about the failure to bring the killer to justice. They found it galling that such a person could still be walking the streets, having never owned up to what they had done. And what other harm might that kind of person have caused to others down the years? The kind of person who carries a loaded shotgun and is prepared to fire it indiscriminately, what else had they done since they killed Lorcan O'Byrne in 1981? The O'Byrne family began asking the Garda Commissioner to help them. The family heard about the setting up of the Garda Cold Case Unit. "I contacted senior Gardaí and asked if Lorcan's case could be included, could be reviewed," Niall O'Byrne tells me. "I met with Christy Mangan from the Cold Case Unit and after I went through the whole case with him he agreed to take a look at it. Two weeks later Christy told me there was enough to fully re-open the case."

Before the Cold Case Unit ever got to visit John Meredith he took his own life. It was a pure coincidence that within weeks of the Unit being set up in late 2007 John Meredith shot himself. He was 55 years old and was terminally ill at the time. In previous years he had tried to contact Lorcan O'Byrne's family, he wrote to them seeking forgiveness. A Garda told him to stop trying to make contact, the O'Byrnes wanted nothing to do with him.

John Meredith may have been genuinely remorseful for what happened to Lorcan O'Byrne. On the surface, it would appear that his later work in developing a group for ex-prisoners in Dublin was evidence of a changed character. The real test perhaps would have been if the Cold Case Unit had ever got the chance to speak with him. Meredith had the full story of what had happened on the night of Sunday 11 October 1981. The fact that he wasn't armed himself and simply used his hands and feet to terrorise and assault Lorcan's brother Niall might indicate that he was the lesser of the two criminals. The gunman may have been the leader, the thinker, the boss. Meredith may have been in fear of the other man after Lorcan was killed. While Meredith readily confessed his own role when he was arrested within two weeks of the crime, you have to wonder if he was alive today what his stance would be about the gunman, the cold-blooded killer who got away with it.

Despite John Meredith's death, the Cold Case Unit have a wealth of material to re-examine as part of their review of Lorcan's murder. Gardaí have also built up a significant amount of information from people in the criminal world. With the passage of time, allegiances change, people fall out, people talk.

The murder of Lorcan O'Byrne is one of the oldest cases that the Serious Crime Review Team are re-investigating. Because you have to start somewhere, the Cold Case team took 1980 as a start date to review every unsolved homicide. The detectives also look at cases from the 1970s if they are asked, but most of their earliest cases are from the start of the 80s. While Lorcan's case is one of the oldest, there is another case that precedes it which is also being actively pursued at present.

Four months before Lorcan was shot dead at The Anglers Rest, a 54-year-old mother of three, Nora Sheehan, was abducted and murdered in Co. Cork. Nora was last seen outside the South Infirmary Hospital in Cork city on Monday 6 June 1981. Her body was found on 12 June by two forestry workers at Shippool Wood at Innishannon, 17 miles from Cork city. Nora had been suffocated during the course of a sustained assault and the killer was never brought to justice.

Similar to the murder of Lorcan O'Byrne cold-case detectives believe there is potential for achieving a breakthrough in the case of Nora Sheehan. A number of items recovered by Gardaí during their initial enquiries in Cork in June 1981 are being re-examined at the Forensic Science Laboratory. It's hoped that microscopic material which the killer may have left at the scene of the crime or elsewhere might now be positively identified.

And north of the border, a recent cold-case investigation by the PSNI has led to the solving of another murder case which is now more than thirty years old. Jennifer Cardy was nine years old when she was abducted and murdered while cycling near her home in the village of Ballinderry, Co. Antrim, on 11 August 1981. Her bike was found hidden behind a hedge but Jennifer had vanished. Six days later her body was found ten miles away in McKee's Dam at Hillsborough, Co. Down. This shocking murder was actively re-investigated by the PSNI's Serious Crime Branch in recent years, and a man in his sixties was arrested and questioned about the crime in 2005. In October 2011, this man—Robert Black—was convicted of Jennifer's murder. The court heard he was already serving three life sentences for murdering three girls in Britain in the 1980s.

When I obtained a copy of Lorcan's inquest file from the National Archives, I found official documentation which rightly records the cause of Lorcan's death and his address and age and occupation. But the documentation only allows for a Coroner's Certificate to specify if a deceased person was married, widowed or single. Never has official documentation been so inadequate to properly reflect a tragedy. There is no section to acknowledge that Lorcan was engaged, that he wanted to be married, that he was in love with his fiancée Olive, that only that night he was celebrating his engagement, that they had their whole lives ahead of them. The documentation in Lorcan's inquest file merely records that he was 'single'.

The Cold Case Unit are actively working to bring Lorcan's killer to justice. Based on descriptions given by witnesses, Garda intelligence in the case, and looking at the circumstances of his accomplice John Meredith, it is quite likely that the killer who escaped justice is now in his sixties and from Dublin. As we chat about their memories of Lorcan, both Niall and Ger O'Byrne tell me of how their brother's murder has affected how they have reacted to other violent incidents. On one occasion an armed man hijacked Ger's car, but not before Ger started screaming at him. While other people might be frozen with fear, Ger found he was consumed with anger. Likewise, Niall once witnessed a high-speed car chase with Gardaí in pursuit of a group of people. The 'getaway car' came to a halt near Niall, and he offered his assistance to the Gardaí in keeping the suspects on the ground until Garda reinforcements arrived. It was an instinctive reaction by someone who has previously come face to face with the worst type of people in our society. I ask them their thoughts on John Meredith's apparent remorse for what happened to Lorcan. They don't know if it was genuine or not, but Ger sums it up well. "Meredith may have been remorseful," he says. "But the other man never had any remorse. He never said sorry. Committing a murder didn't faze this man, he has no value on life."

"This case is not solved at all," adds Niall. "Although Meredith was caught, the other guy, the one who shot Lorcan, is still walking around, and has been for the last thirty years."

02 | THE UNSOLVED MURDER OF NANCY SMYTH

After strangling 79-year-old Nancy Smyth to death, her killer set a fire in Nancy's bungalow in an attempt to make her death look like an accident. It was the early hours of Friday 11 September 1987 at Wolfe Tone Street in Kilkenny city. The killer had most likely entered Nancy's home through the front door. Nancy lived alone with just her small pet dog; Nancy's husband Dick had passed away the previous year. After getting into the house, the murderer had either punched or kicked Nancy in the head before strangling her to death in the living room of her home. The attacker then apparently set fire to the sofa which was beside Nancy's body. And then the killer fled the scene, while Nancy's small dog fretted over its owner's body. As thick smoke filled the living room and then other rooms in the house, Nancy's dog died beside her from smoke inhalation.

It is most likely that the killer was not a visitor to the city, but was actually a Kilkenny man. A credible theory is that after he murdered Nancy, the killer would have walked home to his own house in another part of Kilkenny, perhaps further out of the city. Based on all the witness statements which were taken in the original investigation, all the indications are that the murderer of Nancy Smyth knew her in some way, or had known her late husband. It would appear that a young man specifically targeted Nancy because he knew she lived alone, and he knew that, at 4'9" in height and aged 79, she would have been defenceless to an attack. After strangling Nancy and setting fire to her home it is likely the murderer slipped away to walk the streets of Kilkenny to his own home. Over the years he may have come to believe he got away with murder. However, approaching a quarter of a century after Nancy's murder, the Garda Cold Case Unit recently completed a full review of the case and made 200 recommendations, including that all significant witnesses be re-interviewed and all items found or seized during the original investigation be forensically tested once again.

As he walked away from Nancy's home shortly after setting the fire, the killer obviously hoped the bungalow would be engulfed in flames. Certainly the sofa where the fire had started was practically burnt out, but while this had caused thick plumes of smoke to spread throughout the bungalow, the fire was burning itself out in the living room by the time the emergency services were alerted. Although one bedroom window was slightly ajar when the fire service arrived, with heavy black smoke filtering out through it, it seemed that because the bedroom door was tightly shut, the fire in the living room had died out due to a lack of oxygen. So because Nancy's body did not suffer extensive fire damage, the State Pathologist was later able to determine that not only was she dead before the fire was started, but that she had been strangled.

Nancy Smyth was seen arguing with a man at the front of her home just a few hours before she was murdered. A young witness was walking home after a night out with his girlfriend when he saw an altercation between Nancy and a man. The witness who saw this argument was able to provide a significant amount of detail about what he had seen. The witness had earlier left his girlfriend's house in the north of the city at around 12.30 a.m. and arrived at Wolfe Tone Street sometime between 12.45 a.m. and 1 a.m. The witness was heading towards nearby John's Green to get a lift home. He had only begun walking down the top of Wolfe Tone Street when he looked across the road and saw a man knocking on the window of a bungalow. The bungalow was itself distinctive—it was set in off the road with a small garden to the front, whereas other more recently built houses on either side of the bungalow were fronted directly onto the footpath. But it was the commotion at the front of the bungalow that immediately caught the witness's attention.

A man was banging on Nancy Smyth's porch window which was to the left of the front door. The man was shouting something but the witness could not make out what it was. The witness slowed down as the man at the front of Nancy's house continued to bang and shout. Just then the man saw the witness and walked out of the front gate onto the footpath and called over to the witness, asking him if he had a light. The witness crossed the road and would later tell Gardaí that he had been expecting an explanation from the man as to why he was banging on the window of the bungalow. However, the man did not offer any explanation to the witness, who gave the man a light for his cigarette. The man said something to the witness to the effect that he would offer him a cigarette but didn't have a spare one, and the witness said it was okay, that he didn't want one. The witness then walked back across the street and continued walking down Wolfe Tone Street, but looked back towards the house. He didn't know who lived there. As he looked back he saw a woman inside the porch of the bungalow opening the front door.

The witness did not know Nancy Smyth, but from a distance back on the other side of the wide street he was able to tell it was an elderly lady. She began shouting at the man, who was standing on the footpath outside her house. Across the road the witness stopped to observe fully what was going on. He would later tell detectives that the woman was shouting angrily at the man on the path, who began shouting back at her. From the animated tones, the witness heard the woman make some reference to a sister of the man's. The man then said something to the effect that he was going, and the witness began to walk on himself on the other side of the road. When the witness looked back again a short time later the woman had gone back into her house, and the man had walked away to the end railings at the front of Nancy's bungalow. The witness presumed he was witnessing an argument between two people who knew each other and he continued on his journey. A short time later he was at the end of Wolfe Tone Street and onto John's Green and got a lift home from there. It was only when he heard the next day about the murder of a woman in her bungalow at Wolfe Tone Street that he realised the potential significance of what he had witnessed and he made a detailed statement to Detective Gardaí Jim Ryan and Michael Delaney.

The man who the witness saw arguing with Nancy Smyth continues to be of great significance to Garda enquiries. It is quite possible that Nancy knew the person she was arguing with, but perhaps not very well. Nancy was well known in the area, and her late husband Dick had many acquaintances through his interest in keeping pigeons. Ever since the Garda Cold Case Unit re-investigated this case in recent years a lot of its attention has been focused on the man who was seen both banging on Nancy's window and arguing with her at the front of her house just a few hours before her body was discovered inside.

Nancy's body was found shortly after 5.10 a.m. after a passing night security worker spotted smoke coming from Nancy's house and raised the alarm. Members of Kilkenny Fire Service all lived within a few hundred yards of the fire station at Gaol Road and, when they were awoken by their bleepers, they raced to the station. Their fire tender then travelled at speed through the quiet streets and crossed the River Nore to the eastern side of the city, pulling to a halt outside Nancy's home on Wolfe Tone Street. Fire officers Tony Lacey and Martin Cleere put on breathing apparatuses and went to the front door of the smoke-filled house. Together with Garda Pat Starr, who had already arrived at the scene, the firemen used a sledgehammer to break open the door.

Tony and Martin went into the house, and soon found themselves in a room where there was a sofa on fire. Small flames were coming out of the arm of the sofa but the fire itself was almost burnt out. However, the smoke throughout the house was intense, and visibility was practically nil. Conscious that there might be someone who had been overcome by fumes while sleeping, Tony Lacey felt his way to a bedroom at the end of the bungalow. Before he had entered the house he had noticed that the front window of this room was ajar. He did a full search of the bedroom but didn't find anyone in there. Meanwhile Martin Cleere had made his way to the other bedroom at the far side of the bungalow to check there, but there was no occupant of that bedroom either. Tony Lacey was now back in the room containing the burning couch. He moved the couch slightly and that's when he saw Nancy's body. She was lying on her back parallel with the couch and fireplace. The smoke was so thick in this room that Tony couldn't tell if he had discovered the body of a man or a woman. He could just tell it was an adult.

All these years later, Tony's memories of the early hours of that morning are vivid.

When I found Nancy's body I shouted to Martin and it was when we carried the body outside of the house that we saw it actually was Nancy. We knew that it was her home that we were going into that night. Her bungalow was quite unique on Wolfe Tone Street. I remember the intense smoke and the heat of the smoke when we went into Nancy's home. I got the impression that the fire had been burning for a couple of hours and had burned itself out due to lack of oxygen. I actually knew Nancy to see and her husband Dick also. They were two real characters in Kilkenny.

Whoever murdered Nancy Smyth hoped that her home would go up in flames and that all evidence of a murder having occurred would be lost. Nancy Smyth was a smoker, and perhaps the killer hoped that Gardaí would assume the fire had been the result of an accident involving a lit cigarette. If the fire had taken hold and Nancy's body had suffered extensive fire damage, the marks around her neck indicating strangulation would not have been visible. Similarly, the bruising to her head indicating punches or kicks would no longer have been visible either. But for some reason, the fire didn't accelerate as the killer had planned. The intense heat of the fire and smoke plumes didn't cause the windows of Nancy's home to explode, which in turn would have seen the flames grow rather than diminish. One strange thing about the fire was that a bedroom window in another part of the house was partly open, and in different circumstances this might have helped to accelerate the fire. But perhaps the door of this bedroom, which was closed when the fire service arrived, was particularly airtight and kept all outside air away from the fire in the sitting room. Whatever the explanation, the killer failed in his intention to destroy all evidence of the crime.

Even before the fire service arrived at Nancy's house that morning, Gardaí were at the scene. Once Nancy's body was removed to St Luke's Hospital, Gardaí remained at her house, which would eventually become a crime scene. In the immediate aftermath of Nancy's body being found, it was thought that perhaps her death was indeed an accident. Over the following hours, as neighbours stood around expressing their shock, Gardaí soon started hearing reports of the altercation between Nancy and a man at the front of her home just a few hours before she was murdered. Gardaí contacted State Pathologist John Harbison to ask him to conduct a post-mortem examination.

Members of the Garda Technical Bureau travelled from Dublin to assist in a forensic analysis of Nancy's house. Detective Sergeant Willie Hogan took photographs of the scene, Detective Garda Séamus Quinn looked for clues as to the source of the fire and Detective Garda Oliver Cloonan dusted Nancy's property for fingerprints. These officers also attended the post-mortem examination along with local Sergeant Michael Melia.

It was Nancy's nephew Des Murphy who had to identify her body and the memory is still with him. "It was the day after Nancy was murdered, the afternoon of Saturday 12 September, that I went to the morgue to identify her," he tells me.

I went in to the morgue with Sergeant Eddie Geraghty. Nancy was married to my Uncle Dick, who had died the year before. After Dick died, Nancy lived alone at Wolfe Tone Street. Nancy and Dick never had children, but they had extended

family such as myself and other nephews and nieces. They
lived in the house in which Dick and his brother John and
three sisters Alice, Mary and Chrissie—my mother—had
grown up. John later moved to England, and the three sisters
moved out and got married, so it eventually became Dick and
Nancy's home. I will never forget going in to identify Nancy's
body. The entire family hopes that even at this late stage
Nancy will get justice and her killer will be caught.

On the afternoon of Saturday 12 September 1987,
Dr John Harbison carried out a post-mortem examination on
Nancy's body. He saw that Nancy had suffered burn injuries all
along the left side of her body. Her left arm and leg were
scorched and blistered, and her back and the left side of her
head had also been damaged by the fire. However, Dr Harbison
soon established that the burn injuries to Nancy's body had
occurred when she was already dead.

When he studied the back of Nancy's neck Dr Harbison
found an intermittent thin pressure mark. It was a faint bruise
which extended for three inches. On the front of her neck he
found further evidence of bruising across Nancy's thyroid
cartilage, or Adam's apple. Dr Harbison also observed a bruise
to the side of Nancy's left eye and another bruise to the right
side of her head. As he continued the post-mortem,
Dr Harbison found several injuries to Nancy's thyroid cartilage.
The right lower horn of the cartilage was fractured. Upon
further examination the pathologist established that there was
no trace of soot in Nancy's larynx or trachea.

Dr Harbison completed his examination at 7.30 p.m. and
travelled to Kilkenny Garda station and took part in a
conference chaired by Chief Superintendent Tom Sloyan,
accompanied by Superintendent Vincent Duff. The State
Pathologist told the assembled Gardaí it was his view that

Nancy Smyth had died from asphyxia due to strangulation. The nature of the internal injuries to Nancy's neck, coupled with the visible bruising to the front and back of her neck, led Dr Harbison to the view that it was more likely Nancy had been manually strangled rather than with a ligature. Dr Harbison further stated that Nancy had also suffered two head injuries which were consistent with being punched or kicked. The death of Nancy Smyth was now officially a murder investigation.

Soon after Nancy's body had been removed from her home that Friday morning, her dog's body was also found in the sitting room. The body of the small dog was taken to a vet on the Hebron Road in Kilkenny, and when a post-mortem examination was carried out on the following day, it was established that the dog had died from smoke inhalation. It was a poignant scene to imagine. The faithful dog had stayed beside Nancy as she lay dead on the ground, and as smoke filled the bungalow from the burning sofa beside them, the dog had eventually died.

Just a few hours before Nancy was murdered she had gone out for a social drink. She went into a pub on the eastern side of Kilkenny city at around 9 p.m. and chatted away with staff at the pub and with other customers. The owner of the pub would later recall how Nancy had enjoyed a rum and blackcurrant, and a Paddy whiskey and white lemonade. Ever since her husband of 29 years had passed away in October of the previous year, Nancy was coming to terms with living alone, and she was making the effort to get out of her home and socialise, as she and Dick had done as a couple. Nancy was well known in the locality, she was a Kilkenny woman, though not from the city originally. The youngest of nine children, Nancy had grown up in Castlecomer and her parents had both died when she was very young. Nancy had later moved to Bray in Co. Wicklow and Shankill in south Dublin to get work. She also spent time in England before returning to Co. Kilkenny and settling down for good. She married local man Dick Smyth two days after Christmas Day of 1957. Although they had no children, the couple had many relatives and Dick's interest in pigeons also opened up a wider social circle in Kilkenny. The couple's home at Wolfe Tone Street was one of the oldest buildings on the long road which linked the area around the local swimming pool and park with John's Green and the nearby train station off the Dublin road. The larger part of the historic city was over the River Nore a few minutes' walk to the west.

The owner of the pub where Nancy socialised on the night of Thursday 10 September later dropped her home. Nancy had still been in the bar at closing time and the owner had offered her a lift. He had seen that Nancy, although not very drunk, was a little merry and he rightly wanted to make sure she got home safely. It was sometime around 12.10 a.m. or 12.20 a.m. when he dropped Nancy home. On the journey Nancy spoke about her late husband and asked after the driver's family. The man made sure Nancy got in her door and when she was safely inside the hallway he bid her goodnight and went back to his pub to help finish closing up.

It was about half an hour after the pub owner dropped Nancy home and headed on his way that a young man was both seen and heard banging on the window of Nancy's house. Because a witness also saw Nancy at her front porch remonstrating with this man we know that Nancy was certainly alive as it approached 1 a.m. The expert opinion of the fire service was that the fire in Nancy's home had been set quite some time before her body was found shortly after 5 a.m., so it is reasonable to assume that Nancy was strangled sometime closer to 1 a.m. than 5 a.m. Nancy was still in her outdoor clothes when her body was found, so she had not had time to change for bed before her killer struck. It would also appear that her killer had pulled the front door shut as he left the house after killing her. When the fire service had later broken down the front door with a sledgehammer to gain entry, the door had given way quickly. This implied that the inside bolt had not been on. The logical conclusion was that the door had been pulled shut by someone going out the front door.

While we can assume that the killer brazenly walked out the front door, how he actually got into the house is still unresolved. It is possible that Nancy still had her front door open after having words with the young man seen banging on her window shortly before 1 a.m. It is also possible that the killer had entered the house through the bedroom window which was slightly ajar. Because Nancy's home was on a curve in the road and set back from the footpath, with a small garden in front, people living in the nearby houses would not necessarily have seen any activity at the front of Nancy's home. While the angle of the house ordinarily gave Nancy some privacy, it also inadvertently gave a killer some measure of cover.

Detectives have long sought to establish a clear motive for the murder of 79-year-old Nancy Smyth. Two motives which have still not been ruled out are sexual assault and robbery. Thursday would have been pension day and perhaps the killer wanted to steal Nancy's money, which she would have collected earlier. Equally, the possibility that Nancy was the intended victim of a sexual assault has also been actively considered by the Garda Cold Case Unit. Looking at all the circumstances of the case, and based on their intelligence, this is a motive which they cannot discount. However, it is also possible that there was no clear motive, and that perhaps the killer simply wanted to cause hurt and inflict pain and he chose Nancy Smyth because she lived alone and was defenceless.

It is the opinion of detectives who carried out the original investigation, and also the opinion of cold-case detectives, that Nancy's killer was from Kilkenny. Gardaí do not believe the killer lived on Wolfe Tone Street or any of the immediately surrounding streets, but it is felt, however, that the killer had to be from the wider Kilkenny environs. The logic of this theory is that there were no reports of any suspicious vehicles in the area. It is assumed that the killer arrived at Nancy's house on foot and also left on foot. If he was walking to the safety of his own home after committing the murder it is perhaps less likely that the killer would have headed towards the busier main part of Kilkenny city to the west of the nearby river. It's more likely the killer stayed in the shadows and walked along quiet streets east of Wolfe Tone Street. Another possibility is that the killer may have returned to the scene to watch the aftermath of the fire, when Gardaí had cordoned off the scene and news had broken in the media of the murder investigation.

As Gardaí began their investigations they considered if the murder might be linked to an incident on the far side of Kilkenny city. On the night of Thursday 10 September, just hours before Nancy was murdered, a woman was attacked in her home by a masked man who stole £5. However, detectives eventually formed the view that the incidents were not linked in any way.

Detectives spoke with a young man who said he had been the person arguing with Nancy outside her home. He initially denied he had been anywhere near Wolfe Tone Street, but later he confirmed he had walked down the street in the early hours of 11 September. He did not live anywhere near Wolfe Tone Street, but said he had been out drinking in a pub earlier that night and was later walking by Nancy's house and that she had been arguing to herself when he first came up Wolfe Tone Street. The young man said he had then argued with Nancy for up to a half an hour. He said she opened and shut her front door at least three times. His explanation for arguing with Nancy was that if anyone argued with him he would argue back. He confirmed he had stood inside her front gate but he said he did not go into Nancy's home and that he had no physical contact with her. He confirmed that as he stood outside Nancy's home he had asked a man who was passing by on the other side of the road for a light for his cigarette. The young man told Gardaí he had later walked home at around 2 a.m. and that he did not meet anyone on his journey home.

The murder of Nancy Smyth was one of a number of killings of women in the Republic of Ireland in 1987 which would not be solved. The year saw a spike in the number of murders committed in Ireland and it is purely coincidental but somewhat disturbing that a number of women were killed in 1987 and their killers were never brought to justice. The circumstances of each killing was entirely unique, but little did anyone know at the time that all the murderers would get away scot free.

On 1 April 1987 a 76-year-old woman, Lilly Carrick, was beaten to death in a laneway off Gardiner Street in Dublin city. Lilly was a widow and was walking home after missing her bus. Her killer beat her about the head, fracturing her skull. DNA was obtained from the crime scene but Lilly's murderer has never been brought to justice. As detectives were continuing to investigate this murder, 29-year-old mother-of-two Antoinette Smith vanished from Dublin on 11 July after earlier attending the David Bowie concert in Slane. It would be 3 April of the following year before her body was found buried at Glendoo Mountain near Glencree in Co. Wicklow. It is believed she was the victim of a random killer or killers.

A number of murders as a result of the Troubles also stretched Garda resources in 1987. Mary McGlinchey was shot

dead while bathing her two young sons at her home at
Muirhevnamore in Dundalk on the evening of 31 January 1987.
Mary was the wife of INLA leader Dominic McGlinchey, who
was in prison at the time of his wife's murder. (He himself was
shot dead in Drogheda in 1994 and similarly his murder
remains unsolved.) Two INLA members were shot dead during
an ambush at a hotel in Drogheda on 20 January in what was
an internal feud. On 3 May a man disappeared after going to a
funeral along the border. His body was found in December
buried under the floor of a disused cow shed in Co. Monaghan.
And a member of the RUC was also murdered in the Republic
of Ireland in 1987. Samuel McClean, who was from Letterkenny
and had almost 20 years' service with the RUC, was shot dead
by a two-man gang near his family's property at Convoy in Co.
Donegal on 2 June. Samuel was one of two RUC officers
murdered in Co. Donegal whose killers were never brought to
justice. (Fellow officer Harold Keys was visiting his girlfriend
in the county in January 1989 when they were ambushed and
Harold was shot 23 times.)

Nineteen-eighty-seven was also the year that father-of-four
Brian McGrath vanished from his home at Coole in Co.
Westmeath. The 43-year-old's body would not be found until
November 1993, when Gardaí excavated a field next to Brian's
house, after his daughter bravely came forward to give details
of the murder she had witnessed six years before. However, it
would be 2008 before advances in forensic science would
confirm that the body was indeed missing man Brian McGrath.
His wife Vera was later convicted of murder and is now serving
a life sentence. A man was convicted of manslaughter and jailed
for nine years. The Brian McGrath case was the first major
success for the Garda Cold Case Unit, and gave hope that other
historic unsolved murders might see similar advances. In
Nancy Smyth's case, there was a similar hope of a

breakthrough. The circumstances of every case were different, but in Nancy's case, just like the Brian McGrath case, the feeling has always been that the person responsible is still alive and might still be brought to justice.

On Tuesday 15 September 1987, four days after Nancy's body was discovered at her home in Kilkenny, Gardaí arrested a man in his mid-twenties. The arrest was made in Kilkenny and the man was held at the local Garda station and questioned by teams of detectives. The man was questioned throughout Tuesday afternoon and into the late evening, and again the following day. With an arrest having taken place so soon after the murder, people naturally wondered if there might be substantial progress in the case. However, after being held for two days the man was released. His was the only arrest to be ever carried out in the murder enquiry.

Two months after the murder of Nancy Smyth, Co. Kilkenny was again the centre of national attention when a major security operation saw the arrest of Dessie O'Hare, who was wanted for the kidnap and mutilation of Dublin dentist John O'Grady. O'Hare and other members of the newly formed Irish Republican Brigade had kidnapped Mr O'Grady in Dublin on 13 October. He was held at hideouts in Dublin and Cork before being rescued by Gardaí in Dublin on 5 November. During his ordeal, the tops of John O'Grady's two little fingers were chopped off by his kidnap gang, which was led by Dessie O'Hare. A manhunt continued for O'Hare across Ireland for three weeks after John O'Grady's rescue, before intelligence was gathered which led to his capture in north Co. Kilkenny during a shootout on 27 November. Detectives from Kilkenny and Tipperary joined with members of the Army in mounting a roadblock, which led to O'Hare's arrest. Another gunman was shot dead during the operation that led to the capture of Ireland's most wanted man. O'Hare was later given a 40-year prison sentence but has since been released as part of the Good Friday Agreement. The work done by Gardaí from Kilkenny in helping to bring Dessie O'Hare to justice was admirable. Their sense of satisfaction with being involved in such an arrest was tempererd somewhat by the ongoing investigation into the murder of Nancy Smyth, which had by now stalled with no sign of an early breakthrough.

The murder of Nancy Smyth was not the first time a killer tried to hide his crime by setting fire to his victim's home, and it wouldn't be the last. Co. Kilkenny was again the scene of a most horrific case in December 2008, when three innocent lives were taken by a killer and arsonist. In the early hours of Christmas morning of that year, 30-year-old Sharon Whelan was strangled to death in her home in Windgap in the south of the county. Sharon had been renting a farmhouse where she lived with her two daughters Zsara and Nadia, who were just seven and two years old. Sharon did not know her killer—a 23-year-old man, Brian Hennessy, who was a postal worker and lived in Windgap village. He went to Sharon's isolated home and, after strangling her, he spent a number of hours in the house before he then set at least two fires to try and cover his tracks. He then callously walked out the door as the two little girls slept in the house. Both Zsara and Nadia died from smoke inhalation. Brian Hennessy is now serving one life sentence for the three murders. Hennessy was caught through DNA evidence. It was the quick thinking of brave neighbours of Sharon's who removed the three bodies from the burning farmhouse which later allowed pathologist Maurice Murphy to determine that Sharon was dead before the fire was set, and a major criminal investigation led to the capture of a triple-killer.

Some of the detectives who investigated the murders of Sharon, Zsara and Nadia could remember the unsolved case of

Nancy Smyth. Once Brian Hennessy was identified as the culprit for the murders in Windgap, it was clear that there was no link whatsoever with Nancy's case. The two cases showed that two separate killers had struck in the county just over twenty years apart and both had used arson as a means to try and hide evidence of murder. If Sharon Whelan's neighbours had not managed to remove the three bodies from the burning farmhouse before it was too late, the evidence of murder might have been lost and the deaths might have been blamed on an accidental fire. Similarly, if the fire set in Nancy's home in September 1987 had taken hold fully, it might have been wrongly assumed that there was nothing suspicious about her death.

The one major difference between these two cases is that the murderer of Sharon and Zsara and Nadia was caught, and caught quickly. The people of Co. Kilkenny could breathe a sigh of relief that a dangerous killer was off the streets. There was to be no such feeling in the aftermath of Nancy Smyth's murder. Her killer would remain free to roam the streets.

The Cold Case Unit have continued to carry out a full review of Nancy Smyth's case. There are hundreds of recommendations which the Unit have made about new angles to explore, old witnesses to re-interview, original crime scene material to be located and examined.

Nancy Smyth is buried at St Kieran's Cemetery in east Kilkenny, not too far from Nowlan Park GAA grounds. The use of the term 'city' to describe Kilkenny comes from a medieval charter it received over 800 years ago. The city is dominated at the south end by Kilkenny Castle, while the western bank has become a hub for arts, crafts and design which have all led to sizeable tourist numbers, even in the midst of a recession. The continued successes of Kilkenny's hurlers also give a sense of excitement to the busy and compact Kilkenny city.

The house where Nancy Smyth was murdered is still there on Wolfe Tone Street. Less than half a kilometre away Nancy is laid to rest with her husband Dick. Gardaí investigating the murder of Nancy Smyth need evidence, they need people to talk. Nancy Smyth's final resting place is in Kilkenny, and the chilling possibility is that her killer may still walk these streets.

03 THE UNSOLVED MURDER OF INGA-MARIA HAUSER

Eighteen-year-old Inga-Maria Hauser had hardly set foot on the island of Ireland when she was murdered and her body hidden in a forest in Co. Antrim in April 1988. The teenager was on the trip of a lifetime to Britain and Ireland, having set off from her home in Germany at the end of March. A confident and self-sufficient young woman, Inga-Maria had travelled alone, using an InterRail ticket to set off from Munich. From the south of Germany she travelled north, going to Holland where she got a ferry to England on 31 March. She was due to meet up with a friend in Wales, but just before Inga-Maria had left Munich the friend told her she now couldn't meet until 9 April. Inga-Maria wasn't deterred from her plans and decided to do a week of sightseeing on her own before meeting her friend in Cardiff. When she arrived in England she stayed in London for two days and then travelled by train to Bath, Oxford, Cambridge, Liverpool and then to Scotland. She went from Inverness to Glasgow and then to Stranraer. Inga-Maria still had four days before she was due to meet her friend in Wales so she decided to get the ferry from Scotland to Northern Ireland, travel by train from Belfast to Dublin and then get the ferry back to Wales in four days' time. It was a whistle-stop tour for a young woman who had developed a great love of British and Irish people and their cultures. Inga-Maria arrived in Northern Ireland on the late evening of 6 April 1988 but she never made it to Belfast. Instead, she was taken by her killer or killers to Ballypatrick Forest in north-east Co. Antrim where she was sexually assaulted and beaten. During the attack her neck was broken and her body was left face down in a remote part of the forest, just off a dirt-track.

Cold-case detectives have a massive clue which they are actively pursuing as part of ongoing efforts to solve this most brutal murder. Police now have a full DNA profile from a person they describe as a 'crime scene donor'—it is male DNA found where Inga-Maria's body was recovered, and advances in forensic science in recent years mean that the DNA profile is a full profile. Back in 1988 the sample could only give a match of 'one in 2,000', meaning one in every 2,000 men would have similar DNA to the 'crime scene donor'. But now, advances in science have moved the mathematical certainties so far on that the DNA found at the crime scene can provide a one in a billion match. All the Police Service of Northern Ireland have to do now, and what they have been trying to do in recent years, is find that mystery person. "Inga-Maria's case is one that we carry with us all the time," says the current senior investigating officer Detective Superintendent Raymond Murray.

It is wonderful to now have a full DNA profile from the crime scene, but it is also frustrating at the same time, because we have not yet matched that profile to any individual. It is forensic science which is currently leading us in particular directions, and as more and more people are eliminated as the

possible crime scene donor, the pool shrinks and you wonder
how close you might be getting. We feel we are very close to an
answer, I believe we are all around this, but these cases are
marathons and you have to dig in for the long haul.

It was Raymond Murray's colleague, Detective Inspector
Tom McClure, who made the breakthrough in 2005 that has
given this murder investigation an amazing impetus. The
detective carried out a review of the case, looking in particular
at possible forensic opportunities. He knew that DNA had been
found at the scene in Ballypatrick Forest in 1988, but back then
forensic science was nowhere near as advanced as it is today.
One of the frustrating aspects of DNA sampling is that when
you raise a DNA profile you can effectively destroy the sample,
so the sample raised in 1988, which could only give a one in
2,000 match, was quite possibly not going to be any use in
trying to raise a new, more exact profile. Tom McClure looked
over the full crime scene and the list of all the materials, which
had been kept safe over the previous seventeen years. He
suggested that certain items should be re-examined to see if
further DNA could be sourced. The scientists later came back
to inform him he had been right, they had now found a new
DNA sample which could be analysed with the latest
technologies. The new DNA profile was raised under a process
known as Second Generation Matrix Plus (SGM+), the standard
that experts currently work to in Britain. The sample matched
the original DNA found in 1988, which had been raised under
the Single Locus Point process, but the newly raised sample also
now allowed for a one in a billion match with whoever had left
their DNA where Inga-Maria's body was found. "The first thing
we did in 2005 was race down the road and run the sample
through our own DNA database, but there was no match,"
Raymond Murray tells me. "At that time the Northern Ireland

and the UK databases were not one unified database, so we then ran it through their computers, but again there was no match. Everybody was disappointed. We've also gone to Interpol and a number of countries with databases have checked it out but still there was no match."

At her home in eastern Munich, I meet Inga-Maria's mother Almut. Now in her early seventies, she has been kept up to date by the PSNI with the recent and ongoing developments in her daughter's case. Detectives have written to Almut in German, outlining the work which has been going on. With the assistance of a translator, Nele Obermueller, Almut tells me she is heartened to know that her daughter's unsolved murder is being pursued. "It is good that police have this lead which they are working on. I cannot get my hopes up too much. The crime was so long ago. It was and still is unbelievable."

Almut showed me around her apartment, pointing out all the paintings on the walls which Inga-Maria had done. She was a very talented artist, both with paint and pencil sketches. One painting is of a girl walking through long grass on a summer's day, she's wearing a straw hat with a pretty bow. Another image is entirely different, it's a black and white sketch which she did in school depicting the subject of war. There are headstones in the centre of the image, with a dark sky above and distraught relatives in the foreground. "Inga-Maria was in her second last year at Oskar Von Miller high school here in Munich," says Almut. "She was in 12th grade when she decided to travel to Britain and Ireland. Inga-Maria was a kind, sociable, conscientious young woman. When her friend said she couldn't meet up as soon as they had originally planned, Inga-Maria decided to travel on anyway and do sightseeing. She wanted to see Ireland, she had spoken about wanting to explore Ireland. She rang home every day at the start of her trip, and then the phone calls stopped."

As well as phoning home during her time in England and Scotland, Inga-Maria was a prolific writer and sent numerous postcards to her friends during her trip in early April 1988. Having grown up in a large city, she was also streetwise. In one of her postcards sent from England a few days before her murder in Northern Ireland she wrote: *'You probably cannot imagine how much England pleases me. The people here are so lovely that you don't need to worry. I cannot imagine anything bad happening to me.'* On another postcard which she later sent from Scotland she drew a small sketch of the Loch Ness monster. *'I have just arrived in Inverness at Loch Ness where the monster lives but I have certainly not seen it yet,'* she wrote. *'My journey has run without a hitch so far. And it really is indescribably beautiful here. Unfortunately my money is slowly running out.'* As well as sending postcards Inga-Maria kept a diary of her travels.

One entry records *'the day after tomorrow I'm going on to Ireland. I'm looking forward to that the best.'* Inga-Maria's last diary entries are on 6 April 1988 and record her travel up to and including being on the ferry: *'Going to Glasgow now. Snowy mountains, wild landscape … Went from Glasgow to Ayr and then to Stranraer to get over to Ireland. Saw the sea, beautiful and mysterious. Wonder where I stay tonight, need more money.'*

Inga-Maria arrived in Northern Ireland at 9.40 p.m. on 6 April 1988 when the ferry, MV *Galloway Princess*, docked at Larne, having left the Scottish port of Stranraer just over two hours previously. Inga-Maria was dressed as a typical backpacker. She carried a large blue rucksack on her back and also had a distinctive canvas bag on top of the rucksack. The canvas bag was green but had a lot of prominent red, blue and yellow colouring with stars and circles motifs and the letters 'USAF'. She also carried a green shoulder bag and had a pair of white runners hanging by the laces from her rucksack.

A total of 422 people are believed to have travelled on the ferry from Stranraer to Larne that evening. Many of those people were located back in 1988 or have been identified since then, but there are still a number of passengers who were on the same ferry as Inga-Maria who have never made themselves known. There were around 100 vehicles on the ferry, both cars and lorries. Some of those vehicles and their drivers have never been positively identified. Inga-Maria boarded the ferry in Scotland as a foot passenger and one assumption is that she similarly walked off the vessel when it docked in Larne. This is the logical conclusion, given the fact that the train station was just a short distance away within the port. This is where Inga-Maria would have planned to get a train to Belfast. Despite the late hour she might have planned to stay in a hostel in Belfast and maybe travel to Dublin the next day, or perhaps the day after that. But something happened to stop Inga-Maria even making it to the train station in Larne. She was either abducted or accepted a lift from someone, perhaps someone who told her they would drop her in Belfast. If she accepted a lift it's possible she sat into a vehicle as the ferry docked. While there are reported sightings of Inga-Maria during the two-hour ferry crossing, it's still not clear whether she left the docked vessel by foot or in a car or lorry.

While it's logical to assume that Inga-Maria's plan was to travel to Belfast and then to Dublin, perhaps she changed her mind and willingly accepted a lift from someone she knew was driving further north from Larne. Inga-Maria had seen some stunning scenery in Scotland and perhaps she made a decision to find a hostel in north-east Antrim and then do some sightseeing the following morning. Maybe Inga-Maria had heard about the Carrick-a-rede Rope Bridge or Rathlin Island or the many other scenic spots on Ireland's most north-east edge, where you can see across to Scotland's Mull of Kintyre.

Perhaps Inga-Maria fell into conversation with someone on the ferry who told her of all the tourist spots she could visit in this corner of the island of Ireland, and maybe they offered to drive her to a hostel.

Inga-Maria either willingly took a lift or she was abducted. If she was abducted, it would appear that it happened in Larne at the same time as other passengers were leaving the port for their onward journeys. If Inga-Maria willingly took a lift, the person or persons into whose vehicle she entered may have either told her they were taking her further north, or they may have lied to Inga-Maria and told her they were bringing her to Belfast, but instead of heading south from Larne, they turned north. It was now dark outside, and Inga-Maria may not have even known which way she was being brought, and may not have suspected anything until it was too late.

Inga-Maria was not a hitch-hiker, she was self-sufficient and confident, but she used public transport to get around. From the ferry terminal exit, it was less than a minute walk to Larne train station. She had an InterRail Pass and she loved travelling that way. Detectives have long considered what might have happened to divert Inga-Maria from her intention to get the train. Is it possible that Inga-Maria was abducted either before the ferry had docked, or as she disembarked, or as she walked towards the train station? There are so many possibilities which police have considered. Is it possible that Inga-Maria felt ill and had to sit down and accidentally missed her train before a predator killer struck?

Amid all the uncertainty about what happened to Inga-Maria once the *Galloway Princess* docked in Larne, one thing is now apparent. Detectives believe that Inga-Maria met her violent death within minutes or hours of arriving in Northern Ireland. Although her body was not found in Ballypatrick Forest until 20 April, developments in pathology and other tests have now led the PSNI to the view that Inga-Maria was murdered soon after arriving at the port in Larne. This would tie in with the fact that Inga-Maria's last diary entry was on 6 April 1988 as she travelled across the Irish Sea on the ferry. She did not send any more postcards after this date and her camera, which was later found close to her body, showed that she never took any photos in Northern Ireland.

An examination of the crime scene at the most western part of Ballypatrick Forest Park, which is forty miles from Larne, indicates Inga-Maria's neck was broken where her body was found. It is possible that the full attack occurred at the forest, that Inga-Maria was sexually assaulted and beaten at this location before being murdered. But it is also possible that there is another crime scene or crime scenes. If Inga-Maria was abducted, the vehicle in which she was driven from Larne to Ballypatrick Forest might well have held forensic evidence. It is also possible that she was taken to another location before being brought to her death in the forest. There is nothing to firmly indicate this, but in the absence of much of the detail, police must keep their minds open to all possibilities.

Almut Hauser and her husband Josef became very concerned when Inga-Maria stopped ringing home after 6 April. It just wasn't like her not to be in contact. On the first week of her trip abroad she had been phoning every day, describing all the places she was visiting. When she failed to meet up with her friend as arranged in Wales on 9 April, it was very clear that something was terribly wrong. And then, on her mother's birthday, 20 April, the worst fears of Inga-Maria's family and friends were realised.

A sheep farmer out on his rounds made the shocking discovery. It was Wednesday evening, 20 April 1988, and as the man walked in an isolated part of Ballypatrick Forest he discovered Inga-Maria's body. The teenager was lying face down, and her clothing had been disturbed by her attacker. Her body lay in a grassy area close to tall trees at the end of a dirt-track in the deepest part of the forest. Inga-Maria's backpack, and her two smaller bags and her shoes were all strewn nearby. She had suffered blunt force injuries to her face and head, and a pathologist would later determine that her neck was broken. It was possible that a weapon had been used to inflict the head and face injuries, or Inga-Maria may have been punched or kicked.

Police were quickly able to identify Inga-Maria from her diary and travel documents, which were found with her body. Within a short time detectives had established that Inga-Maria had arrived in Larne on the night of 6 April. A medical opinion was initially given that Inga-Maria had died close to the date her body was found on 20 April and this meant she might have been held hostage somewhere for almost two weeks before being murdered. However, as part of a cold-case review sparked by the discovery in 2005 of a full DNA profile from the crime scene, police carried out a fresh assessment of Inga-Maria's most likely date of death. The PSNI studied the footage of the crime scene from April 1988, and they conducted tests in Ballypatrick Forest in April 2007. Inga-Maria's body had been remarkably intact when it was found; it had not been subject to any animal interference and this had led to some people thinking she might only have been dead some hours or days before she was found on 20 April. Establishing a precise date of death was essential in prioritising which people would be asked to give DNA samples to compare to the full profile which police now had. Some people might have been in Co. Antrim on 6 April but not later in the month, and vice-versa. In an effort to get a definitive conclusion on the most likely date of Inga-Maria's murder, the PSNI asked a botanist to study the growth of nettles at the crime scene and compare crime scene images with the nettle growth of April 2007. Detectives also asked an entomologist from Queens University in Belfast to assist in studying fly activity and animal activity in the forest. Over the course of the month of April 2007 it was established that the location where Inga-Maria's body was found was a particularly cool environment with very little fly activity and no animals. On comparing the topography of the area with how it appeared in April 1988, it was clear the appearance of Inga-Maria's body was consistent with it having been in the forest since the earlier part of that month. From the pathology report, detectives knew that Inga-Maria's hair was clean when her body was found, and again this was consistent with her having been murdered shortly after arriving in Northern Ireland, rather than her having been held captive anywhere. The logical assumption, and what all the scientific and general evidence now points to, is that Inga-Maria was driven to her death at Ballypatrick Forest Park on the night of 6 April or early hours of 7 April 1988.

Whoever murdered Inga-Maria had very detailed knowledge of Ballypatrick Forest. The location where Inga-Maria was found is remote, it is in the western part of the forest, the furthest point from entrances, all located off the A2, which links the coastal town of Ballycastle with the villages of Cushendall and Glenariff further down the coast. By day Ballypatrick Forest Park is a beautiful mix of mature forests, wildlife trails and picnic sites. To the north is Glenmakeeran River and to the west are low-lying mountains. By day the forest is a popular spot for tourists and locals alike but by night, it can be a dark and lonely place, and not somewhere anyone might venture alone. Police who have studied the crime scene, and profilers who have been asked to give their assessment, have both come to the conclusion that the killer of Inga-Maria Hauser knew the forest very well. Or if there was more than one killer, at least one of them knew the location almost like the back of his hand. Assuming Inga-Maria was brought to the forest under cover of darkness, the killer or killers would have had just their vehicle's headlights and the light of the moon to manoeuvre their vehicle down a rough track, then attack and murder Inga-Maria, and later drive their vehicle safely away. There were other isolated locations closer to the main road where the killer could have brought Inga-Maria, but he (or they) chose to go to the furthest point within the forest. This indicates a confidence of someone who knew the area and who went to the extra trouble of driving a further distance into the forest. Where Inga-Maria's body was found was not somewhere a roaming killer with no links to Co. Antrim might choose to commit a crime; it was more likely the attacker had some close link not only to Antrim, but specifically to Ballypatrick Forest Park.

In March 2011 the PSNI issued another major public appeal for assistance and disclosed more details about their ongoing enquiries, saying they were 'tantalisingly close' to making significant progress in solving Inga-Maria's murder. The detectives involved in the current investigation have lived the case for the last few years. Knowing they have a full DNA profile from the crime scene which, despite massive efforts, they have been unable to match, has left them both frustrated and enthused. They haven't made the breakthrough yet, but they feel they are so very close. It has been one of the largest DNA screening processes in the history of policing but still the 'crime scene donor' has not been identified. In March 2011 the PSNI focused their appeal on Co. Antrim, in particular the rural area east of Ballymoney. "I cannot rule out the possibility that more than one person was involved in Inga-Maria's death," said Detective Superintendent Raymond Murray.

I also have a report that a man in the rural area east of Ballymoney was seen soon after the murder in April 1988 with scratches on his face and that there was concern in the community that he had some sort of involvement. I am asking for information, as opposed to statements or formal evidence. I recognise that some people may still feel uncomfortable talking directly to police, perhaps because of their past, or their allegiances. The important thing is that we bring this investigation to a successful conclusion, primarily for Inga-Maria and for her family who have suffered too much for too long but also for the people of north Antrim who will continue to have this lengthening shadow hanging over them until the killer or killers are caught.

In the year that Inga-Maria Hauser was murdered, 106 people lost their lives as a result of 'the Troubles'. Nineteen-eighty-eight was one of the most violent years in Northern Ireland and it was a year which also saw Troubles-related deaths in the Republic of Ireland, Gibraltar, Holland, Belgium and England. However, 95 of the 106 deaths that year due to 'the Troubles' occurred in Northern Ireland. On the very day that Inga-Maria Hauser arrived in Larne on the ferry from Scotland, an IRA bomb had exploded under a car in Co. Fermanagh close to the Cavan border. A 51-year-old father of five who was a part-time member of the Ulster Defence Regiment was killed. Less than a week after Inga's body was found in Ballypatrick Forest the IRA killed two more people. A 23-year-old man was shot dead as he collected dustbins in Co. Tyrone on 26 April. The father of one was also a part-time member of the UDR. On the same day a 20-year-old British soldier was killed in an IRA booby trap bomb while he was on patrol in Co. Tyrone. The previous month had been one of the most violent and bizarre in the history of the Troubles. On 6 March the SAS shot dead three IRA members in Gibraltar. Their funerals were being held on 16 March at Milltown Cemetery in Belfast when a UFF gunman launched an attack and killed three men. Two of those shot dead were civilians while the other man was an IRA member. His funeral was being held three days later when two British soldiers in plainclothes drove into the cortège in west Belfast. The car was surrounded and the two men were pulled from the vehicle and taken to waste-ground a short distance away and shot dead. The moments leading up to the deaths of the two soldiers had been captured by television crews who had been filming the funeral of the IRA member. The harrowing scenes were broadcast on television screens around the world and Northern Ireland was at one of its lowest of many low ebbs.

It was into this environment that Inga-Maria Hauser chose to visit Ireland. The 18-year-old German was not deterred by news reports of violence, shootings, bombings, maimings and murder. She saw a different Northern Ireland, and wanted to soak up the culture and meet ordinary people. While Inga-Maria's murder had nothing to do with the Troubles, it seems that her killer used the surrounding mayhem to operate under the radar. While the RUC conducted a major investigation into Inga-Maria's murder, they were faced with dozens upon dozens of other murders to investigate and there was also the fact that a significant number of nationalists would not engage with police at all.

The PSNI represents a new era in policing in Northern Ireland. It's not just about a name change, it's about changing mindsets, and the new police service has been embraced by communities on both sides of the old divide. "We have come across paramilitaries as we have continued our screening process," Raymond Murray tells me.

We know who they are and they know who we are. That's the way it is, they have still given their DNA sample like anyone else. They've been co-operative and they are anxious that Inga-Maria's murder is solved. We believe that Inga-Maria's murder was discussed amongst paramilitaries. We think that they had their suspicions. We are not where we were in 1988. A lot of water has flown under the bridge and perhaps it is time, be it through whatever means, either direct contact with police or through intermediaries or whatever, for that seam of information to come through. Could it be the key bit? These are rural communities in east Co. Antrim, they are close, they are tight-knit. People talk and people know every blade of grass in a hedgerow. They know when something isn't right.

Raymond Murray tells me that he is not necessarily looking for people to stand up and give evidence in court.

Because we have the DNA profile from the crime scene, we don't necessarily need someone to give evidence. It would be very nice if they would and it's the best way, but we don't need that for the case to stand up in court. We don't need written statements, what we need is the piece of information which helps us put all of this into proper perspective, that might help us understand the chain of events that brought Inga-Maria from Larne to Ballypatrick Forest, and that we learn what happened on that journey, be it on the coast road or an inland road en route which completes the picture.

In 1988 the concept of using DNA to identify an individual was in its infancy and there was no DNA database in Northern Ireland. The DNA process that was used in the late 80s was known as Single Locus Point and the material found at the scene of Inga-Maria's murder allowed for a 1 in 2,000 match. The science involved was nowhere near as discriminating or as sensitive as it is today. But with the profile that was raised back then police went and took swab samples from seventy men who had been nominated for testing as part of the investigation. Most people co-operated and voluntarily gave a sample of their DNA. However, all of those who were tested came back negative, and the investigation eventually hit a brick wall. Because DNA profiles are raised through 'destructive sampling', the profile originally raised under the Single Locus Point couldn't be compared to the developing technologies of Second Generation Matrix Plus which allowed for an astronomical advance in comparing samples. Police investigating Inga's murder found that they had a DNA sample which couldn't be compared to the thousands upon thousands of profiles which had by now been placed on databases for Northern Ireland and for England, Scotland and Wales. It was only in 2005, when Detective Inspector Tom McClure carried out a forensic review of the case that he found more DNA from which to raise a profile. It was a massive breakthrough and one which has kept Inga-Maria's case to the fore ever since.

Detectives have long been aware of the possibility that the name of the killer or killers may be in the investigation file somewhere. It may have been someone spoken to during door-to-door enquiries but who never raised the suspicions of police. Or the killer may have given a witness statement, or may have been stopped at a roadside checkpoint. There are many high-profile murder cases throughout the world where it turns out the killer was in the mix very early on but simply wasn't identified as the culprit until much later. So once the PSNI had their new DNA profile which would allow for a one in a billion match, they consulted with a behaviourist at the National

Crime Operations Faculty in England. He gave detectives certain parameters so as to 'score' every male who featured in any way in the case. The higher the score the higher the possibility that someone might be the type of person who should give their DNA sample. It might be that they had lived in the area of Larne or east Antrim, or that they had worked driving a vehicle around Northern Ireland, or had come into the mix in some other way. Detectives built up a matrix of what they called 'male nominals' and eventually went and took voluntary swabs from 1,000 men. Police put a huge effort into prioritising which people should be sampled, but after completing what is one of the largest such 'voluntary swab' procedures, not one of the men was a match for the 'crime scene donor'.

"One of the issues of working with DNA is that the science is advancing so quickly," says Detective Superintendent Raymond Murray.

Once we didn't get a match from the 1,000 men that we prioritised for sampling, we then got high-level approval from our head of Crime Operations to ask the DNA overseer in England to do a familial trawl on the database. This is where a certain process can be used to search for siblings or a parent or child of the crime scene donor. Basically if his DNA is not on the database, the science is so advanced that we can possibly identify a close relative of his if they are on the database, and perhaps they can in turn lead us to the man we wish to identify. We did 500 such tests, we did a third of that number of tests looking for a brother or sister of the donor and the other two thirds looking at the parent and child list, but again we didn't get a match. Just as we are wondering what we are going to do now, the scientists tell us about a new development called Y-STR DNA which relates to the male chromosome. Your Y-STR DNA should be the same as your father, grandfather, your brothers, your sons. This new science allowed us to eliminate not just individuals but entire male lines in a family.

But before they could do any test under the Y-STR analysis, scientists had to again raise a new profile from the crime scene DNA material. There was by now just a small amount of the crime scene stain left but the Forensic Science Service in England managed to raise a profile.

Each time you raise a profile it is destructive sampling, but we managed to get a sample under this new method of Y-STR DNA. Again we don't get a match with anyone, but what we do get are 'inconclusives'; at the last count we had 44 men who were 'inconclusives'. If you are a male, your Y-STR DNA should be passed directly to your son, and half your SGM+ should also be passed to him, but every so often, and we've been quoted a figure of one in every 300 generational events, something happens and the DNA changes slightly, it mutates. So what the scientists have told us is that within those 'inconclusives' it is unlikely that it is a match but it may be a mutation and they cannot be totally eliminated. Within those 44 samples, there are some that are as absolutely close to the Y-STR profile without being an actual match. That is something we have to consider and have long considered. In one particular case over in England it turned out that one of the 'inconclusives' in a DNA trawl was indeed a male relative of that 'crime scene donor' who was being sought.

It is a distance of 40 miles from Larne to Ballypatrick Forest. The most direct route is on the A2, which travels along the coast through Ballygalley, Carnlough and Cushendall before heading inland slightly. Just a few miles on and a turn off to the left is Ballypatrick Forest. Driving within the speed limit, and allowing for a number of vehicles leaving Larne from the ferry that evening, it is likely that a straight journey to Ballypatrick Forest would have taken about an hour. There is also another possible route to the forest, which is less direct but which police have also had to consider. Whoever drove Inga-Maria away from Larne could have driven west towards Ballymena before heading north on the A26 heading for Ballycastle on the north coast. This journey would have brought Inga-Maria close to Cloughmills and Loughguile and then through Armoy before the driver could have gone through Ballycastle and travelled south to Ballypatrick Forest. It's a more roundabout journey involving a distance of almost 50 miles and a journey time of 80 minutes. It seems less likely that this is the way Inga's killer travelled, but it's a possibility nonetheless. Even if it wasn't the way Inga-Maria was brought to the forest, it could have been the route which served as a return journey for the killer or killers as they made their escape.

Whatever vehicle the killer or killers used to travel into the depths of Ballypatrick Forest, it was quite possibly a particularly sturdy vehicle. It would have been driven along dirt-tracks within the forest in darkness, and a killer who gave enough thought into travelling that far into the forest may well have felt secure in that his vehicle was reliable in difficult terrain; perhaps it was a jeep, or a truck or a van. As detectives strive to keep an open mind on what may have occurred, they have also considered that the vehicle which brought Inga-Maria to her death in the forest may not have been the same vehicle that she was either abducted in or accepted a lift in at Larne. Is it possible that Inga-Maria was taken to some location before she was transferred into another vehicle and then taken to her death in Ballypatrick Forest?

The PSNI has long pondered these types of questions, with detectives having brainstorming sessions, trying to think 'outside the box'. The fact that the 1,000 men who were prioritised for giving DNA samples failed to unlock the mystery has led officers to analyse and re-analyse the case. And they are learning new information all the time, in doing recent house-to-house enquiries and carrying out the recent voluntary sampling of men in the locality. Every piece of information is put into the mix. "The screening process has been good not only in terms of the forensic investigation, but also in terms of building up information," says Raymond Murray. "It's like an onion, layer upon layer of information. Who was in the docks, who was in the forest, who was in a particular place in Co. Antrim, what people were driving lorries, what people were driving cars. The account has grown substantially since 2005."

Back in Munich, Almut shows me more artwork that her daughter did in school. Inga-Maria was just two months short of her nineteenth birthday when she left for her trip to Britain and Ireland. She hadn't decided what she wanted to do when she left school and she had one full year left in high school before she had to make up her mind. One of her favourite subjects was English and she spoke it very well, and had been very much looking forward to practising it when she headed off from Munich on her InterRailing adventure. Almut tells me that the original family home is just up the street. Inga-Maria was the younger of two daughters.

In August 2006 Almut's husband Josef died at the age of 67. In 1988 he and his wife had travelled to Northern Ireland to take their daughter's body home and to meet police and make a public appeal for help in catching Inga-Maria's killer. "My husband was a very good man, very good father and very good husband," says Almut, as she looks at his Memorial Card. "Josef and I were both from Vorchdorf, a town in northern Austria. We met in school, I was the one who later pursued him. We moved to Germany for financial reasons and settled in Munich. Josef is now laid to rest here in Munich with Inga-Maria, I visit them every day."

Northern Ireland has thousands of unsolved murders, most of them linked to the Troubles. The Historical Inquiries Team was specifically set up to review more than 3,200 deaths attributed to the conflict from the late 1960s to 1998. There is an understanding in Northern Ireland of the need to get answers for families who have been bereaved. That feeling is also reflected in the many other cold-case murder investigations which the PSNI has undertaken in recent years. One of those cases is the murder of nine-year-old Jennifer Cardy, who was abducted while cycling near her home at Ballinderry in south Co. Antrim in August 1981. Six days after her disappearance Jennifer's body was found ten miles away at McKee's Dam near Hillsborough. A massive investigation was put in place at the time by the RUC, and in recent years detectives from the PSNI's Serious Crime Branch carried out a full re-investigation. In October 2011 a Scottish serial-killer was convicted of Jennifer's murder. After murdering Jennifer in 1981, this man had murdered three other girls in Britain during the 1980s.

Another cold case which has seen renewed investigations is the disappearance of 15-year-old Arlene Arkinson, who vanished on a night out in August 1994. It is feared that Arlene was murdered and her body secretly hidden either in Co. Tyrone or in Co. Donegal. In August 2011 it was confirmed that the PSNI planned to begin new searches for the missing teenager, using specialist search equipment.

The potential for huge developments which forensic science can have in a cold-case review was clear in a remarkable case solved by the PSNI in 2008. For twenty years the person who battered and strangled 66-year-old Lily Smyth in her apartment in Belfast had escaped justice. But the killer had left a small bloodstain on a towel in Lily's apartment and tiny amounts of his blood on her clothing. A full cold-case review had begun in 2005 and advances in forensics led scientists to finally identify the stain on the towel as being that of William Stevenson, who had lived in the same flat complex as Lily. Stevenson's blood was subsequently found on items of Lily's clothing which had been kept safe for two decades, and the probability of a match was given as one in a billion. In October 2008 Stevenson was given a life sentence and told he would serve a minimum of 25 years for a murder he had committed twenty years before.

The person who left their DNA at Inga-Maria Hauser's crime scene has never been detected in any other criminal investigation. This means he has not been convicted of any crime in Northern Ireland, England, Scotland or Wales. Detectives have considered that perhaps the crime scene donor is dead. But even if he is, the developments in familial DNA mean he could still be identified through his relatives. The crime scene stain is a permanent fixture in the investigation, and establishing its owner is crucial in moving the investigation forward.

The PSNI have liaised with Gardaí to see if the DNA found at Inga's crime scene matches anyone on files in the Republic. One major hindrance in this work is the continued lack of a DNA database in the Republic, despite repeated promises by successive Governments. While the crime scene was in rural north-east Antrim, it is still possible that people south of the border have information about the case. Perhaps they were on the ferry that night, or know people who were.

The murder of Inga-Maria Hauser is the only murder of its kind to have occurred in Northern Ireland. Many visitors were killed in violence linked to the Troubles, but no other tourist was sexually assaulted, murdered and their body hidden by an opportunistic random attacker, similar to what happened to Inga-Maria. However, in the Republic of Ireland there are a number of tragic cases of women who came to the Republic of Ireland to either visit or live and who fell victim to murderers. One of those women was also from Munich. Twenty-three-year-old Bettina Poeschel was on a holiday in September 2001 when she decided to visit the historic Newgrange site in Co. Meath. She got a train from Dublin to Drogheda and then began to walk towards Donore, three miles from Newgrange. Bettina failed to return that night and her body was found 23 days later during a Garda search. Her murderer was a convicted killer from Drogheda named Michael Murphy. He had previously served a sentence for the manslaughter of another woman. He is now serving a life sentence for Bettina's murder. Another murder which was committed by a known violent offender occurred in October 2007, when Swiss student Manuela Riedo was murdered in Galway by local man Gerald Barry. Manuela's murderer is now serving a life sentence for strangling his victim to death; he is also serving a life sentence for raping a French student in Galway in the same year he committed murder.

The murders of Bettina Poeschel and Manuela Riedo were committed by men with a history of extreme violence who lived local to the areas where they committed opportunistic attacks on visitors to Ireland. A major difference between these solved cases and Inga-Maria Hauser's unsolved case, is that the 'crime scene donor' who left his DNA at Ballypatrick Forest has not surfaced in any other criminal investigation in Northern Ireland or anywhere else where DNA databases have been checked.

In the 1990s six women disappeared in the Leinster area, and they have never been found. It is feared that these women may have been killed and their bodies hidden. There has been no clear evidence to show a serial killer is responsible for any of these cases. Indeed in three of the disappearances— Fiona Pender in Co. Offaly in 1996, Ciara Breen in Co. Louth in 1997 and Fiona Sinnott in Co. Wexford in 1998—it's thought the victims may have known their killers. But in the other three cases—the disappearance of American woman Annie McCarrick in 1993, Jo Jo Dullard in Co. Kildare in 1995, and an 18-year-old woman in Co. Kildare in 1998—it's believed random abductors may be responsible. And there are also three unsolved murders of women whose bodies were then hidden, which may have involved random attackers. Marie Kilmartin vanished from Port Laoise in December 1993; her body was found hidden in bog water on the Laois-Offaly border in June 1994. Patricia Doherty disappeared in Tallaght in December 1991; her body was found buried in the Dublin Mountains the following June. And the oldest such unsolved case occurred when Antoinette Smith disappeared in Dublin in 1987; her body was found buried in the Dublin Mountains on 3 April 1988—co-incidentally Antoinette's body was found while Inga-Maria Hauser was travelling through Britain en route to Northern Ireland. There is nothing to indicate that Inga-Maria's killer was responsible for any of the unsolved disappearances and murders which Gardaí have so far failed to solve, but even if there is no link, it is clear that there were a number of similar type murderers operating on the island of Ireland in the late 1980s and into the 1990s.

One issue which the PSNI have long considered is why was Inga-Maria's body left so that it was eventually found. Although the killer or killers went to great lengths to bring Inga-Maria to a remote spot in Ballypatrick Forest, once they had murdered the teenager, they simply left her body there, with all her belongings strewn around. They didn't try to bury her body, or hide it in any other way. Did they panic, were they running out of time, were they expected to be somewhere, were they late for a workshift, or late with a delivery of goods, or would their wife or another family member be asking where they could be?

Northern Ireland has seen a number of cold-case murder trials in recent years. Some of those cases have involved murders which occurred as a result of the Troubles. Some trials have resulted in convictions, and others in not-guilty verdicts. No matter what the verdict in any particular case, at least evidence has finally been tested in court and a verdict given.

The Courts of Justice have also seen non-Troubles-related cold cases come before them. One of the most remarkable such murder cases only actually came to light because one of the killers—Colin Howell—finally confessed in January 2009 that he and his lover Hazel Stewart had murdered his wife Lesley and Hazel's husband Trevor Buchanan in May 1991. For almost eighteen years, it was believed that Lesley and Trevor had committed suicide by inhaling exhaust fumes in Co. Derry. It was only when Colin Howell suddenly told all that it was realised that a double-murder had actually taken place and that both Lesley and Trevor had been poisoned by their cheating spouses. Howell later pleaded guilty to murder and Hazel Stewart was convicted of murder by a jury in 2011 and similarly given a life sentence.

Before his arrest, double-murderer Colin Howell was a pillar of the community. A respected dentist and a church-goer, his friends and the wider community were left stunned by his revelations when he finally confessed in 2009. A case such as this begs the question—is it possible that Inga-Maria Hauser's killer is also a pillar of the community, someone who has all the appearances of being a law-abiding citizen, someone who has lived a lie since 1988?

In Almut's apartment she keeps a scrapbook of all correspondence from Northern Irish authorities relating to her daughter's case. There is a letter in German written by an RUC officer shortly after the murder to update the Hauser family on the investigation. There is also a letter in German sent by the PSNI in recent times to update the family on the ongoing work to try and identify the full DNA profile discovered in 2005. And there are other letters from 1988—correspondence from the funeral directors in Northern Ireland who cared for Inga-Maria before she was brought home to Germany, and contact from Germany's Honorary Consul in Northern Ireland. The coroner for North Antrim wrote in May of that year to say that an inquest into Inga-Maria's death could not be held due to ongoing police enquiries. In February of 1989 Moyle District Council wrote to say that still the inquest could not be held because the police investigation was continuing. The letter expressed the optimism that authorities were 'hopeful of positive action'. To this day Inga-Maria's inquest has not been held.

The unsolved murder has been featured twice on the BBC *Crimewatch* programme, once in 1988 and the second time in 2005. In the second appeal, then Detective Superintendent Patrick Steele appealed to people who had made anonymous contact with police some years before to get back in contact. Getting the appeal broadcast throughout Britain was important and still is. While the killer may have had detailed knowledge of Ballypatrick Forest, that didn't mean he was originally from Co. Antrim. He could just as easily have come from England, Scotland, the Republic of Ireland or anywhere else. In his appeal Patrick Steele spoke of all that had been taken from Inga-Maria. "If she was alive she could be living in

Ireland, or she could be teaching English in Germany. Her whole life was stolen from her."

Detective Superintendent Raymond Murray and Detective Inspector Tom McClure and their colleagues are still actively working on the case, but they also hope for the magical 'ping'— where someone is caught for some other crime and their DNA is put on the database and all of a sudden they finally learn the identity of the crime scene donor. "We would love if that was to happen, that a newly taken DNA sample would suddenly match our profile," says Raymond Murray.

But while we hope for that to happen, we are working to actively identify this person. We are looking abroad too and asking police forces in the United States, Canada, New Zealand and Australia to check if our unidentified profile matches any profile they may have. We choose those countries because they are the traditional destinations for emigrants from Ireland. But working with the international police community is an exercise in itself, each country has different rules and standards in relation to DNA.

As well as running the DNA profile against the databases in Northern Ireland and beyond, the police investigation has now seen over 2,000 people who are not on any database giving their DNA samples for the purposes of elimination. These are people in Co. Antrim and beyond who have voluntarily given their samples when requested by the police. As well as the SGM+ screening and the Y-STR familial trawl of DNA databases, detectives are also now looking at women who are on DNA databases, to see if any of their male relatives should be asked to give a DNA sample. This line of enquiry has developed as forensic science is now so advanced that certain female DNA profiles can be identified which show some similarities to the crime scene stain. Because of the way DNA characteristics are inherited from parents, there is a possibility that within that particular female group there may be a male relative of one of the women whose DNA profile could match the DNA from the crime scene. The PSNI has been contacting some women who are on the database to reach out to their male relatives and ask them to provide DNA samples for the purposes of elimination.

The PSNI still have Inga-Maria's backpack and her sleeping bag and other materials found with her body. Each item is safely guarded, each a potential piece of evidence if the suspected killer or killers are ever brought to trial. Inga-Maria was a bright, confident and friendly young woman who met her violent death over 1,000 miles from home. "It sits apart, it sits apart from the Troubles," says Detective Superintendent Raymond Murray. "The murder is completely out there on its own. People are still very animated about it, it is viewed as a stain on the community, and that is the message coming across to investigators. There is something about an act of brutality perpetrated on a visitor who came to our shores for all the best reasons. She came to Northern Ireland at a time that it was in a state of conflict, yet she still came to see and to listen and to soak up the culture and the folklore, and somebody killed her."

Almut's front-facing ground-floor apartment looks out on one of the busy streets in Munich just east of the River Isar. As I sit with her and our translator, Almut shows me more paintings that Inga-Maria did in school and she shows me more photographs of her daughter. One of the sketches that Inga-Maria did was a two-dimensional self-portrait. She also made an elaborate papier mâché collection of puppet faces. Her sense of humour also comes across in a painting of a woman who is riding a bike which is far too small for her.

Almut has two grandchildren from her other daughter. She worked as a nurse but is now retired and keeps active by playing badminton. Almut has not visited Northern Ireland since 1988. She knows the PSNI are doing all they can to catch Inga-Maria's killer and she is grateful that they still remember her daughter. As we finish our interview Almut shows me another photo of Inga-Maria smiling at the camera. "That is my daughter," she says proudly. "Isn't she lovely."

04 | THE UNSOLVED MURDER OF BROOKE PICKARD

Forty-two-year-old Englishman Brooke Pickard was abducted by a group of armed men at a beach car park in Co. Kerry at around 11.20 a.m. on Friday 26 April 1991. He has not been seen since. It's believed Brooke was lured to the car park near White Strand beach on the Ring of Kerry by someone he knew. Garda investigations to date suggest Brooke was helping someone who had apparently run out of petrol, when a group of armed men suddenly appeared from the side of a vacant holiday home. It's known that five minutes before he vanished, Brooke and another man bought £3 worth of petrol from a pump at O'Leary's shop in Castle Cove, the small village where Brooke, his wife and four children had been living for almost eight years. After buying the petrol, which he poured into a large can, Brooke and the other man got into Brooke's blue van and drove a short distance down to the car park at White Strand. It would seem Brooke believed he was simply helping someone who needed to get their car started, but within seconds of arriving at the car park Brooke was attacked, bundled into his own van and driven away.

Just moments before the abduction, a young girl who was riding her pony on the main road nearby saw Brooke and his passenger drive into the car park. The girl didn't recognise the passenger but had seen someone like this man walking in the village a short time earlier. However, the girl knew Brooke and he gave a wave and a smile and said hello. Brooke was well-known and well-liked in the area. He was a Yorkshire man who fell in love with Ireland and together with his wife Penny had renovated a farmhouse to fulfil a dream of raising their family in the countryside.

The young girl was moving slowly on horseback as she watched Brooke drive over to an orange-coloured car in the car park. Suddenly she saw a masked man running out a laneway at the side of the holiday home nearby. He was wearing a balaclava and was beckoning with his hand to someone behind him. The man was moving quickly towards Brooke's van. All of a sudden the masked man saw the girl and he stopped and stared at her. He was only about 15 yards away. The girl, now very frightened, turned around on her pony and headed away immediately. She would later tell her friends what she had seen, but they assumed it had been children playing. It seemed so absurd to think that armed and masked men would be found in the middle of the day in the sleepy Kerry village of Castle Cove.

The sighting of Brooke Pickard by this young girl is the last definite sighting of him. From information gleaned during the subsequent Garda investigation detectives now believe that within seconds of parking his van in the car park, Brooke was attacked, beaten and bundled into his own van. Detectives have information to suggest that up to five men may have been involved in attacking Brooke and that he put up a strong fight, and was only subdued when he was struck on the head with the butt of a gun by one of the gang. Both Brooke's van and the orange car were driven out of the car park a short time later. Brooke's van would later be found burnt out 27 miles away in a remote forested location close to Knocknagapple Mountain. The orange car which is believed to have been used to entice Brooke into the car park was later abandoned in the grounds of Limerick Regional Hospital. It had been taken to Co. Kerry from Co. Kilkenny without its owner's consent.

A group of men from Northern Ireland are suspected of being involved in the abduction of Brooke Pickard. The attack was not the work of a paramilitary organisation, but some of those involved may have had previous involvement with the IRA or INLA many years before. Gardaí still wish to question at least five men with addresses in Belfast. However, investigations also suggest there are a number of people living in Co. Kerry and Co. Cork who also have information about what happened to Brooke Pickard on that Friday morning over twenty years ago. These include foreign nationals who have made Ireland their home, and Irish people also. A total of 12 people were arrested during the original criminal investigation, including two women, but no charges were brought. Brooke Pickard is still officially a missing person, but his family and Gardaí both fear he was murdered soon after his abduction and then secretly buried.

I met Brooke's wife Penny in England where she now lives. Penny was forty years old when her husband vanished without trace. Their four children—Lisa, James, Crohan and Dan— were aged 15, 11, 7 and 5. The impact of Brooke's disappearance on the entire family has been immense. Penny and Brooke were both from Leeds, and moved to Co. Kerry because they wanted a complete change of lifestyle, a fresh start and wanted to live in the countryside. They worked hard to build up the farm and they very much enjoyed life in Ireland. "I met Brooke in 1979," recalls Penny.

I was actually moving from Leeds to a nearby town, and I needed a removal man with a van. That's how we met and soon after we began going out. Brooke was a very cheerful man, a hard worker, a real grafter. We decided to make a life somewhere in the countryside. We initially thought of moving to north-west Scotland because my parents had a holiday home there. We both loved it up there but Brooke was concerned about the harsh winters. We looked at a map and found that southern Ireland had similar terrain but a much milder climate. Neither of us had ever been to southern Ireland, we had no links there. But we just fell in love with Co. Kerry. We went and looked at the south-west peninsulas and we both fell in love with the same part of the same Kerry peninsula.

Brooke and Penny settled on a beautiful location on the Ring of Kerry between Waterville and Sneem. The farm, with its mature trees, elevated location and sea views, was the type of place they had always dreamed of. The nearby village of Castle Cove had a shop and pub, a church, friendly people, country air and wonderful views. Brooke had asked an auctioneer to suggest locations where they might get five acres of land, a ruin and a stream. Of all the locations they were shown, both Brooke and Penny fell in love with a spot at Behaghane, just a mile outside Castle Cove. And so in 1983 they bought an old but sound farmhouse in need of a lot of work, complete with five acres, where they would soon keep all types of farm animals. To the back was a mountain range, to the front was the view down to the coast just a short distance away. And on a clear day you could look right across where the expansive Kenmare River met the Atlantic Ocean and see the next peninsula to the south, where the Slieve Miskish Mountains held court. It was perfect. In November 1983 the family moved in. "The first few years were incredibly basic," remembers Penny.

The previous owners had put in beams to build an upstairs but hadn't completed it. We had come over that July and put in an upstairs before moving in. We piped water from the well in the back field down to the house. It was maybe two years before we got a bathroom and a flush toilet. We didn't get mains electricity for many years after that. But it was a wonderful home. There was a single-storey cow shed adjoining the house, and Brooke took the roof off, capped the stonework and built it up to two storeys. Over the years we added further extensions. It wasn't finished but it became a wonderful spacious home.

The Pickards kept a busy farm. They acquired more fields and they kept goats, chickens, ducks and geese. They also had ponies, and Jersey cows and a few sheep. They had a Jersey bull named Goliath, and they kept a vegetable patch and planted fruit trees. Penny shows me some photos of Brooke, and in one he is smiling for the camera with a large shovel resting on his shoulder. Dozens of large blocks are piled high to his right and he is wearing wellies, jeans and jumper. It is a simple picture, but conveys the hard worker and happy character that Brooke was. In another photo he stands proudly with his arm around his youngest son Dan, who is standing on a stone wall outside their home. James and Crohan are also smiling in the picture, as is their older sister Lisa who is leaning on a half-door looking at her Dad and brothers.

Penny Pickard spent the day of Friday 26 April 1991 doing housework and farmwork, painting a room, and reading the Bible and praying. Normal things, normal pleasures and normal chores on what was to become the last normal day Penny and her children would have.

On the day Brooke disappeared Penny had no reason to suspect anything was wrong, as he wasn't expected back until evening. When Brooke left the house that Friday morning he was due to go and cut turf for the whole day. On a previous occasion there had been a problem with the vehicle and he had not returned home until very late because he'd had to unload the turf and fix the problem before loading it all up again. So when Brooke failed to show up on the evening of Friday 26 April 1991, Penny thought the same thing might have happened as before. It was an era before mobile phones so there was no way to contact Brooke, and Penny eventually went to bed. She had cooked a leg of lamb for dinner, and Lisa, James, Crohan and Dan had stayed up with their Mum waiting for their Dad until around 10.30 p.m. before going to bed. Eventually Penny turned off the oven and went to bed herself after 1 a.m. She was very concerned but could only think Brooke must be on his way. It was when she woke the following morning at 7 a.m. that she realised Brooke had not come home at all. She woke her daughter Lisa who suggested she ring John, the neighbour that Brooke had been due to go cutting turf with. Penny rang John and he told her Brooke wasn't with him, that he had never shown up the previous day. Penny immediately knew something was badly wrong. Brooke was a stickler for punctuality, for keeping arrangements. It was completely out of character for him to fail to keep an arrangement. However, Brooke had previously gone away to England without telling anyone in advance, but leaving a note. Penny rang family and friends in England to check if Brooke was there but they had not seen him. She also began asking around the neighbours in Castle Cove, to see if anyone had seen Brooke, and eventually she met the father of the young girl and heard about masked men being seen with Brooke at the car park at White Strand the previous day.

Sergeant Michael Griffin took the call at Caherciveen Garda station. A neighbour was ringing on behalf of Penny Pickard. Penny's husband was missing since the previous day, and she had just been told about armed and masked men being seen with Brooke in the car park at White Strand. The people who had first heard the girl's story had assumed it had merely been children playing, but now it was becoming clear that Brooke Pickard was missing and the armed and masked men at White Strand car park were very real. It was now more than 30 hours since Brooke had last been seen.

Immediately upon receiving the phone call Sergeant Griffin and Detective Garda Dan Coughlan travelled to Penny's house and they spent the following hours piecing together what was known about Brooke's last movements. Gardaí immediately began a major criminal investigation, and over time would build up a detailed picture of what had most likely happened to Brooke. There are gaps in the story but, based on solid detective work, good eyewitnesses and the discovery of Brooke's van in the Kerry Mountains, much is now known or suspected about the abduction and most likely the murder of Brooke Pickard.

Brooke left his home shortly before 11 a.m. on Friday 26 April 1991. He was looking forward to spending the day getting a trailer-load of turf to heat the house. A neighbour of his was giving him the turf from a bog near Waterville as a payment for work Brooke had done earlier in the week when he had transported a calf from Castle Cove to a woman in Kenmare. Brooke had told his neighbour John that he'd meet him around eleven that Friday morning. When Brooke said goodbye to Penny it was a normal day, nothing yet out of the ordinary. Brooke came back into the house twice, once to get a shovel, and the other time thinking he'd forgotten a shopping list which was actually in his pocket. He was wearing blue overalls and brown leather working boots. He got into his blue diesel Ford Transit van, it was a distinctive van with a long wheel base and had an English registration number YNP 231W. As he headed down the lane towards the village, he stopped and called to another neighbour, Brian, to give him the name of a farmer who had some animals for sale. Brian would later tell Gardaí that Brooke was in good form, was his normal self. Brooke said goodbye to Brian and headed for John's house across the other side of the village. By chance, from a good distance John actually saw Brooke leaving Brian's. From his house John had a clear view across the village and could make out the blue van coming down the lane from Brian's house. He expected Brooke to arrive at his door within a few minutes as they had arranged. However, Brooke never showed up. Having left Brian and driven down the lane on his own, and either just before or soon after he pulled onto the N70 Ring of Kerry road to enter the village, someone stopped him and apparently asked for help in getting petrol for their car which was at White Strand car park.

It's believed that the person who stopped Brooke had previously been in the area. They did not live locally, but perhaps knew the best spot to stop Brooke's van so as to limit the chances anyone might see them. And it must have been someone that Brooke somehow knew. It must have been someone that he felt comfortable helping. Brooke was the kind of person who might have helped anyone but the circumstances and the geography indicate that Brooke was assisting someone he knew. The orange car in the car park was situated more than a kilometre to the east of Castle Cove village, while Brooke's house was just over a kilometre to the west of the village. Any person who had simply run out of petrol at the beach could have gone to the nearby pump and got petrol to bring to their car. But someone had effectively sought out Brooke and had asked for his assistance. Brooke was a good mechanic and perhaps the person knew this. Maybe they made up a story about the car experiencing some other trouble which Brooke might be able to help with, or that there was someone else in the car who wished to speak with Brooke. Whatever the lure that was used, it doesn't appear that Brooke was under duress when he picked up his passenger, nor when he stopped a few minutes later and got the petrol in a can from the BP pump at O'Leary's shop in the village. Nor did he seem under any pressure as he and his passenger drove into the car park at White Strand. The way Brooke waved to the girl on horseback and said 'hi' was typical Brooke. It seems that until he pulled his van up behind the orange car at the end of the car park Brooke had no idea of the imminent danger he faced.

Gardaí believe they know exactly the actual orange car which was parked in the car park and which was apparently used in the abduction. Thanks in particular to the excellent observation of one witness, detectives believe they not only know the make and model of the car, but the actual car itself. Sometimes a witness can be particularly observant, or have a sixth sense about something. One such person was a woman who was in Castle Cove less than fifteen minutes prior to Brooke's abduction and who noticed an orange car parked in the car park at White Strand. There was something about the car that seemed out of place. It was just a feeling that the woman had. The woman's husband had seen the car earlier in the morning at around 10.15 a.m. and noticed three men in it. He was then out with his wife a short time later and saw the car again. It was parked at the White Strand car park near a block of timber which was on a trailer. The woman got a pen and the nearest thing she could find to write on, and so on a copy of *The Kerryman* newspaper she wrote down the licence plate of the orange Toyota Corolla that seemed out of place.

She also jotted down the time, it was 11.10 a.m. The man and woman continued on about their day, but they later saw the same car driving fast near Castle Cove village. When the couple subsequently heard about the disappearance of Brooke Pickard they immediately told Gardaí what they had seen and handed over the copy of *The Kerryman* with the licence number of the orange car written on it.

As Garda investigations continued, it seemed a number of people had seen the same car that morning. White Strand car park is well below the level of the nearby N70 road and is shielded from a significant portion of the main road by a wall, but some people walking or driving past still got a glimpse into the car park and noticed some activity. One man actually saw Brooke's blue van and the orange Toyota Corolla in the car park at around 11.20 a.m. but he didn't see any people. About ten minutes later another man was passing by and glanced into the car park and saw about five or six people down the end of the car park. Another man also saw the orange car in the area and he had a particularly good memory of it. It was a four-door model with a towbar fixed to it, and it had a red rear number plate.

The orange car that it is believed was used by the abductors had been taken without its owner's knowledge from north Co. Kilkenny. Sometime after Brooke was abducted the car was left in the grounds of Limerick Regional Hospital. It was a 1980 Toyota Corolla and there were a number of stickers on the car, including one for the *Italia* 90 soccer World Cup. The car was later forensically examined and it was established that it had been recently cleaned both inside and out. Brush fibres were found at the windows of the car which looked like plastic automatic car-wash fibres, and there was very little dust or debris inside the car. It appeared that after the car had been used in the abduction of Brooke Pickard, someone had gone to great lengths to try and remove any trace of evidence from the vehicle.

It's possible the Toyota Corolla was indeed suffering some genuine engine trouble on the day Brooke was abducted. When later examined the Corolla had dirt in the carburettor and was cutting out. A number of witnesses who had seen a similar car on the Ring of Kerry on Thursday 25 April, the day prior to the abduction, described seeing an orange car parked awkwardly on the side of the road. The witnesses all saw the car close to the village of Sneem, nine miles east of Castle Cove. They later told Gardaí that the way the car was parked made them think it had broken down. The car these witnesses saw was very like the car used in the abduction. It had a red rear number plate, a towbar and was an orange Toyota Corolla. This opens up the possibility that the armed gang were in the Co. Kerry area at least one day before they abducted Brooke. Perhaps they had been carrying out reconnaissance or perhaps they were meeting with one or more local people to finalise plans for the abduction.

The fact that the car believed used in the abduction was later found to be cutting out also opens up the possibility that Brooke had indeed believed he was going to White Strand car park to help fix a car. It is just a theory, but given the fact that Brooke was a good mechanic, perhaps the fact that the Toyota Corolla was giving trouble was a convenient inconvenience. Perhaps the gang decided to use a truthful reason to entice Brooke down to the car park. Perhaps the plan involved making sure he brought his van as well. Perhaps Brooke bought the petrol en route to the car park in case that was the simple problem with the car. Perhaps the person who had waved him down as he drove onto the main road was actually being genuine in saying he had car trouble. Perhaps the abduction was a spur of the moment decision by other people who had been in the car and were waiting. However, if this is the case, why has the person who drove into the car park with Brooke never come forward to say what happened? That man's failure to identify himself and say what he knows has led Gardaí to strongly believe that he was part of the abduction plot, and that coincidentally, the getaway car later broke down completely and was abandoned in Limerick.

The investigation into the disappearance of Brooke Pickard was essentially a criminal investigation from the moment Gardaí were alerted. Once Sergeant Michael Griffin took the phone call at Caherciveen station which first raised the alarm, detectives knew they were dealing with an armed abduction and possible murder. A large team of Gardaí was assembled, led by Chief Superintendent Donal O'Sullivan and Superintendent Thomas Lally. A major search was undertaken throughout Castle Cove and beyond for Brooke, his blue van, and the orange Toyota Corolla. A thorough search of the coastline was conducted, and the army helicopter was used to search the nearby mountainous terrain. A full description of Brooke was issued to the local and national media—slim but fit, short cropped grey-brown hair, grey-brown stubble, would normally wear wire-rimmed glasses for driving, a distinctive nose, square jaw bone and Yorkshire accent. Brooke had previously worn a full beard but had recently shaved it off and wore stubble instead. The appeal also included the information that Brooke smoked rolled-up cigarettes and had a pleasant manner.

Within days of Brooke's disappearance, much information was coming to light. There were now suggestions that another abduction attempt had been made on the same Kerry peninsula within a few hours of Brooke's disappearance. Information was coming into the investigation team suggesting another man had managed to escape from armed men when he realised he was about to be abducted. It was quite possible that there might be a link between the two. It's a lead Gardaí are still actively following.

There was also talk that at least one person might have seen Brooke fighting back against the men who attacked him. There was a rumour that a man had seen Brooke being struck on the back of the head with a firearm and then being bundled into his own van. Extensive interviews of all local people led to information suggesting that men from Northern Ireland had previously visited the area. A number of people in Cos. Kerry and Cork were also nominated as perhaps having more information than they were giving. In the first few days of May 1991 a number of people were arrested in connection with Brooke's disappearance. The investigation into the abduction of Brooke Pickard was soon unearthing information of other suspected criminal activity in the south-west of the country. It was becoming apparent that the investigation would be very complex and time-consuming. Assistance was sought from the Crime and Security Branch at Garda Headquarters, and two experienced officers, Detective Superintendent Tom Connolly and Detective Garda Bernie Hanley, travelled to Kerry to assist in the case.

Gardaí spoke at length with the young girl who had been on horseback when she saw the masked man in White Strand car park. Despite her young age, her recall was very good. The orange car was parked facing towards the beach, she remembered. The masked man who had suddenly appeared from the side of a vacant holiday home was wearing a balaclava which had holes for the eyes but no hole for the mouth. He was wearing a blue jacket with white stripes from the shoulders to the sleeves. He seemed to be hunched up but running and was beckoning with his right hand to someone behind him.

The girl also gave as much information as she could about the man she had earlier seen walking in Castle Cove and who was quite possibly the man that had later been in the passenger seat of Brooke's van as it had entered White Strand car park. The girl remembered he was wearing a white jumper and he might have had a moustache. She had seen him walking near the creamery stop in the village. She did not recognise him.

As friends and neighbours sought to comfort Penny, her daughter and sons, Gardaí continued extensive searches along the coastline. They walked for miles both east and west of Castle Cove, but there was no sign of Brooke and no sign yet of his van. However, the Toyota Corolla was soon located in Limerick because the licence plate had not been altered by the gang which had taken it from Co. Kilkenny, so detectives soon built up a picture of how it had been taken to Co. Kerry and, some time after Brooke's abduction, the Corolla was then abandoned in the grounds of Limerick Regional Hospital. A search of the car did not reveal any clue as to what had happened to Brooke. Gardaí continued to search around Co. Kerry but it was like looking for a needle in a haystack. But then, on Thursday 16 May—twenty days after Brooke was abducted—his van was found burnt out 27 miles from his home.

It was 3.35 p.m. when Garda Tom O'Connor received an anonymous call at Caherciveen station to say there was an abandoned van near Shronaloughane Forest, deep in the mountains north-east of Waterville. Garda O'Connor immediately told his colleagues and one hour later Gardaí found what was left of Brooke's van at the end of a track at the entrance to a wood in the townland of Derreennageeha, just south of Shronaloughane. The van had been driven as far as it could along a dirt-track off the winding, hilly country road. A large tree had long ago fallen across a section of the dirt-track and so the van had been abandoned about 300 yards in off the road, where it could go no further. It had then been set on fire. The number plate was still on the van—YNP 231W—this was

Brooke Pickard's van, last seen three weeks previously at White Strand car park.

Garda enquiries would later lead them to believe that the person who made the anonymous call alerting them to the burnt-out van had merely been passing by and saw the van. This person did not have any involvement at all in what had happened to Brooke. There had been a good deal of media appeals about the missing Ford Transit van so the person who made the call may have rightly believed they had found Brooke's van, but didn't want to have anything further to do with the case. They had done their civic duty by alerting detectives about their chance discovery.

The scene at Derreennageeha was immediately sealed off and a team from the Garda Technical Bureau arranged to travel to the forest from Dublin the next day. Detective Sergeant Edwin Hancock from Ballistics, Detective Garda Moses Morrissey from the Fingerprint section, Detective Garda Peter O'Connor from the Photographic section and Detective Eamon Murphy from the Mapping section each had a very precise and important job to do. The discovery of Brooke Pickard's van was a tangible lead. The abductors might have left trace evidence at the scene, either inside or outside the vehicle. The van had been badly damaged by fire, but a number of items were removed for further examination. One of the first things found in the van was the exploded remnants of a round of ammunition. It was a bullet designed for use in a revolver. A technical examination by Detective Sergeant Hancock showed that the round had not been fired from a weapon but it had exploded with the heat of the fire in the van. The detective found the casing of the round also in the rear of the vehicle.

Other items were removed from the van, each a potential clue to what had happened to Brooke, each a normal everyday item which gave an insight into Brooke's hard-working lifestyle.

Gardaí removed one brown leather boot from the van, and a pair of orange and yellow coloured boot laces. The head of a garden fork was found, along with a hacksaw, a chainsaw, shovel, spanners and pliers—all items Brooke used for work on the farm. Two religious medals were found in the debris along with some buttons and a number of 2p coins.

As the forensic search of the van was continuing, a major search of Derreennageeha Forest was also being conducted. Detectives were very conscious that Brooke might have been driven in the back of his own van to the remote forest high in the mountains and then murdered. It was possible that his killers had then tried to hide his body nearby. On 17 May a large team of Gardaí walked through the forest looking for any clue, any piece of clothing, any trace of violence, any trace of Brooke. Even with the assistance of search dogs, officers were faced with a massive search area. The forest where Brooke's van had been found comprised 400 acres. There were a number of other forests and mountains in the area where Brooke's attackers could have hidden him. It was assumed that Brooke's van had been driven to its final destination from the Waterville direction, so a full 12-mile stretch of road was searched for a width of 50 yards on both sides. Despite extensive searches no trace of Brooke was found.

If Brooke was killed, there is no way to definitively say how he met his death. There are some suggestions that he was struck on the head with a firearm as he was being abducted. This may have rendered him unconscious or could have caused a fatal injury. The discovery of a bullet in Brooke's van would certainly lend to the theory that the abductors carried weapons which were fully loaded. However, there was no evidence of a weapon having been fired—the bullet found in Brooke's van had exploded due to the fire that was set—but its discovery does lend weight to the theory that Brooke may have been forced to walk at gunpoint from his own van after it came to a stop at Derreennageeha. Perhaps he was transferred to another vehicle, but it is quite possible that he was forced to walk deep into one of the forested areas in this remote part of Co. Kerry. Although his abduction was not considered the work of a paramilitary organisation, history has shown that such groups would force people they abducted to walk quite some distance from any road before they were executed and buried in unmarked graves in remote locations. Perhaps the abductors of Brooke Pickard did the same thing. The more you look at the case, the more you have to wonder if the answer to Brooke's disappearance lies within a mile or two of where his van was found abandoned and burnt out.

There were only two ways for Brooke's abductors to drive his van from Castle Cove to Derreennageeha Forest. Gardaí later drove both journeys and, based on all the information they have, one theory is favoured over the other. While it is technically possible that Brooke's van could have been driven east of Castle Cove along the Ring of Kerry towards Sneem and then high up into the mountains, this journey would have been more awkward and taken almost an hour. The more logical route for the abductors would have been to come out of White Strand car park and turn left, heading west along the Ring of Kerry through Castle Cove and passing just a short distance from Brooke's home, which was up a hill to the right. Keeping on the N70, the van would have driven through the village of Caherdaniel before entering the coastal town of Waterville. From there the van would have taken a right and driven high up the mountains, eventually passing over Lisatinnig Bridge close to the source of the River Inny. Just a mile further on is Derreennageeha Forest, which lies at the foothills of two impressive mountains—Knocknacusha and Knocknagapple. The journey from Castle Cove through Waterville to this location is almost 27 miles and takes 45 minutes. It's much quicker and more convenient than coming from the east. There are no houses for miles. Derreennageeha Forest is one of the most remote places you could find. And it is here that Brooke Pickard's van was set on fire. It is also entirely possible that it is here or very close to here that Brooke was murdered and his body hidden.

If Brooke Pickard's body lies hidden in this part of Co. Kerry, only a major search using the latest technology may find him. An extensive search of the terrain in 1991 did not locate any trace of Brooke, but search techniques and expertise have developed and improved significantly in the last twenty years, and specialist equipment has also advanced. A full and extensive new search of the terrain around Derreennageeha must be undertaken.

Penny Pickard has never been to the spot where her husband's van was found abandoned. She knows generally where it is, some miles north-east of Waterville, but she has found the prospect of going there too upsetting. She remembers the fear she and her children felt when news came that Brooke's van had been found. "It was very scary. We were very much expecting that the Gardaí were going to find Brooke's body imminently. We were also very surprised that it had taken three weeks to find the van and it had only been found by chance. It was a very disturbing and sinister feeling when Brooke's van was found."

Although Gardaí suspect men from Northern Ireland were involved in Brooke's abduction, detectives believe the gang must have had assistance from someone in Co. Kerry. The location where the van was abandoned was too remote, too out of the way to have been the sole work of outsiders. When you consider that the Toyota Corolla was found abandoned in Limerick, it seems the gang wished to get out of Kerry as quickly as possible. Going to Derreennageeha Forest without local assistance might not be a wise move for people who didn't know the area, and who might run the risk of getting lost in the mountains. It seems logical that someone led them to that spot, someone who perhaps travelled in Brooke's van, or drove in the Toyota Corolla, or perhaps in another vehicle. Someone who knew Co. Kerry, who knew where to hide the van, and perhaps where to hide Brooke. Perhaps that person didn't physically travel to the forest but had given a map to the abductors indicating a well-concealed hiding place high in the mountains. The location where Brooke's van was abandoned ties in with the belief of Gardaí that one or more people living in Co. Kerry may have been part of the plot to abduct Brooke.

In the first few days and weeks after Brooke's disappearance, friends from Sneem and Caherciveen rallied around Penny and her children. A friend came to man the farm and cooked meals for Lisa and Penny. Other friends had kindly taken the boys into their home to keep them safe, away from the trauma and to leave Penny free for what seemed like endless, if vital conversations with Gardaí. As the weeks passed, Penny was trying to keep things going for her children. And all the while she was hoping Brooke would suddenly reappear. It was a very traumatic and stressful time.

As weeks turned into months and eventually years, Penny and her four children were left in limbo. All the indications were that Brooke had been murdered, but in the absence of his body being found, there was no real certainty about what had happened. Although a dozen people had been arrested, no charges were brought and there was no trace of Brooke. Detectives wanted to interview at least five men from Northern Ireland but they were no longer in the Republic of Ireland. The Garda investigation eventually wound down and the media moved on to the next story. Penny was now faced with bringing up the family by herself.

The one thing that kept me going was my foundation of trust in, and reliance on, God. I cried out to God for help in 1985 at a time of family stress. My prayers were quickly answered, and I avidly read the Bible and committed my life to the Lord. Back then, Brooke and I started to rebuild our life together. The foundation laid in my life at that time greatly prepared me to still find peace, strength and hope during the ensuing tragedies and traumas.

Amid the emotional turmoil there were also practical problems, which can affect any family of a missing person. In Brooke's case the problems were particularly acute because family assets were in his name.

"When someone goes missing presumed dead all their assets are frozen for seven years," explains Penny.

It's seven years before you can begin the process of having a missing person declared legally dead. So we had this unfinished house to maintain and the whole farm to maintain and our capital was frozen in the bank. I couldn't have sold the house even if I'd wanted to, as it was frozen too. It actually took 14 years before money was freed up for the family. That period was extremely difficult. It was frustrating that there was money in the bank, but I couldn't use Brooke's money to maintain his own assets. We were in financial hardship.

In January 1994, another tragedy struck the Pickard family. Less than three years after Brooke disappeared, the eldest child in the family, Lisa, passed away following a road traffic accident.

She was just 17 years old. Lisa had been seven when the family had moved from England to Castle Cove. She loved the country life, with her pet chickens and later her ponies. At seventeen, she was making plans for university. She was a very strong, capable person, fun-loving, with a great sense of humour. She was well loved within the community and her loss was massive. Lisa is now laid to rest near Castle Cove.

A file was sent to the Director of Public Prosecutions by Gardaí investigating Brooke's disappearance. Detectives believed that up to five men had been present when Brooke was abducted and some of those men were armed. Having interviewed a number of people in the south-west of the country, Gardaí believed the abduction might have been related to an attempt to steal money which the gang believed Brooke had in his possession. Although a number of men from Northern Ireland were known to have visited Castle Cove prior to Brooke's abduction and were believed to have carried out the attack, there was no evidence that the abduction was carried out by an illegal organisation. The investigation had been hampered because a number of the suspects had returned to Northern Ireland and were beyond the reach of Gardaí. Having studied the file in late 1991 the DPP decided no charges could be brought at that time.

As part of their enquiries, Gardaí examined Brooke's one brush with the law during his life in Ireland. It was in December 1988 that he and another Englishman were arrested in Dún Laoghaire in Dublin after detectives found Brooke's friend in possession of a modified starting pistol. A court later heard that Brooke had been owed £4,000 by a man who in turn was owed money by others. Brooke and his friend had gone to try and collect the debt from these other people and the gun had been brandished. "He lent money to someone and was angry that he hadn't got it back," recalls Penny. "He went to retrieve the money and took someone with him. The person who owed him the money claimed he had had it taken from him by two others. Brooke and his friend went to try and retrieve the money from these two people but one of them called the Gardaí and took Brooke's number plate. It was a foolish venture that he had gone on and the courts recognised it as such. He eventually received a suspended sentence. He never got his money back." Detectives are satisfied that this incident had nothing to do with Brooke's abduction two and a half years later.

Penny tells me that after Brooke's abduction his family still held out some hope that he might turn up alive. The family were clutching to things, trying to make sense of what was a mystery. Penny recalls Brooke had always liked a song by comedian Billy Connolly called 'John Stonehouse Went Swimming'. The song told the true story of how a British MP faked his own death in 1974 by leaving a pile of clothes on a beach in Miami. John Stonehouse was trying to escape charges in England of theft, fraud and deception. It was initially thought Stonehouse had tragically drowned in Miami before he was found by Australian police living under an assumed name in Melbourne. He was later extradited and served a prison sentence in England. Brooke really liked Billy Connolly's musical take on the story. After Brooke disappeared himself, his family wondered if he too might have headed off somewhere to start afresh. He had left home twice before without any prior notice but had left a note behind each time to say he had gone away. On one of those occasions he had travelled to England. Brooke's family knew him best, and knowing him the way they did, they wondered if he might have gone away again. Maybe he was somewhere like South America? Maybe he had somehow faked his own death? However, over time such thoughts by the Pickard family faded somewhat. No matter what way you considered it, you couldn't get away from the fact that an armed gang had been seen abducting Brooke from White Strand car park. Everything after that was speculation, but when he was last seen Brooke was in imminent danger.

Co. Kerry has been the scene of another mysterious disappearance of someone who came to make Ireland their home. On the afternoon of 2 July 1978 a 26-year-old Dutch woman named Leidy Kaspersma vanished just a few miles south of Kenmare. Leidy was last seen by her English boyfriend after she got out of their car and began walking along the road near where they were living. She has not been seen since. Neither has there been any trace of the cream woollen shoulder bag she was carrying or matching jacket she was wearing along with brown boots and brown corduroy jeans. Leidy had fallen in love with Ireland on a previous visit and had decided to move permanently to Co. Kerry. She was only living a few weeks in the county when she vanished without trace. Although it is possible that Leidy chose to go missing, or met with an accident while walking in the mountains, it is feared that she may have been abducted and murdered. It is a sobering thought that if Leidy died as a result of an accident or was secretly hidden in the mountains, there has been absolutely no trace of her. Despite thousands of visitors to Co. Kerry every year there are many parts of the county which are still rarely if ever inhabited. If Brooke Pickard was killed and buried close to Derreennageeha, he may only be found in a planned and extensive search. Likewise perhaps only a major search of land from Kenmare south to the Cork border may unearth the mystery of what happened to Leidy Kaspersma more than thirty years ago.

Brooke Pickard's disappearance is one of dozens of missing persons cases which are similarly baffling. Brooke's case is obviously a criminal investigation but there are other non-criminal cases which are equally mystifying. Less than a week after Brooke disappeared in Co. Kerry a couple in their sixties vanished from their home in Fermoy in Co. Cork. The couple have not been seen since nor has their white Toyota Cressida car been located. It's just another example of how people can simply vanish without trace, and how even vehicles can apparently just disappear.

In May 1996, the Pickard farmhouse at Castle Cove suffered a major fire. There was no-one at home at the time, so thankfully no-one was injured but damage to the property was major. By the time the fire was extinguished, only one-fifth of the building was left standing and that was badly damaged. The dream home of Brooke and Penny and their children was no more. Life was now so much different to the expectation and excitement they had felt when they arrived in Co. Kerry in 1983. There were great emotional ties to the farm and the area, with more than a decade of memories, and it was where the boys had grown up. Also, Lisa was laid to rest nearby, and Brooke was possibly buried somewhere in the nearby countryside. But in August 1996 Penny and James, Crohan and Dan moved to England where Penny subsequently divided her time between looking after her children and looking after her own parents in their old age. Her father passed away in 2009, aged 98.

In recent years Penny contacted the WAVE Trauma Centre in Belfast asking if they could help her find her missing husband. The group works with families of 'the Disappeared'—people abducted, killed and secretly buried by the IRA or the INLA. The IRA were responsible for over a dozen such killings in the period from 1972 to 1981. The INLA killed one man in France in 1986 and similarly his body has never been located. For years Penny knew that the men who had abducted her husband had come from Northern Ireland. While Brooke had no involvement in politics he had previously visited the North on one or two occasions. Was it possible he had crossed very dangerous people? Was it possible that IRA or INLA members were involved in his disappearance? If her husband's killing had been sanctioned by a paramilitary group, was it possible that one or more of those might now come forward and give information, safe in the knowledge that they would not be prosecuted? "I had been at a Christian weekend in England and had been talking to a friend of mine," recalls Penny.

I had been describing how my marriage had turned around in many ways through my faith. When it came up in conversation that Brooke had since been kidnapped by masked gunmen and never found, she immediately suggested that we start praying about it again. The very next day I was on a train and heard two church leaders talking opposite me, and we got chatting. One of them was from Northern Ireland and I told him about Brooke and he described the work of WAVE, which a friend of his was involved with, and he put me in contact with them.

Once Penny contacted Sandra Peake in WAVE she was put in contact with the Independent Commission for the Location of Victims' Remains (ICLVR). The Commission has had fantastic success in recent years in recovering the bodies of a number of people who were killed by paramilitaries in the 1970s and early 80s. In 2008, the ICLVR found the body of Danny McIlhone buried in Co. Wicklow. Danny had last been seen in 1981 in Dublin. Since the discovery of Danny's body, the specialist team have also found the bodies of Gerard Evans in Co. Louth, Charlie Armstrong in Co. Monaghan and Peter Wilson in Co. Antrim. Gerard was last seen in 1979; Charlie was last seen in 1981 and Peter vanished in 1973. The Commission's success is partly due to the absolute confidentiality it can ensure—former IRA members or others can go directly to a location where they believe a body may lie and point out the spot without any fear of subsequent criminal charges. The Commission is led by two retired English detectives—Geoff Knupfer and Jon Hill.

Geoff Knupfer met at length with Penny, and the Commission studied the details of Brooke's case at Penny's request, but ultimately they were unable to accept it into their remit. There was no evidence to suggest any paramilitary link to Brooke's abduction. Although the armed gang had apparently travelled from Northern Ireland to carry out the abduction, it seemed the men were criminals and not paramilitaries. The case did not fit the criteria for the Commission's work under the Good Friday Agreement. Geoff told Penny of the newly established Garda Cold Case Unit and suggested she contact them. A team of detectives from the Unit is now actively reviewing the case. The items recovered from Brooke's van when it was discovered at Derreennageeha have been kept safe for the last two decades by Gardaí in Kerry. Detectives from the Cold Case Unit are assessing all the forensic opportunities that still exist, and are assessing all the original witness statements. It is also hoped that the current excellent working relationship between the Gardaí and the Police Service of Northern Ireland will see anyone north of the border who has information being actively pursued. The men involved in abducting Brooke would now be in their fifties and sixties.

There is also a hope that a cold-case review might see other people come forward with information who could not or would not in 1991. For example, it is possible that IRA members in Co. Kerry might have been aware of the presence of men from Northern Ireland who were perhaps trying to pass themselves off as paramilitaries in the area. With the passage of time, there may be someone who can now tell what they know.

At Tralee Garda station I met Detective Sergeant Declan Liddane, who has worked on the case since day one. He is one of the few Gardaí involved in the original investigation who is still serving. He remembers how he met Brooke on one occasion—Brooke called into a Garda station to complain about a truck driver who had been driving dangerously in the area. Detective Sergeant Liddane tells me that Gardaí would dearly love to find Brooke and help bring some form of closure for Penny and her sons.

The whole world has moved on in the twenty years since Brooke's abduction and suspected killing. People now are in different places and I ask anyone who may have information that can give closure to the Pickard family and indicate where Brooke's remains are buried, to do so. Any information supplied will be treated with the utmost confidentiality. I can be contacted at Tralee Garda station, or any Garda or psni officer can get the ball rolling.

One issue which has long intrigued investigators is why, if Brooke was murdered, was his body not simply left in his van in the mountains? Why did the armed gang go to such great lengths to hide the body of their victim? Every minute spent in Co. Kerry was a minute that could lead to the gang being caught, so why would such people spend further time taking Brooke from his van and hiding him somewhere else? There are so many unanswered questions about this troubling case.

Every little thing is analysed and re-analysed. Brooke had worn a thick beard for many years, but a short time before he disappeared he had shaved it off and was sporting stubble when he vanished. Was he trying to change his appearance, was he trying to avoid someone? Did he perceive a threat from anyone? Another issue which remains unresolved—if another man was indeed the victim of an abduction attempt that same weekend on the same peninsula, is there a link? Was Brooke the victim of mistaken identity or was he just one of a number of targets for an armed gang? What was the motive for Brooke's abduction? Did he really have cash that the gang was after, or was it wrongly believed that he did? There are so many questions, which perhaps one day will be answered.

Brooke's three boys, who are now young men, have often found it very difficult to move on. On more than one occasion one or other of them has been approached by strangers who have made suggestions to the effect that Brooke might still be alive, or that everything is not as it seems. None of these strangers has offered any evidence to back up such claims. One of Brooke's sons told me how he received one such approach in a pub in Cork city. Such claims by strangers have kept stirring up thoughts of 'what if', what if Brooke escaped from the abductors, or what if there is some other answer to the mystery. "All the available evidence would lean towards the fact that he has presumably been murdered," says Penny. "But the absolute proof is not there. If his body was returned we could sort things out in our minds once and for all."

Penny goes back to Co. Kerry quite a bit. She currently lives in England but still has strong ties to Castle Cove. Penny has many fond memories of living at the farmhouse.

It's a place with very happy memories for me. The local people are so, so supportive. They were so supportive when I lost my daughter, and when our house burnt down. One friend set up a fund to pay for Lisa's funeral and people gave so generously. It was so amazing how kind and supportive people were. Later, local people even organised a charity race to raise

Lorcan O'Byrne was 25 years old when he was shot dead by armed raiders in his family home above The Anglers Rest pub in Dublin in October 1981. (*Courtesy O'Byrne family*)

Behind the bar at 'The Anglers', Lorcan shares a joke with his mother Bernie.
(*Courtesy O'Byrne family*)

The murder of Lorcan
O'Byrne was one of
the first to be reviewed
by the Garda Cold
Case Unit. (*Courtesy
O'Byrne family*)

An image of The Anglers Rest from a news report within days of Lorcan's murder. The bar and lounge were on the bottom floor and the O'Byrne home was on the top floor. The armed raiders had walked up the steps to the right of picture, and burst in the front door of the O'Byrne home towards the centre of picture. (*Courtesy RTÉ News*)

A Garda forensic expert dusts for fingerprints at the scene of the murder of Nancy Smyth in Kilkenny in September 1987. (*Courtesy RTÉ News*)

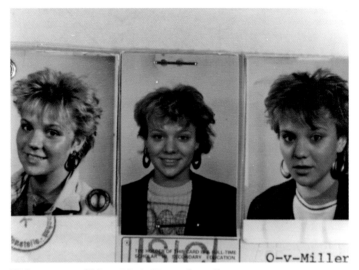

Eighteen-year-old Inga-Maria Hauser from Germany was on an InterRailing trip across Britain and Ireland when she was murdered in Co. Antrim in 1988. (*Courtesy Hauser family*)

Inga-Maria's body was found in this part of Ballypatrick Forest. (*Courtesy Police Service of Northern Ireland*)

Inga-Maria was carrying a distinctive backpack. (*Courtesy Police Service of Northern Ireland*)

An image of Inga-Maria taken before she left Germany. (*Courtesy Hauser family*)

The unsolved murder of Inga-Maria Hauser is being re-examined by the PSNI. (*Courtesy Hauser family*)

Brooke Pickard working at his home near Castle Cove, Co. Kerry. Brooke was 42 years old when he was abducted by armed men at a beach car park in April 1991. He has not been seen since.
(*Courtesy Pickard family*)

Brooke and his wife Penny at their Co. Kerry home. (*Courtesy Pickard family*)

Brooke pictured with his children, James, Crohan, Dan and Lisa. (*Courtesy Pickard family*)

An earlier image in Co. Kerry of Brooke and Crohan. (*Courtesy Pickard family*)

Fifty-six-year-old Grace Livingstone was shot dead at her home in Malahide, Co. Dublin, in December 1992. (*Courtesy Livingstone family*)

An earlier image of Grace on holiday. (*Courtesy Livingstone family*)

Grace had a love of the outdoors. (*Courtesy Livingstone family*)

Grace and her husband Jimmy on a visit to Co. Monaghan. (*Courtesy Livingstone family*)

Jimmy Livingstone has repeatedly called for his wife's murder to be completely re-investigated. In 2011 the Garda Cold Case Unit confirmed it was to carry out a full review of the unsolved case. (*Courtesy Livingstone family*)

Stephen Hughes Connors was 12 years old when he was killed by an arsonist in Tallaght in September 2001. (*Courtesy Hughes Connors family*)

Stephen was always full of fun, full of adventure. (*Courtesy Hughes Connors family*)

Stephen shares a joke with his sister Kelly. (*Courtesy Hughes Connors family*)

This image of Stephen was taken shortly before he was killed. (*Courtesy Hughes Connors family*)

Captured on CCTV: In the early hours of 1 September 2001, a man walks towards the makeshift hut where Stephen Hughes Connors is sleeping. (*Courtesy An Garda Síochána*)

Less than a minute later the man walks quickly away, as the fire takes hold off camera. The reflection of the fire can be seen on the back of the killer's jacket as he flees. (*Courtesy An Garda Síochána*)

money for a headstone for Lisa, when our family finances were still frozen. The support of the local community following the house fire was just wonderful and has left such a deep sense of gratitude for people's kindness. I didn't leave Ireland by choice, it was just that my parents urgently needed looking after in England. Castle Cove and County Kerry are very happy places for me, despite the difficult things that happened there.

There is nothing at White Strand car park to signify this is the location where Brooke Pickard disappeared in April 1991. Castle Cove village, or An Siopa Dubh, is one of many beautiful spots that Co. Kerry has to offer. The surrounding area is a major tourist route during the summer months. Just a short distance off the coast are many small islands including Cammarha, Illaunnanoon, Illaunacummig and Carrigheela. Driving back out of the car park and turning left brings you into Castle Cove, the direction from which Brooke would have driven that Friday morning. He would have come down his laneway to the junction at Behaghane Cross to join the Ring of Kerry road. He would have driven over Bunaneer Bridge, passing the milk collection stand and the local church. The journey would have brought him past the post office and pub before stopping at the grocery shop and petrol pump on the right-hand side where he bought the £3 worth of petrol, which he put in a can before heading to White Strand car park. And soon after he saluted a young girl on horseback nearby, a criminal gang suddenly rushed towards him.

Penny Pickard is now a grandmother. She is in close contact with her three sons, and spends much of her time with her grandchildren. With her own family reared and her parents no longer needing her care, Penny now has more time to ask questions of Gardaí about her husband's case.

We need closure. Brooke's disappearance has impacted upon my sons in so many ways. The first priority in terms of closure would be finding Brooke's body if he has been murdered and secretly buried. It would bring a form of closure for the boys and myself and also for his brother and sister, if Brooke was found and laid to rest. That first priority is to find Brooke. The second aspect of closure would be to find out what happened and why. And the third aspect of getting closure would be for those responsible to come clean with what they have done so that it all can be laid to rest. It has been very hard for my boys to accept the injustice of it all. There have been massive knock-on effects caused to the entire family by what happened to Brooke. My boys have had to live for over twenty years without a dad, and the people responsible are still keeping their secrets. It's a tough thing. It must affect one's world view, it must lend to a view of the world that things are not fair. Whereas I believe that ultimately things are just. I believe that God is a God of justice. The people responsible, in a sense that is God's business. He hasn't finished yet. There is a principle in the Scriptures that whatever evil is done against us, if we're trusting in God and if we are doing everything we can to live this way, that He will turn that evil to the good even in this life. That's one of the reasons I've always had a real sense of underlying peace. Obviously I've still got the sadness of Brooke not being here to see his children grow up and see his grandchildren, but the foundation of my belief is that there will be a purpose, there will be something that comes out of this that will be beneficial. One thing that I have experienced in the last twenty years is the peace, strength and hope that comes when you trust in God.

05 | THE UNSOLVED MURDER OF GRACE LIVINGSTONE

Fifty-six-year-old Grace Livingstone was shot once in the back of the head as she lay face down, bound and gagged, on her bed. Black tape covered her mouth. Similar tape held her hands tightly together behind her back, and her ankles were also bound. It was the afternoon of Monday 7 December 1992, and one of the most audacious and shocking murders had just occurred in a mature and normally peaceful estate in Malahide in north Co. Dublin. The killer has never been identified but there remains a clue which is every bit as valid today as it was then. When the black adhesive tape was removed from Grace's body and forensically examined, a set of fingerprints were found which have never been identified. Grace's husband's fingerprints were also on the tape— Jimmy Livingstone had cut the tape from his wife's wrists and ankles when he found her body—but there were another set of prints which did not match Jimmy's or anyone else known to have been in the Livingstone house after Grace's body was discovered. These mystery fingermarks were on both sides of a section of the black tape—there were impressions of the tops of fingers found on part of the adhesive side, and one finger impression found on part of the non-adhesive side. These fingermarks could well be those of the killer.

Jimmy Livingstone found his wife's body shortly before 6 p.m. The image is seared in his memory. Jimmy and his son Conor and daughter Tara have not only suffered the loss of their Grace, but they have also suffered as a result of years of false suspicion and innuendo peddled by people who wrongly asserted Jimmy was still a suspect for his wife's murder.

The simple truth of the matter is that within a day or two of the murder investigation being launched in December 1992 it would have become clear there was no forensic or factual evidence to maintain Jimmy could have murdered his wife. Jimmy had given his clothing to Gardaí just hours after Grace's body was found, and when the items were forensically examined it was clear there was no evidence of gunshot residue. This showed Jimmy had not been in contact with a recently fired weapon. The doctor who first attended the scene gave an estimation that Grace had been shot dead at around 4.35 p.m. What was without doubt was that Jimmy had been in work in Dublin until 5 p.m. He had driven all the way to Malahide with a work colleague and had not arrived home until sometime around 5.50 p.m. The 999 call was received by emergency services at 5.58 p.m. and not one of the many people who entered the house to assist in the following moments could get the smell of a recently fired weapon. This indicated the weapon had been fired some hours previously. A neighbour who was also a nurse was one of the first people to enter the house. She had checked Grace to try and find a pulse. This neighbour noticed that the blood from Grace's horrific head wound had started to congeal or clot, and this again indicated that the wound had been inflicted some hours before.

Meanwhile, a Garda fingerprint expert would soon find the fingermarks on the tape which have never been identified. While there may be some innocent explanation for the marks, such as that they were somehow put on in the manufacturing process, this seems a remote possibility. The fact that the marks are on both the sticky and non-sticky side of the tape indicates the finger impressions were put on as Grace was being bound and gagged with the tape. What is without doubt is that the fingermarks were certainly not Jimmy Livingstone's.

Another important factor which remains unresolved is that the actual roll of black tape, from which three pieces had been taken to gag and bind Grace, was never found. The tape was strong, similar to 'gaffer' tape which might normally be used to cover wires or cables. Logic would dictate the killer had removed three pieces of tape from the roll during the attack, and had then taken the rest of the roll of tape with him as he left the house. That roll has never been found.

In the first few days of the investigation a number of witnesses gave statements about a man seen close to the Livingstone house at around 4.30 p.m., a time when Jimmy and Conor were both still working in Dublin city. Indeed one witness actually saw a young man at the Livingstone front door at 4.30 p.m. To this day this young man has never been identified. He was spotted standing in the porch and bending down to pick up a pot plant, as if he had just knocked it over. A number of witnesses also reported hearing a distinct sound at around 4.30 p.m., and what they most likely heard was the sound of the murder, the sound of the shotgun being fired. From very early in the investigation there was a wealth of evidence to indicate Jimmy Livingstone did not shoot his wife.

Almost two decades after his wife was murdered, Jimmy Livingstone kindly met with me and did an interview for this book. He and his family have been through a great deal. In

April 2008, he and his daughter Tara and son Conor settled a High Court action they had taken against the State. Part of the settlement was a declaration on behalf of the Minister for Justice that '... *notwithstanding the diligent and exhaustive investigations carried out in this matter, An Garda Síochána can confirm that Mr James Livingstone is entitled to the full and unreserved presumption of innocence.*' It had been a long road for the Livingstones to get that declaration. The family had begun preparing court proceedings in the mid-1990s. During our conversation Jimmy often refers to the second Garda investigation involving a different set of detectives which took place a year after Grace's murder and which effectively cleared him. This investigation involved a fresh team of detectives being despatched from Garda Headquarters to study the case. Led by Detective Superintendent Tom Connolly and Detective Sergeant Todd O'Loughlin, the cold-case investigation surmised that the murder of Grace Livingstone occurred sometime around 4.30 p.m., when Jimmy Livingstone was still at work. "I persisted with my High Court action because unkind reports were being published erratically about the crime, and none of them ever referred to Tom Connolly's investigation which cleared me. That was always played down and the first investigation by other Gardaí was played up. And I wanted to correct that, to have it corrected publicly, and I also ultimately wanted the culprit to be found. I still believe that can be done."

It took until 2008 for the High Court case to actually get into court, and it was then scheduled to last up to eight weeks. But on the fourth day the case was settled to the satisfaction of Jimmy and Tara and Conor. "The State was bloody minded in bringing it that far," Jimmy tells me. "An estimate of my legal fees had been put at €1.3 million if it had gone to an eight-week trial. I assume the State was facing the same. As part of the settlement the State paid my legal fees. If I had lost the case I would have gone to appeal and if I had lost that I was prepared to go to the Court of Human Rights in the EU. I had prepared for giving up everything I had financially. What else would you do?"

On 3 March 1993 Jimmy was arrested under Section 30 of the Offences Against the State Act. It was just less than three months since Grace had been found shot dead. Detectives came to Jimmy's front door at the same house in which Grace had been found at The Moorings in Malahide. He was arrested and taken to Swords Garda station. By that time Gardaí had established that, while Jimmy owned a number of legally held firearms, he was also in possession of two unlicensed guns. Jimmy was a gun enthusiast, it was in his blood. His father had owned guns, and Jimmy had been going shooting since he was a teenager. "I did have an unlicensed firearm, and it was later dealt with in the District Court as a summary matter," Jimmy tells me. "I got a fine of £300, it was a rap on the knuckles. I had an unlicensed revolver, it was a Mark VI Webley revolver from the First World War. I was also charged with possession of another gun which had the capacity to fire corks."

While Gardaí might maintain that they were following the letter of the law in forwarding a file to the DPP in relation to the two unlicensed firearms, the circumstances of his arrest left a sour taste in the mouth of Jimmy Livingstone. In the opening days of the High Court case that Jimmy and his two children took in April 2008, their barrister John Rogers outlined a number of grievances which his clients had with the original investigation which took place in December 1992 and early 1993. Mr Rogers said his client had no motive and insufficient time to murder his wife, and that Gardaí had failed to follow through on other leads, in particular the unidentified man seen at the house at 4.30 p.m. on the day of the murder. The Livingstones argued that Gardai had failed in their 'duty of care' in relation to the case. Because the case was settled on the fourth day without the State outlining its full defence, we don't know what it would have said to each of the individual allegations made by Jimmy. But sixteen years after Grace's murder the High Court settlement was vindication for the Livingstones. Standing with his son and daughter outside the court just after the case was settled, Jimmy welcomed the public declaration by the State that he was entitled to the full and unreserved presumption of innocence. "This has been a long, long haul. After fifteen years we have now established that I am not a suspect for the murder of their mother, and my wife. Those who heard the evidence over the past few days will know what the family has suffered." Asked if his wife would be proud of her family for the action they had taken, Tara and Conor nodded as Jimmy emotionally replied, "I think she would." Conscious that this was an action that the family should never have had to take in the first place, Jimmy Livingstone emotionally told reporters the authorities should now go and find who killed Grace.

When I met with Jimmy to discuss his family's ongoing campaign, he showed me some of the boxes of documents he was given by the State prior to his High Court action. Jimmy knows the case inside out. It has consumed his life ever since he found his wife's body. He has 77 large boxes of documents, containing 17,000 pages of detail about the case. "There are other documents I didn't get copies of, documents where privilege was claimed. I'd say there are between 5,000 and 10,000 documents I was not given. Maybe they had confidential information from informers and the like. I handled a lot of information myself in my time and a lot was formal and a lot was informal."

At the time of Grace's murder, Jimmy was a Senior Inspector of Taxes with the Revenue Commissioners. He worked in the Special Enquiry Branch, tracing people who were evading taxes on a large scale. It would only be in the aftermath of the murder of journalist Veronica Guerin in 1996 that the Garda Criminal Assets Bureau was established. Prior to this, it was people like Jimmy in the Revenue Commissioners who were investigating the wealth of criminals or people with subversive connections.

Jimmy loved his work; he had joined the Civil Service in 1956 aged just 18. He had begun working with the Revenue Commissioners in 1959, and during his career had worked in Dundalk, Castlebar and Dublin. It was in the 60s that Jimmy Livingstone from Co. Monaghan met Grace Vernon from Co. Louth. "I met Grace while I was working in Dundalk, and we got married in October 1968," he recalls. "We lived in Whitehall in Dublin, then Biscayne in Malahide, then we moved to Castlebar for a time and finally we moved to The Moorings in Malahide." The couple's eldest child Tara was born in 1970 and Conor was born two years later. In 1977 tragedy struck when the couple's third child, a little girl, Maeve Elaine, died aged just ten weeks old.

By December 1992, Grace and Jimmy had lived at The Moorings for 16 years. They had been one of the first families to move into the estate when it was first built. The area was home to a number of professional people including Gardaí and nurses. Each two-storey house was detached and there was a distance of four or five feet between each. Every home had a spacious back garden. The Coast Road linking Malahide and Portmarnock was just a short walk away and Grace would often walk the family dog along the coast. Grace and Jimmy loved the outdoors, and they often spent time on a boat they had moored on the River Shannon.

Tara Livingstone was now 22 years old and living in Paris where she was working for an accountancy firm. Conor was twenty, and was studying electronics at the Regional Technical College in Dundalk. He was still living at home in Malahide and while he waited to repeat a term at college in January of 1993 he was working at an amusement arcade—Dr Quirky's—in Dublin city. The family also had two pets, a German pointer gun dog named Shot, and a small black cat called Frisby.

Jimmy and Conor last saw Grace on the morning of 7 December 1992. As they were having breakfast Jimmy and Grace discussed arrangements for travelling to Co. Monaghan that evening. Jimmy's brother Peter, who had passed away in 1987, had been a priest in Broomfield near Castleblayney. That December night there was going to be an anniversary mass in his former parish, and Jimmy and Grace were planning to join Jimmy's cousins in Broomfield as they had done for the previous few years. They arranged to leave Malahide at six that evening to make it to the mass for eight o'clock.

It was a normal morning on what was to become the most abnormal and shocking day. Having finished their breakfast Jimmy and Conor said goodbye to Grace and got into Jimmy's Renault Estate and headed for Chalfont Avenue on the other side of Malahide to pick up Art O'Connor, a work colleague of Jimmy's. Jimmy and Art and two others had begun the carpooling arrangement some years before, but now it was just Art and Jimmy who were still working in the one building. Jimmy and Conor picked Art up at 8.30 a.m. and they headed into town. Conor was dropped off for work at O'Connell Street at around 9 a.m. and Jimmy and Art headed to the Revenue Commissioners Offices at Setanta House on Nassau Street. Jimmy parked his car as usual in the car park. Art worked on the first floor and Jimmy was on the third. They arranged to meet at 5 p.m. to head home.

Grace Livingstone was well known in Malahide. While Jimmy drove a Renault, Grace's car of choice was a Ford Fiesta, registration number XYZ 681. She was a familiar sight at 9 a.m. mass at St Sylvester's Church in the village. Her particular passion was flower arranging. She was a member of Portmarnock Flower Club and Malahide Horticultural Society. Grace and Jimmy both shared a love of the outdoors. Grace would often join her husband when he was going shooting or fishing, and she would gather wild flowers to cultivate at home, or she would gather leaves and moss to make hanging baskets. On a recent trip, they had gathered holly to make wreaths to be sold at the Christmas fairs of both the Church of Ireland and Catholic churches in Malahide.

At about 11.45 a.m. on 7 December 1992 Grace was in her driveway. Her next door neighbour Bernard Owens was also in his driveway and they had a chat, talking about plans for Christmas. Everything was normal. Bernard and his family later headed out to Dun Laoghaire for the afternoon and then on to Bray. Bernard was a Garda, and the following day it was he who would go to the hospital and identify Grace's body to State Pathologist John Harbison.

Another neighbour of Grace's spoke with her at around 1.50 p.m. Anne Watchorne lived across the road and was a good friend. Anne was a nurse and she had helped to care for Grace's sister when she had passed away in the Livingstone home some years before. Anne walked across to Grace's house to give back a basket she had borrowed, and the two women spoke at the front door for around 15–20 minutes. Grace was in good form, and they spoke about a sale-of-work they had helped organise the day before. Grace was wearing a check blouse, wool cardigan and trousers and had some rollers at the front of her hair, with the rest tied back in a pony tail. She told Anne that she and Jimmy were heading to the memorial mass in Co. Monaghan that night. Grace offered Anne some green cuttings and she spoke about making arrangements for dinner.

It was a normal everyday chat. Anne said goodbye to Grace at around 2.10 p.m. and headed back to her own house. Apart from the killer, Anne would be the last person to see Grace alive. Anne collected her daughter and then went to Malahide village, before calling to another neighbour's house and heading home again. It would be about 6.10 p.m. when she would see a flashing blue light in the street and a neighbour would tell her that Grace was dead.

Jimmy Livingstone spent the morning working in his office. At about 12.50 p.m. he dialled home but there was no answer. Grace may have been out in the village, or she may have been out the back in the greenhouse and not heard the phone. Just after 1 p.m. Jimmy met a work colleague, Joe Stone, and they travelled from Nassau Street to go swimming at Marion College in Ballsbridge, as they did every Monday lunchtime. Jimmy returned to the office at 2.15 p.m. or so and stayed on the third floor all afternoon. He left the office just before five o'clock and met Art O'Connor in the car park for the journey home.

Four teenage girls were walking near The Moorings at around 4.30 p.m. The girls were heading home from school, and they stopped at a corner near The Moorings cul-de-sac and continued chatting. They saw a young man coming up the hill and he turned into The Moorings. The girls were only about ten feet away from him and none of them recognised him. He seemed to be in his late teens or early twenties and was tall, about six foot. He wore a fawn trenchcoat which went below his knees. His hair was blond and parted in the middle. He was of thin build and average looking. He had what one of the girls thought was a rich look about him.

At 4.40 p.m. a landscape gardener was finishing work for the evening at a house almost directly across the road from the Livingstone home. He started up his Nissan Vanette to head home. He thought of driving straight ahead and turning the

van at the end of the cul-de-sac but there were two youths
playing football at the end of the road so he decided to do a
quick turn into the driveway of a house across the road in order
to turn his van the right way around. The gardener turned his
van into the driveway of the Livingstone house. As he looked
out of his van he could see straight down to the front door. The
house was only a short distance from the public footpath,
maybe the length of one car, so the gardener had a clear view
ahead of him. It all happened in a matter of seconds but what
this witness was about to see would turn out to be very
significant. He saw a young man standing in the glass-fronted
porch. Because the headlights of the van were turned on, the
gardener got a clear look at the man. He would later describe
him as about 20 years old, or early twenties. He had dark,
collar-length hair and was of thin build and average height. The
young man reminded the gardener of a student. His hair was
dark, but somewhat long and bushy. The witness saw the man
bending down and picking up a pot plant as if he had knocked
it over. The man glanced around into the focus of the
headlights. The gardener saw the outer porch door was closed
but the inner door was opened. The hall light might have been
on. The witness turned his van and headed out of The
Moorings. It would be on that night's nine o'clock news that
he would hear about a murder having occurred in the Malahide
cul-de-sac. It would be the next day when he returned to work
that he would realise the killing had happened in the house in
which he had seen the young man at the door.

Jimmy and Art headed home from Dublin in the evening
traffic. They didn't pick up Conor because he was working late,
and was going to get the train home. The two men chatted
about work and they arrived in Malahide sometime around
5.45 p.m. Jimmy dropped Art at his house and Art would later
recall that after he arrived into his house, he put away a step-

ladder and some other items into his garage before looking at the clock in the house and seeing it was ten to six.

Jimmy drove from Chalfont Avenue along by the Estuary towards Malahide village, passing under the railway bridge and travelling along Strand Street, before turning up James's Terrace and passing the Garda station. Just over an hour later Jimmy would be back at the Garda station trying to do everything to assist detectives investigating his wife's murder.

Jimmy turned left to drive along the Coast Road before taking a right turn into the Seapark Estate and then two more right turns bringing him into The Moorings. Jimmy turned his car in the cul-de-sac so that he and Grace would be ready to drive to Monaghan after dinner. His wife's car was parked as normal in their driveway, reversed into place as Grace always left it. But very quickly other things began to appear out of place. Jimmy noticed the porch light was not on, and the dog was not at the front of the house where he would normally be. Both the porch and inner front door were closed and locked. Jimmy opened the doors with his key. It was now some time around 5.50 p.m.

To this day Jimmy Livingstone relives over and over the discovery of his wife's body. Having entered the front door Jimmy saw there was no light on in the kitchen. The plan he and Grace had made that morning was to have dinner as soon as he got home and then head for Monaghan. The curtains in one particular room were closed, and that was very unusual. Grace had previously asked that those curtains not be closed at all because she had potted plants in the window which needed light. Jimmy saw that the kitchen table was not set. He looked in every room downstairs but Grace wasn't there. He checked the back door but it was locked with the key on the inside. The dog would later be found in the back garden.

Jimmy walked from the kitchen to the hallway, turned on the landing light and went upstairs. As he arrived at the top he saw his rifle case containing his rifle lying on its butt against a bedroom door. As a gun enthusiast Jimmy had a number of guns in the house. As well as his .22 rifle, he had a number of shotguns and other firearms. Jimmy was a member of Fórsa Cosanta Áitiúil—the reserve Defence Force. He was an FCA Commandant, attached to McKee Barracks on Dublin's northside.

When he saw the rifle resting against the door-jamb Jimmy became anxious. The gun was normally stored away; it shouldn't be out like that. Everything seemed strange in the house. Jimmy entered the master bedroom. He didn't put on the light, thinking that perhaps Grace had been feeling unwell and had maybe gone to lie down. With the light from the landing Jimmy saw the outline of Grace lying on the bed. She was lying on her front. Jimmy walked to the near side of the bed and put his hand on Grace's forehead. Jimmy's hand immediately became moist and he instantly thought Grace had vomited. The bedclothes were moist too. Jimmy withdrew his hand and turned on the bedroom light. It was then he saw that it was blood on his hand.

Jimmy ran from the house to raise the alarm. He didn't know it at that stage but his wife was already dead. He ran to Anne Watchorne's house across the road but Anne didn't hear the door. He went to the next house, to Margaret Murphy. Margaret was a retired nurse, and the Murphys and Livingstones had known each other for 17 years. Margaret's son answered the door to Jimmy and quickly got his mother. Jimmy ran back to his house and by the time Margaret ran after him he was already on the phone to the emergency services. The 999 call was logged at 5.58 p.m. Margaret went upstairs into the bedroom. She immediately saw Grace lying face down on the bed. Margaret saw that Grace's hands were tied behind her back and her ankles were also tied with some type of black material. Jimmy was now in the bedroom too. He took a small scissors from his pocket and cut the binds which were holding Grace's hands and feet together. There was a substantial amount of blood on Grace's head and neck and in her hair. Margaret could see the blood had started to congeal and Grace did not appear to be still bleeding. Margaret wrapped a blanket around Grace in the hope of keeping her warm if she was still alive. Grace was still lying face down and neither Margaret or Jimmy could yet see her face. Margaret moved Grace's head to clear her airways and it was then that she saw Grace's mouth was also taped.

Margaret tried to find Grace's pulse but there was none. She advised Jimmy to call 999 again. It was a most surreal and horrific situation. Jimmy looked in presses and said that some of his guns were missing. He also mentioned that he believed he knew who had attacked Grace, he mentioned a person living along the border who was under investigation for tax fraud. But still Jimmy didn't know Grace was dead. Fr John Keegan, a family friend, arrived within minutes. By now word was spreading through The Moorings that something awful had happened at the Livingstone home. An ambulance crew soon arrived too, followed by Dr Barry Moodley, who was Grace's GP. Dr Moodley examined Grace where she lay on the bed and at 6.35 p.m. he pronounced her dead. Jimmy became very upset and began to shout and Margaret Murphy brought him out of the bedroom and eventually over to her own house across the road. He tried to contact Conor who was heading home from Dublin city, but he had just left work. Jimmy wanted to go and collect his son from the train station, but he was persuaded not to. Gardaí asked Jimmy to accompany them to the Garda station and make a full statement to assist their enquiries. Jimmy was still in shock but readily agreed; he wanted to do everything he could to help the investigation. Less than an hour after he had discovered Grace's body Jimmy entered Malahide Garda station and he spent the next eight hours being interviewed by two detectives.

When Margaret Murphy and Dr Moodley both attended to Grace in her bedroom they noticed her body was warm to touch. The bedroom itself was warm. Margaret had noticed that the blood from Grace's horrific head wound had started to congeal. This would indicate Grace had been shot quite some time before the alarm was raised. When Dr Moodley examined Grace's body at 6.35 p.m. he formed an opinion that she had died around two hours previously. State Pathologist Dr John Harbison attended the scene at 11.30 p.m. He was told Grace's body was warm when found. He took a number of temperatures and formed an initial opinion that death may have occurred closer to 6 p.m. When Dr Harbison's finding was put to Dr Moodley, the Livingstone GP said he was happy with his original view based on his experience.

Not one person who entered the Livingstone bedroom once the alarm was raised got a smell of cordite. If a shotgun had recently been discharged in the bedroom there should have been a distinct smell, but there was none. Jimmy Livingstone didn't get such a smell, neither did Margaret Murphy, Fr Keegan, Dr Moodley, the ambulance crew nor the two Gardaí who were the first officers at the scene.

The Livingstone house was quickly sealed off. Later that evening the murder weapon was found. It was one of Jimmy Livingstone's legally held guns—a hammerless DBBL shotgun. It was found abandoned under a hedge in the front garden of the Livingstone home. The outline of a most audacious and brutal crime was emerging. The murderer had entered the house sometime that afternoon, taken one of the shotguns that was in the house, murdered Grace in her bedroom, and then dropped the weapon in the front garden as he made his escape.

In the hours after his wife's body was found, Jimmy Livingstone remained at Malahide Garda station, giving a detailed statement, outlining how he had found his wife's body. He remained in the station until the early hours of Tuesday morning and gave Gardaí details of a number of revenue investigations he was currently involved in. Jimmy believed the murder was most likely linked to the work he was doing.

Conor Livingstone got the train home from Dublin to Malahide that night after a long day's work in the amusement arcade in Dublin city. Conor didn't have a mobile phone so there was no way anyone could make contact with him until he got home. He got off the train in Malahide and began walking home through the village, still unaware that his mother had been murdered. He was walking past Malahide Garda station en route to The Moorings when someone saw him and broke the news to him that his mother had been shot dead in their house. Tara was contacted in Paris and told the awful news. Just four months earlier Grace had visited her daughter in France and they had spent three weeks together, including going on a wonderful trip to Switzerland. Now Tara was being contacted by the Irish Embassy in Paris and told the news about her mother's murder.

Members of the Garda Technical Bureau carried out an extensive examination of the house. The tape which had been across Grace's mouth and tied to her wrists and ankles was carefully examined. Every person who had been in the house that evening was fingerprinted. A Garda fingerprint expert examined the tape—he found Jimmy Livingstone's print where he had cut the tape from his wife's body. But there were other unidentified impressions on the tape which were not Jimmy's. There was a finger mark on the non-sticky side and the impressions of the tips of fingers on the sticky side. The tape was labelled and put into storage. To this day those fingermarks have not been identified. They were checked against all known fingerprints the Gardaí have in their system, but no match was found. These prints remain a real clue.

Jimmy Livingstone was doing his utmost to help Gardaí. He outlined all the firearms he had in the house, including two for which he didn't have the required licences. One was from the First World War and the other was an air gun. He mentioned a number of suspected criminal or subversive figures who the Revenue Commissioners were investigating. One suspected senior member of the IRA was under investigation in relation to smuggling activities. Jimmy gave all the information he could about all the people who might possibly have a grievance with him.

Some days after the murder of Grace Livingstone the IRA issued a statement denying responsibility. History has shown that such denials cannot always be taken at face value, but it is the considered view of many experienced investigators that the murder of Grace Livingstone did not fit with an IRA operation. It just didn't fit—what was the motive? Was it to stop Jimmy Livingstone carrying out a particular investigation? If so, why not claim responsibility, or why not expressly say this was the case? Why not target Jimmy directly? Or why not simply give a warning of some sort? Although the organisation didn't always stick to its stated policy of not firing on Gardaí or the Defence Forces or other servants of the Irish State, the murder of Grace Livingstone does not seem to fit the bill of an IRA killing.

Perhaps the murder was the work of an organised criminal gang. There were certainly ruthless gangs which were capable of such an attack. Over ten years previously, in January 1982, Dublin criminal Martin Cahill had obtained a bomb and placed it under the car of Dr Jim Donovan, head of the Forensic Science Laboratory. Dr Donovan survived the explosion but suffered long-term physical injuries. On another occasion Cahill shot a Social Welfare official in both legs when his dole was stopped. Such violent actions showed that Dublin-based gangs were prepared to target civil servants who were simply doing their jobs. It was entirely possible that Jimmy Livingstone's work had incurred the wrath of some psychopath whose criminal wealth was being examined. But if this was the case, the basic question remains—why was Jimmy's wife targeted, why was he not targeted himself?

Another theory is that the murder was perhaps not sanctioned by a subversive group or criminal gang, but was perhaps carried out by someone who was trying to join such a group, and who wanted to prove they were capable of clinical murder. There is nothing to prove this, it is simply one of the many theories to try and explain what type of character might have committed such a callous murder.

Perhaps the most likely scenario, however, is that it was a psychopathic young man acting on his own initiative who carried out the murder. This begs the question whether he knew his victim, or was Grace simply the unfortunate victim of a random burglar. There was no sign of a break-in, but perhaps Grace answered the front door to someone who initially looked innocent. Perhaps Grace was punched and quickly disorientated, then forced upstairs and bound and gagged. Perhaps the burglar then found the guns in the house, and for some reason decided to shoot Grace as she lay face down on her bed. Her clothing had not been disturbed so sexual assault was not a motive for the murder. Was the killer someone who was high on drugs, who forced his way into the house with perhaps simply theft on his mind, but whose plan changed when he saw the weapons?

It would appear the killer had brought a roll of black tape with him. The tape was unusually large, it was about two inches wide. The origin of the tape, the place it was manufactured, was never identified. But what type of person carries black tape with them? Did they carry it with the specific intention of using it to tie someone up?

Maybe the killer knew that there were weapons in the Livingstone house. Maybe he knew his victim, maybe he was invited into the house, or maybe he was a stranger who for some reason didn't cause Grace any suspicion when he called to the front door before he suddenly struck out. There are so many theories, but in the absence of fact, theories are all we have …

The day after the murder the landscape gardener who was working across the road returned to work at The Moorings. He had seen on the previous night's news that there had been a murder in the cul-de-sac where he had been working. As he pulled into the estate he saw that the house where he had seen the man standing in the porch the previous afternoon was the house which was now sealed off. He immediately spoke to a Garda and gave a description of the man he had seen. He told of seeing the young man picking up a large pot plant in the porch. The gardener pointed out a large leafy plant on the left-hand side of the door. That looked like the plant the unidentified young man had touched. The witness was later asked if it might have been Grace he had seen in the porch, but the gardener was adamant it was a young man. Four teenage girls also gave statements about a young man they had seen near The Moorings. He wasn't a local, they didn't recognise him.

Four of Grace's neighbours gave statements outlining how they all, independently of each other, heard a loud sound at around 4.30 p.m. on the day of the murder. One woman likened the sound to what you might hear if someone struck an empty oil tank. One of the women had experience of guns where she had grown up in the countryside and she said she knew the sound of a firearm when she heard it. She believed the sound she heard at 4.30 p.m. on the day of the murder was a gunshot.

The gardener who had seen the unidentified youth at 4.40 p.m. on the day of the murder had told Gardaí that he didn't see any car in the driveway of the Livingstone home. This raised the possibility that Grace had gone out for a drive and later come home not knowing there was an intruder in the house. Had someone been watching Grace's movements that afternoon and waited until she had gone out of the house before breaking in? But there was no sign of a break-in, no damage to the front or back door. For every theory it seemed there was something to knock it back. What was without doubt was that Grace's car was parked in the driveway as normal by the time Jimmy came home that evening.

As investigations continued it was established that a young man had called to a number of houses close to The Moorings cul-de-sac that afternoon and represented himself as a collector for a recognised charity. When Gardaí checked with that charity they discovered it did not have any registered collectors in the Malahide area on 7 December 1992.

As the investigation continued, Gardaí sent a file to the Director of Public Prosecutions in relation to the two unlicensed firearms which Jimmy Livingstone had at his home. In the hours and days after Grace's murder, Jimmy had volunteered all the information he had about the guns he kept. To this day he is still very upset about his arrest under Section 30 of the Offences Against the State Act in March of 1993. He was later summonsed to appear at Swords District Court and in November 1993, approaching the anniversary of his wife's murder, he was fined £300. Asked by journalists outside the court if he was surprised he had been prosecuted, Jimmy thought about his wife's unsolved murder and solemnly said he hoped the authorities "now had other things to do".

It was in late 1993 that a Deputy Garda Commissioner asked a new team of Gardaí to carry out a cold-case review of the unsolved murder of Grace Livingstone. Detective Superintendent Tom Connolly and Detective Sergeant Todd O'Loughlin from the Crime Branch at Garda Headquarters were despatched to Malahide to carry out a root-and-branch review of the case. Both men were much experienced and well-respected officers. Tom Connolly had been part of the team which caught English serial killers John Shaw and Geoffrey Evans in the late 1970s. Shaw and Evans had abducted and murdered women in Co. Wicklow and in Co. Mayo and had planned to commit further murders but were caught by detectives before they could kill again. Connolly had also helped to solve the murders of three Irish soldiers by a fellow soldier in the Lebanon in 1983. Todd O'Loughlin had worked on many serious crime investigations, and would in time be one of the main detectives to investigate the murder in 1996 of journalist Veronica Guerin.

The two detectives read the complete case file, including witness statements. The cold-case review looked at every one of the original reasons that Jimmy Livingstone was initially considered a suspect, and the cold-case team concluded none of the reasons were credible. Central to the cold-case investigation was trying to ascertain the time of Grace's murder. The sound heard by four women in their respective homes in The Moorings at 4.30 p.m. needed to be further investigated. Det. Supt Connolly arranged for two members from the Ballistics section of the Garda Technical Bureau to carry out a test at the Livingstone home. Jimmy Livingstone invited the officers into the house and gave them every assistance. The cold-case team arranged for the four women to be in their homes and in the exact same locations as they had been on the day of the murder. The Gardaí from the Ballistics section went to the bedroom where the murder had occurred and set up a large chest stuffed with cotton wool to use as a 'gunshot chamber' to safely fire the gun. The Garda then fired a shotgun into the chest. This test was to see if the four women could hear the sound—was it similar to what they had heard on the day of the murder. The test was carried out at 4.30 p.m. on a particular day, but the weather conditions were different to what they had been on the day of the murder. A near gale was blowing on the day of the test, and none of the women heard the gunshot. The Gardaí arranged for a second test to be carried out on another day when weather conditions were similar to what they had been like on 7 December 1992. A shotgun was again fired in the bedroom where Grace had been murdered. Three of the women heard the shot this time. The fourth woman wasn't available, but a Garda stood at her home and he too heard the shot. Crucially, the second investigation team asked the women if the sound was similar to what they heard on the day of the murder. It was the exact same sound, they said. As one woman described it, it was like someone banging an empty oil drum.

A short time after the gun was test-fired, Det. Supt Connolly asked retired nurse Margaret Murphy to enter the bedroom and she said she could get a strong smell which she did not get on the evening Grace's body was found. The smell was evident in the hall once you entered the house. A Garda who had attended the crime scene on 7 December 1992 also entered the bedroom and he too said there was a distinct smell of a discharged firearm which was not there when he attended the original scene. The Garda Ballistics officer who fired the test-shot gave his clothing for testing and it was found to have gunshot residue.

This test firing of the shotgun was not absolute proof in itself. You cannot precisely replicate an original situation, and when people are listening out for a sound perhaps they are more likely to hear it. But the fact that the sound the women heard during the test firing was the same as the sound they heard at around 4.30 p.m. on the day of the murder was hugely significant. When you take into account the following pieces of information—an unidentified man had been seen at the Livingstone front door at around 4.40 p.m. on the day of the murder; an unidentified youth was also seen in The Moorings at around 4.30 p.m.; the blood from Grace's wound was congealed by 6 p.m. indicating she had been shot earlier that afternoon; Dr Moodley's belief that Grace had died around two hours before he examined her body at 6.35 p.m.—it all leads to the conclusion that the murder happened sometime around 4.30 p.m. on 7 December 1992. At that time Jimmy Livingstone was still working in his office in Nassau Street.

The second investigation team led by Tom Connolly also found there were a number of cars which had been seen in the Malahide area on the day of the murder which had never been traced. Det. Supt Connolly went on the *Crimecall* programme on RTÉ television on Monday 16 May 1994 to specifically appeal for assistance in tracing the man seen near the Livingstone house on the day of the murder, as well as help in tracing vehicles. The programme got a number of calls, including one from a man who said that at 4.40 p.m. on the day of the murder he had been parked in the car park near the seafront at the Coast Road. He was parked about 200 yards from the pedestrian entrance of The Moorings and he saw a man run from this pedestrian entrance and get into the only other car which was in the car park. The witness said this man drove off in the direction of Malahide village. He was described as about 25 years old, about six foot tall, of slim build, with long hair to his collar and was wearing an overcoat. The car he drove was described as an old Fiesta, bronze or orange colour with a green visor stuck onto one of the windscreens.

Another car which remains of great interest is an Opel Kadett or Fiat 127 which was driving erratically coming from the Malahide direction on the afternoon of the murder. One driver had to swerve to avoid this car and became so annoyed that they followed it from the Swords area all the way to Drogheda where they lost sight of it. The car had a registration number beginning with either HZV 9 or NZV 9.

Two other cars in the area that day were a white BMW which was seen speeding in the Seapark estate, and a black car with red stripes also seen driving at speed in the area. And then there was a red-coloured car with a hint of orange parked on the Coast Road at around noon that day. The car was facing towards Portmarnock. A woman who was walking by noticed a man sitting in the driver's seat of the car. What was unusual was that he didn't seem to be doing anything except looking at the woman through the car mirror. He seemed to be looking at the woman weirdly, and she remembered he had dark collar-length hair.

Det. Supt Connolly and Det. Sgt O'Loughlin carried out extensive efforts to identify the source of the black tape used to gag and bind Grace Livingstone. Their enquiries took them to other countries to try and establish the origin of the 2-inch wide tape which was considered to be particularly strong tape, possibly normally used for binding carpet. But the manufacturer was never found, nor was the actual roll from which the three sections of tape had been taken to constrain Grace. Expert opinion was given that each manufacturing machine gives a particular defined cut to the edge of the tape it produces, but the machine which made the tape used by the murderer was not located.

The fingermarks left on the black tape remain a very real clue which may yet yield results as forensic science advances. While Gardaí may one day get a 'hit' on the fingerprints, they also know that there is always a possibility that the killer left a trace of their DNA on the tape. If the killer was sweating, for example, perhaps they left their DNA on the adhesive side of the tape. It's the same principle which is applied by forensic scientists when they take 'sellotape lifts' of items to check for DNA profiles. The three sections of black tape found on Grace's body could yet prove crucial.

Perhaps in time we will all have to give our fingerprints as part of the process of introducing biometric passports. Such passports allow for a microchip which can contain a facial scan of the passport holder, and could in theory also hold a thumbprint or full handprint of the passport holder as another identifier. If we had something like that in this country, a number of criminal investigations such as the murder of Grace Livingstone might see a breakthrough. This assumes that the person who left fingermarks on the tape was the killer and that furthermore they are Irish.

The second investigation team which began its work in late 1993 came across a number of young men from Britain who were in the Malahide area on the day of the murder. Garda enquiries brought them to Wales and England, but of the individuals that they located, the fingerprints on the black tape did not match any of them. However, it remains a possibility and an active line of enquiry that the killer may not only have been a visitor to Malahide, but may have been a visitor to Ireland.

Tom Connolly retired from An Garda Síochána in mid-1994. His last major case was his re-investigation of the murder of Grace Livingstone. Detective Sergeant Todd O'Loughlin continued to work on the case for a number of years, following up on trying to find the unidentified young man seen in the porch of the Livingstone home at 4.40 p.m. on the day of the murder. O'Loughlin also worked on trying to locate and interview people who had been in the Malahide area and had not been identified during the initial investigation. He also carried out extensive enquiries over the following years to try and find the source of the black tape used to gag and bind Grace Livingstone. However, following the murder of journalist Veronica Guerin in June 1996, Todd O'Loughlin was one of a number of experienced detectives who were assigned to catch the criminal gang which had carried out the audacious and cold-blooded murder on Dublin's Naas Road. In time O'Loughlin and his colleagues would succeed in breaking up a major criminal network involved in the multi-million euro business of importing drugs into Ireland. It was one of the biggest criminal investigations in the history of the State, leading to the setting up of the country's Witness Protection Programme and the successful prosecution of a number of major criminals, including one who was convicted of murdering Veronica Guerin.

Todd O'Loughlin is now retired, but the work he and Tom Connolly did in 1994 and in subsequent years on the Grace Livingstone case laid the groundwork for any future cold-case review. Jimmy Livingstone tells me that he has been in contact with the newly established Garda Serious Crime Review Team to ask them to carry out a full re-investigation of the case. "There are very specific lines of enquiry such as that black tape and the fingerprints which are even more valuable today because technology has advanced," says Jimmy. "That's something that must be done now. The application of current technology to all the physical clues. And every single statement that was made needs to be cross-checked. Through the High Court case I have righted the wrong which was done to me and Tara and Conor, but there is still the duty of the State to care, and that is why I want the Cold Case Unit to investigate this thoroughly."

As part of his efforts to get answers, Jimmy has engaged the services of one of Britain's leading cold-case experts— Mick Burdis, a retired Detective Chief Superintendent who served as a police officer in England for over 40 years. During his service, Mick was personally involved in investigating over 100 murders and served on a number of national working groups which defined the standards for managing major incident rooms. Mick now works as a consultant, giving advice to various police forces and individuals about best practice in major crime investigations. He was asked to give his opinion on best international practice by the Barr Tribunal, which investigated the shooting dead by Gardaí of John Carthy at Abbeylara in Co. Longford in 2000. At Jimmy Livingstone's request he has examined the murder of Grace Livingstone in detail over the last number of years, and has joined Jimmy at a number of recent meetings with the Garda Cold Case Unit.

There are many questions for the Cold Case Unit to ponder in their review of this unsolved murder: What forensic tests have been done on the black tape taken from Grace's body? What forensic tests have been done on the light switches which were taken from the Livingstone home in 1992? What forensic tests have been done on the murder weapon? What work has been done to trace all the people known to have been in The Moorings on the afternoon of 7 December 1992? What is the complete list of items removed from the Livingstone home and garden as part of the original investigation, and what forensic tests have been done on these items? What has been done to try and establish the country, city, factory which made the black 'gaffer' tape found on Grace's body? What has been done to try and trace the person, purporting to have important information, who made a number of anonymous phone calls to Malahide Garda station about the case in the weeks after the murder?

One of the issues which has been considered is the potential for gathering fresh information that a new round of house-to-house enquiries might reveal. The murder of Grace Livingstone was so shocking that, over two decades later, most people in the locality would still remember exactly where they were and who they were with when they heard the news. It is clear that not every single person in every single house in Malahide was spoken to by Gardaí as part of the original investigation. In addition, many of the questionnaires filled in by householders in December 1992 are very short on detail. A fresh round of house-to-house enquiries might well reveal a lot more information which could help the cold-case review. The Cold Case Unit knows that it must have the resources in place to deal with any information which might be gleaned in this way, or indeed which might be gleaned from any fresh appeal for information.

Jimmy Livingstone still lives in Malahide, but not in The Moorings. He left there some years ago and now lives alone elsewhere. He no longer keeps guns in the house. He shows me file upon file relating to the unsolved murder of his wife. Grace is buried in Malahide along with their baby girl Maeve, who died aged just 69 days old in 1977. Conor and Tara both live in Dublin and Jimmy sees them regularly. Jimmy is now a grandad.

In Jimmy's living room there is a photo of Grace taken at Vernon in northern France. They were on holidays and were delighted to come across a town with the same name as Grace's maiden name. In the holiday snapshot Grace poses at a large sign with the name of the town. It is a simple photo, now one of many treasured memories.

After Grace's murder Jimmy continued working with the Revenue Commissioners. He retired in July 1998 after more than 42 years' service. He subsequently gave evidence to the Dáil Public Accounts Committee and was later given an award on the recommendation of the Committee for work he had done in countering the complicity of a number of banks in tax evasion.

The murder of Grace Livingstone is one of a number of murders of women which occurred in the late 1980s and early 1990s which have never been solved. The circumstances of Grace's murder are unlike any other; she was the only woman who was bound and gagged in her home and then shot dead. Gardaí often look for a pattern in murder cases to try and ascertain if the same killer may be responsible for a number of murders. Such a pattern emerged, for example, in relation to the disappearance of a number of women in Ireland from the late 1980s to the late 1990s. But there was no crime like the murder of Grace Livingstone. Detectives checked in Britain and beyond to try and find similarities with other murders, but no links were found. However, such a line of enquiry must be continuously pursued. The modus operandi of using the thick black tape to gag and tie up Grace must also be continuously checked with other police forces. What if the killer used a similar means of attack and constraint in another country?

To this day it is not known where Grace was when the killer first struck. Was she in the kitchen about to start getting dinner ready? Was she elsewhere downstairs? Did she unwittingly answer the door to the killer? Did he get into the house under false pretences? Was Grace asleep upstairs when she was attacked? What was the motive for the murder? If the motive was burglary, why was nothing taken? So many questions, and the only real certainties are that the killer was someone who knew how to load and fire a shotgun, and who it appears entered the house armed with a roll of black tape which they used to tie up and gag Grace before shooting her dead. Perhaps there was more than one person involved. If Grace was first attacked downstairs, perhaps being punched or struck with a weapon, maybe two attackers carried their victim up to her bedroom.

The coastal village of Malahide is normally a peaceful place. Per head of population it has one of the lowest murder rates in the country. But it is the place where one of the most callous murders occurred, and the fact that this killing remains unsolved continues to traumatise many.

Jimmy Livingstone may well publish his own book some day. He has most of it written already. He started it many years ago, and it outlines his campaign for justice for Grace and justice for the rest of the family. But the book has no ending yet. Jimmy will wait and see what happens with the current Garda Cold Case Unit review before deciding his next step.

Jimmy remembers that on the day of his wife's funeral, the priest who celebrated the mass offered prayers for the investigating Gardaí that God would guide them in their duty with regard to the horrible crime. Two decades later, that prayer remains the wish of the Livingstone family.

The review currently being undertaken is perhaps the last chance the Livingstones will get to see Grace's killer brought to justice. Jimmy is now in his seventies and is every bit as determined today to see justice done as he was in 1992. He says he has managed to keep going due to the support of his family. He mentions his solicitor and good friend Gerry Charleton as also being particularly supportive from day one. "Having settled the High Court case, that's a step forward. I don't know how many more steps there are. I will keep at this with whatever time the Lord will leave me in this world. That is what I will do. I owe that to Grace."

06 | THE UNSOLVED MURDER OF STEPHEN HUGHES CONNORS

Stephen Hughes Connors was just 12 years old when he was killed in an arson attack in the Dublin suburb of Tallaght in the early hours of 1 September 2001. Stephen was one of two young boys who were sleeping in a makeshift den at Rossfield Avenue and they were both fast asleep when the den was set on fire by a man who has not yet been brought to justice. Stephen lived elsewhere in the Rossfield estate; the house he shared with his parents and younger sister and brother was just around the corner at Rossfield Park. Stephen's parents thought he was staying in a house in the nearby Brookview estate that night. They'd no idea he had instead headed for home but as he had passed by the den he had decided to join his friends inside. He and a number of other local children were very proud of the den, it was their private space away from adults and older teenagers. Stephen had never slept there before, but he had been in it during the daytime. The den was made up of a number of wooden pallets, and had a covering for the roof. The children had got a two-seater sofa and a foam mattress which they had placed inside. They had also sourced some carpet remnants and floor mats. The den was near the front of the Rossfield estate, close to where the old shops had been. It was set in the front garden of a now disused building. Not everyone approved of the den, but for many parents it was a place where they knew their children were playing within yards of their own homes, a place where children should have been able to play safely.

It is not very often that the events leading up to a killing are captured on camera. However, by chance, the person who set the fire which claimed Stephen's life was caught on video. The footage is dark and grainy, but the man is seen entering the front garden and walking towards the den at around 5.10 a.m. The den itself is just out of vision on the footage, but what is without doubt is that when the man leaves the den a short time later, a flash of light is reflected on the back of his jacket. This seems to be some form of explosion as the fire takes hold in the den. These are the moments Stephen Hughes Connors lost his life.

There is also more information from the video camera which was recording all night from the bedroom of a house nearby. At about 5.01 a.m.—nine or ten minutes before the fire took hold—the man is seen approaching the den for the first time. He walks along the footpath from within the Rossfield estate and turns left into the driveway where the makeshift den is housed. Intriguingly, he has a dog with him on the first occasion. The dog wanders around on the road outside while the man walks towards the den. We don't know what he was doing because the den is not in vision, but a short time later the man emerges from the driveway and walks back into the Rossfield estate as the dog follows him. When the man reappears at the den and sets the fire at 5.10 a.m. or so, the dog is not with him. The video camera footage which captured all this information had been set up by a man who was trying to catch someone who had previously damaged a vehicle of his. What he captured in the early hours of a September morning were the moments before, during and after the death of a young boy.

When I meet Stephen's parents Billy and Liz, the loss of their eldest child is evident. Stephen was a joker, a chatterbox, he had a great sense of humour, was naturally funny. In his twelve years, six months and three weeks of life, Stephen left countless memories for his parents and his sister Kelly and brother Gerry. Kelly was eleven years old when her brother died, while Gerry was just four. Stephen's two youngest brothers weren't born when he was killed. But Johnathan and Jason are constantly asking about the older brother they never knew. Jason is the image of Stephen, he has the same red hair, the same smile and the same sense of fun.

The loss suffered by Stephen's family has been compounded by the failure to see the person who set the fire brought to justice. A major investigation was undertaken by Gardaí in Tallaght in the weeks and months after Stephen's shocking death. A total of 1,190 'jobs' were assigned to officers to follow up on various lines of enquiry. A total of 450 witness statements were taken. The video camera footage clearly showed the arsonist walking back within the Rossfield estate along Rossfield Avenue after setting the fire. This is the same journey the man had taken ten minutes previously after he had first approached the den while a dog wandered beside him.

Gardaí received a great response from the local public who were appalled at what had happened in their midst. But the first investigation did not lead to any significant breakthrough. Then in 2006, following pressure from Stephen's family, a fresh investigation was undertaken. A team of detectives based themselves at Lucan in west Dublin to carry out the cold-case review. Among the lead detectives was Christy Mangan, who now heads up the Garda Cold Case Unit. It would be 2007 before that Unit was officially established, and Mangan and his colleagues used the same investigative principles on Stephen's case. They carried out a full review of all original witness statements and carried out fresh interviews. The cold-case review led to the arrest of a man and woman in April 2006. The woman was arrested in the Tallaght area and the man was arrested in Ballyfermot. A file was later sent to the Director of Public Prosecutions but no charges were brought.

The fact that the cold-case review led to some apparent progress is what heartens but also frustrates Stephen's family. The arrests in April 2006 were the first to be conducted in the case. It's believed the woman was questioned on suspicion of withholding information while the man was questioned on suspicion of having set the fire at the den. The fact that a file was sent to the DPP was also significant, but when it was later decided that no charges be brought, Stephen's family were left back at square one. Sitting with the family in their home they tell me that they believe the cold-case review of 2006 should form the basis for a new re-investigation.

Amid many tears Liz tells me of the horrific moments she discovered her eldest child was dead.

I remember I was in bed and I heard a hard knock at the door and it was my sister and she told me there was a fire at the old shop and everyone was saying that Stephen was in it. I said it couldn't be Stephen because I knew where he was. He was supposed to be staying in a house in Brookview. We drove down to the front of Rossfield Avenue and there were fire-brigades there and two Gardaí and I got out of the car and I told them it couldn't be my son. Everyone was saying it was but I knew where he was. I sat down on a wall and was wondering how

this mix-up could be happening. Then Stephen's friend came
over to me. He had been in the den when it was set on fire and
had managed to escape. He told me Stephen had been with
him. I don't remember anything after that.

Stephen's friend did everything he could to save him. Both
boys had been asleep in the den when the fire took hold. Both
boys woke up terror-stricken. Stephen's friend, who was two
years older, managed to get up onto the top of the den. He went
to pull Stephen up, but Stephen collapsed from smoke
inhalation. "When you look at that video and see that man
walking up to the hut and walking away with the flames behind
him," begins Liz, as she shakes her head in anger and
bewilderment. "To think that Stephen and his friend were in
there asleep. To think of those two little boys asleep. Imagine
the fear they felt waking up. You couldn't begin to think about
it. And to think that someone could do that and that it doesn't
affect them, or that they haven't given themselves up."

Liz last saw her son alive on the previous evening. There was
a carnival in nearby Fettercairn and she brought the three
children over. Stephen arranged to stay over in a house in the
nearby Brookview estate, and Liz agreed as long as he was back
home early the next day. Liz was due in work at 9 a.m. and
wanted to bring Stephen with her. They said goodbye and Liz
and the rest of the family headed home, leaving Stephen with
some of his cousins. Later on it appears Stephen changed his
mind and headed for home instead. But as he passed by the
den at the entrance to the Rossfield estate he saw a number of
his friends 'camping out', and he decided to go into the den. It
was a normal 'adventure' for a 12-year-old boy. He was just a
few hundred yards from home, and Stephen probably thought
he'd be back at his house bright and early, in plenty of time to
go with his Mam to her work.

At around 10.30 p.m. on Friday 31 August 2001 the owner of 4 Rossfield Avenue pressed the record button on a video camera he had set up in the front bedroom. The video was trained out the window and angled slightly left so that it focused on the front garden below, and the main road nearby. The owner of number 4 no longer lived at the house, but he still had some vehicles which he kept in the front driveway. On this night he had a van parked in the drive. He had previously been the victim of criminal damage caused to one of his vehicles as it was parked outside. The man wanted to catch whoever it was, and decided to record through the night. He had a 24-hour tape which he placed in the machine. By sheer chance the video was also focusing on the entrance to the disused property next door where wooden pallets had been assembled by local children to make a den. When the owner of number 4 pressed record he then locked up the house and headed home, completely unaware that his actions were to prove crucial in launching what is an ongoing criminal investigation.

If the video camera had not been recording next door, we might never have known that 12-year-old Stephen Hughes Connors was killed by an arsonist. The cause of the fire might never have been determined. In the initial hour or two after the fire broke out, it was considered a possibility that the fire might have begun accidentally. It was initially speculated that maybe a candle had been lighting in the hut and it had fallen over. But once the video tape which was found in the house next door was analysed the truth emerged.

Stephen's sister Kelly was just eleven years old when her older brother was killed. They used to walk to school together. They had gone to St Mark's Primary School in the Springfield estate a mile or two away. They had actually been in the same class and made their First Holy Communion together. Stephen had been kept back a year in school. He was diagnosed with dyslexia and later moved to St Thomas' Primary School in Jobstown. Stephen would have been due to start sixth class just two days after his death. His four-year-old brother Gerry was due to start Junior Infants in nearby St Brigid's.

"I have loads of memories of Stephen," Kelly smiles as she tells me. "We had a shed out the back and he used to bring out an extension lead and would listen to the radio with his friends out there. He was a messer, always joking, always making people laugh. He had red hair and freckles and a cheeky smile. His friends used to slag him because I was the same size as him even though he was a year and three months older. I went to counselling after Stephen was killed. All Stephen's friends went too. He knew everyone. He would hang around with girls who were a few years older than him too."

Liz also smiles and agrees. "The older girls would have thought he was cute and they would 'mother' him. He didn't play sports but he was into music and animals. He loved listening to Bob Marley. He loved horses and dogs. He was always bringing home stray animals, and buckets of frogs!"

Sergeant Ian Lackey was on duty at Tallaght Garda station in the early hours of Saturday 1 September 2001. At 5.20 a.m. he received an emergency phone call from a man living in the Rossfield estate. The man said he had seen smoke coming from a boarded-up house at the entrance to Rossfield Avenue. Immediately Sergeant Lackey logged the call on the Command and Control System. Fire services were now en route to the scene. Two uniformed Gardaí—Brian Sourke and David Kennedy—who were in a patrol car in the area also raced to the scene. The two Gardaí arrived at Rossfield Avenue at 5.23 a.m. followed three minutes later by the fire-brigade.

Two fire tenders, D71 and D72, attended the scene of the fire. Fire officers from the local fire station on the Belgard Road were assisted by colleagues from Dolphins Barn. Stephen's friend was by now being cared for by a number of neighbours. He told Garda Brian Sourke that his friend Stephen was still inside the makeshift hut.

It took the fire service ten minutes to fully extinguish the fire. Two firefighters went into the hut to completely extinguish the blaze. The team was led by Chief Fire Officer Michael McGoldrick. At 5.45 a.m. the Chief Fire Officer told Gardaí the fire service had discovered the body of a young boy at the back of the hut.

Sergeant Ian Lackey had by now arrived at the scene. He instructed Gardaí Brian Sourke and David Kennedy to immediately preserve the scene. Quite quickly, Sergeant Lackey was told there appeared to be a video camera set up in the house next door. Fire officers had earlier forced open the door of number 4 as part of their efforts to fight the nearby fire. Sergeant Lackey located the camera which led to a video cassette recorder. He removed the video cassette and kept it safely, later giving it to Detective Sergeant Colm Featherstone. Right from the start, Gardaí were following best practice in sealing off the scene and preserving any evidence which would indicate how the fire had started. It would soon become apparent that the fire at the hut was the work of an arsonist and a criminal investigation would begin.

It was later that day that Stephen's body was removed from the scene. The crucial work of a forensic analysis at the scene meant it was some seven hours after his body was discovered before Stephen could be taken from the hut. At 12.30 p.m., as investigating Gardaí and fire officers stopped their work and watched in silence, Stephen's body was removed from the hut at Rossfield Avenue. Stephen was taken to the mortuary at Tallaght Hospital and State Pathologist Dr John Harbison would later determine that Stephen died as a result of inhalation of fumes and smoke caused by fire.

Gardaí looked at the video tape which they had taken possession of from number 4 Rossfield Avenue. The time display on the tape was out-of-synch by close to 13 hours. Where the tape display showed a date and time for 31 August, in real-time the tape was recording events in the early hours of 1 September. This was quickly established by looking at the images of the fire services and Gardaí arriving at the scene of the fire, and then working back from that.

The tape showed that just after 5 a.m. that morning a man walked quickly from the direction of within the Rossfield estate and turned left into the disused driveway which housed the makeshift hut. A dog was with the man but it didn't enter the driveway. The makeshift den was out of vision, but the video footage showed the man leaving again about a minute later, and apparently beckoning to the dog to come with him. The dog quickly follows the man who walks back within the Rossfield estate. About ten minutes later the man returns. This time the dog is not with him, and he seems to be carrying something in his right hand. It's very difficult to see, but perhaps this was some type of device to start the fire, or some form of accelerant. The man again walks up to the hut and is out of vision for about a minute. He then comes into vision and is halfway down the driveway when the light of the fire taking hold clearly illuminates the back of his jacket. He again turns to the right and heads back within the Rossfield estate. He turns back to look at the den, and he would have clearly seen that the fire had very quickly taken hold.

The tape also shows that at around 4.52 a.m. two girls went up to the den. They don't stay very long and are seen heading across the road within the Rossfield estate. These girls had gone to see who was in the den and "hang out" but when they realised that Stephen and his friend were asleep they headed home. The two young girls are perhaps extremely lucky. They left the hut less than ten minutes before the unidentified man first arrived there, and twenty minutes before the hut was actually set on fire.

Despite the early hour, the video footage shows there was quite a degree of activity in the area on the night Stephen was killed. Just as the fire takes hold and the arsonist quickly walks out of vision, a car can be seen in the distance driving along Brookfield Road. Indeed, there were a number of people driving in the locality at that time, including delivery men who were starting their early-morning rounds, and others who were heading home after finishing night shifts. "After Stephen was murdered I used to go out at that hour to see who was out at that time of the morning," says Liz. "I wanted to see how many people I'd meet, and I was amazed at the number of people who were out. So, how no-one saw anything that morning I don't know, I can't understand."

On the day Stephen was laid to rest Gardaí stopped the traffic all the way from the local St Aidan's Church to Bohernabreena Cemetery. The church was packed, and Stephen's friends were invited to sit up at the altar. It was a cold day, but at one stage a ray of sunshine came out. Liz breaks down as she tells me Stephen was buried in a white coffin with white and yellow flowers. "In the church I didn't want them to take the coffin. I just wanted to keep him there beside me."

At the time of Stephen's killing the family were on a waiting list to be moved by South Dublin County Council. Stephen's Dad, Billy, had suffered an injury 11 months previously and at that time was in a wheelchair. The family needed a bigger house onto which they could build an extension. Five weeks after Stephen's tragic death, the family were offered a new house in the Bawnlea estate in Jobstown, about a mile from Rossfield, and they moved there.

Nine days after Stephen was killed, the terrorist attacks occurred at the Twin Towers in New York and the Pentagon in Washington. Every other newsworthy story was swept away as much of the world focused on the unfolding story in the United States. The Garda *Crimeline* programme which had been due to be aired on the night of Tuesday 11 September was put back to the following night. Gardaí appeared on the rescheduled programme and on the following month's programme appealing for information on the man who had set the fire. Detective Inspector Séamus Kane appealed to the man's partner or mother or father or whoever was close to him to contact them. He also asked the man himself to come forward and explain his actions. A £5,000 reward was also offered by Crimestoppers for information which would solve the case.

Stephen's parents Billy and Liz didn't have a Christmas tree that December. They didn't do Christmas, they were too distraught. Two Gardaí from Tallaght visited the family on Christmas Day and brought some toys for Kelly and Gerry. Over the following years a number of Gardaí would provide help and advice to the family and Liz and Billy are grateful to all of those officers. One detective, Paul Connolly, went around with Liz to all the houses in Rossfield and helped to hand out leaflets appealing for people to come forward with information. In recent times Stephen's family have been in contact with detectives John Stack and Tom McManus and Superintendent Eamon Dolan in Tallaght as efforts have continued to try and catch Stephen's killer.

Thirteen months to the day that Stephen was killed, Liz gave birth again. "Having Johnathan gave us a reason to get up in the morning," Liz tells me. "We simply had to get up, and then we had a Christmas tree that year, in 2002. Jason was born a year later. It was our way of coping and carrying on." Billy and Liz are together since 1987. Billy is from Clondalkin and Liz is from Fettercairn. They find strength in each other and in their four remaining children. Billy tells me Stephen is looking down on them all.

On 4 April 2006 a woman in her early thirties was arrested in the Tallaght area by detectives carrying out a cold-case review of Stephen's killing. The woman was questioned on suspicion of withholding information. She was subsequently released without charge. Almost a week later, a 45-year-old man was arrested in Ballyfermot and questioned on suspicion of having caused the fire at Rossfield Avenue which claimed Stephen's life. Stephen's family knew a review of the case had been going on, and they clearly remember getting a call shortly after 7 a.m. in April 2006 to say a man had been arrested in connection with the case. All that day the family waited for news, and then that evening came word that the man was being released and a file would be sent to the DPP. And so there followed more waiting, this time for weeks. "We were eventually told that there was not enough evidence to bring a case to court," remembers Liz. "You think you are getting so close, you think this might be it, that all your questions will be answered, and then it's taken from under you."

Until the person who started the fire at the makeshift den is brought to justice, we don't know what his mindset was that night. Did he know there were children in the den? Why did he set the fire? Why did he go to the hut the first time, and then return to the hut and start the fire ten minutes later, having apparently left his dog somewhere nearby? Did he later confide in anyone about what he had done? How many people are there who know more than they are saying?

One question which remains to this day is what happened to the dog which was sighted on the video camera footage. Is it possible that Stephen's killer later killed the dog and secretly buried it somewhere to try and hide his own identity?

The Garda investigation also utilised the VICLAS (Violent Crime Linkage Analysis System) computer system to assess if the crime had any similarities with other incidents. All information was fed into the computer to assess if the crime was the work of a pyromaniac. Detectives also arranged for the grainy video footage to be sent to an internationally renowned company in England to see if it could be enhanced. The advice was that it was not possible to improve the quality, but Stephen's family believe this is an avenue which should be revisited as new technologies emerge. Liz has written to the FBI to ask if they might be able to assist, pointing out that tapes even from the time of the assassination of US President John F. Kennedy in 1963 have been enhanced in recent years.

Over two years before Stephen died, there was an unrelated horrific arson incident in Tallaght. It was in July 1999 that Sergeant Andrew Callanan was on duty at Tallaght Garda Station when a man set fire to the public foyer. Sergeant Callanan bravely tried to use a fire extinguisher to stop the man, but he received fatal injuries as a result. A man was jailed for 15 years in July 2001 for arson, and was later given a concurrent 15-year sentence for the manslaughter of Sergeant Callanan.

Another despicable case of arson caused horrific injuries to a young brother and sister in Moyross in Limerick in September 2006. The four-year-old and six-year-old were in their mother's parked car when a group of youths set it alight. Three youths were later jailed for the attack. The two children have since shown remarkable strength and courage in recovering from their ordeal. A difference between this case and Stephen's is that, not only did the children in Limerick survive, but those responsible were brought to justice.

Stephen's death is one of a number of cases of unsolved killings of children to have occurred in Ireland in recent decades. Forty years before Stephen lost his life, a five-year-old boy—Tommy Powell—was found beaten to death in a disused graveyard at Camden Row, a street located between the old Meath Hospital and Wexford Street in Dublin city. Tommy lived with his family at Cuffe Street near St Stephen's Green and had last been seen playing in the area on 20 June 1961. His body was found at the disused St Kevin's Cemetery the following day. Despite extensive enquiries at the time Tommy's killer was never caught.

Ten-year-old Bernadette Connolly was abducted and murdered in Co. Sligo on 17 April 1970. Bernadette was attacked while cycling her bike near her home on a Friday afternoon. Her body was found 112 days later hidden at a bog fifteen miles away on the Roscommon-Sligo border. One of most intensive murder enquiries was undertaken, but Bernadette's abductor and killer was never identified. In recent years, her family have asked Garda authorities to conduct another review of this disturbing case.

And then there are the cases of two long-term missing children who vanished in this country in the most baffling of circumstances. Mary Boyle was just six years old, going on seven, when she vanished from Cashelard near Ballyshannon in Co. Donegal on the afternoon of Friday 18 March 1977. Mary's case is one of the oldest missing persons cases which still remains open. Another case which continues to be actively pursued is that of Philip Cairns, who was 13 years old and had only recently started secondary school when he was abducted from the roadside while walking back to school in Rathfarnham in south Dublin on 23 October 1986. A massive investigation, which continues to this day, has so far failed to find Philip.

Each death or disappearance of a child has deep effects on the entire family. Every case is different, the circumstances of each are unique. One common thread is that while trying to come to terms with the unexplained loss of a child, parents must keep going for their other children. In time, those children take up the mantle to fight for justice. The failure to catch the people responsible for causing such pain, the failure to get answers, to get that justice, only adds to this terrible burden.

Back at the Hughes Connors home in Bawnlea, Liz tells me the family suffer Stephen's loss every single day. "To the general public I just ask anyone with information, no matter how small, to come forward. If you heard anything or saw anything, even in the aftermath, please come forward. And please don't assume that the Gardaí know something. If there's a chance you have information, please come forward. Every day we are living this, and it is as bad now as it was when Stephen died. Every Christmas, birthday, anniversary."

Stephen's sister Kelly says some people must have information about the person responsible. "People must have been talking after it happened. People must know more. Don't assume Gardaí know everything. They don't. They need information."

If Stephen was alive today he'd be an uncle. Kelly has a little boy—Cillian. Kelly is now in her early twenties and works as a hairdresser. Stephen's brother Gerry is in his mid-teens and the two younger brothers who Stephen never got to meet—Johnathan and Jason—are eight and seven. If Stephen was alive today he'd be in his twenties. Who knows what he'd be working at. From the sounds of it, he could have become a full-time comedian, or maybe he'd be working with animals. Liz shows me an A4 sheet of paper with the heading 'Fact File' on which Stephen had recorded his favourite things. His favourite subject in school was PE, his favourite TV show was *The Simpsons*. He wrote that he had orange hair and blue eyes and was aged 12.

The year after Stephen was killed, a memorial stone was put up on the footpath outside the entrance to the disused driveway where an arsonist struck at Rossfield Avenue on 1 September 2001. The black marble heart-shaped memorial stone features gold lettering which reads: *Erected In Memory Of Our Most Beautiful And Precious Son, Stephen Hughes Connors, Who Tragically Died Here On 1st September 2001, Aged 12 Years. From Your Loving Family.* The bottom of the stone features the line '*How Could I Have Protected You In This Crazy World*'.

The memorial stone is a great comfort to Stephen's family and is respected and watched over by the local community in Rossfield. Liz tells me she found it difficult at first going back to the Rossfield estate when they moved away in late 2001. "In the weeks and months after Stephen was killed I couldn't go back. But I find that I can now, I think it's because I have the memorial stone there. I still have friends and family in the area so we do go back, and we keep the stone clean and we lay flowers. Where the stone is, it will always be Stephen's place. As long as that plaque is there Stephen will be remembered. It is so upsetting to think of what happened to Stephen at that location, but you can't think like that. I've seen firemen stop at the stone and kneel at it. Strangers to the area all stop and look at the memorial."

Tallaght is one of the largest urban areas in the country, with a population of over 100,000 people. Of the murders which have occurred in the area in recent decades, Gardaí have solved quite a number. These include the shooting of Joseph Cummins in the old village on St Stephen's Day 2001 and the murder of a fifteen-year-old girl in Killinarden in 1988—the first case in which DNA evidence was used. Detectives have also shown a dogged determination to pursue criminal cases many years after a murder has occurred. This determination saw a murder charge being brought against a man from Belfast in 1997 for the murder of Garda Patrick Reynolds who was shot dead in Tallaght in 1982. The man was subsequently found not guilty of the charge by the Special Criminal Court.

There are also a number of murders in which no-one has ever faced trial. The double-murder of Catherine Brennan and Eddie McCabe on 24 November 1995 is one of those unsolved cases. Catherine had taken a lift with Eddie to the Primo garage near The Square Shopping Centre in the early hours of that Friday morning to buy cigarettes. The CCTV footage from the garage shows that Catherine bought cigarettes at 4.08 a.m. The murders occurred over a kilometre from the garage about 12 minutes later. Eddie was found shot dead on the ground at the back of his car on Cookstown Road. He had been shot twice. Catherine was found shot dead in the passenger seat. At least eight people, including two women, were later arrested and questioned about the murders, but no charges were brought. The murders of Catherine and Eddie left two families devastated. Catherine was a 29-year-old mother of two. Eddie was a 35-year-old father of four. The file on the case remains open at Tallaght Garda station.

The file on the killing of Stephen Hughes Connors is also kept safely at Tallaght station. The original video cassette which recorded the scene near the crime is part of that file. There are a number of officers still serving in Tallaght who worked on the original case. Other Gardaí more recent to the area know this is a crime which has devastated a community, and they share the same resolve to never let it rest. But while Gardaí say they remain determined to pursue the person responsible, they need information, they need people to talk.

As I chat with Stephen's Dad Billy in their back garden in Bawnlea in Jobstown, one of his younger sons comes over to ask him to pump up a tyre on his bike. This is a busy house, a welcoming home. With one teenage boy and two younger boys still to rear, there are constant sounds of laughter and chatter. The family are well known in the area. Liz runs a crèche at the nearby Tallaght Leisure Centre. "Before this happened we were just like any other family," says Liz. "Myself and Billy were both working to try and give our kids a better life. We were an ordinary family. The first five years after Stephen died I didn't go out much. If I went for a walk I'd find the quickest way home. I found it difficult to talk to people. Everyone around knew Stephen and it is a comfort to have friends and neighbours supporting us. Everywhere you go there are memories. That was tough at first, but now I find it comforting."

As the family show me more photos of Stephen, Liz smiles. "Stephen really really really loved life. He was so adventurous. He got his red hair from Billy's side of the family. Our youngest, Jason, is very like Stephen, the image of him. We talk to Johnathan and Jason a lot about Stephen, he is still part of our family and we tell them they have a big brother up in heaven. Gerry talks about Stephen all the time. Stephen's death had a huge effect on both Gerry and Kelly."

Gerry and Kelly and the rest of the family have set up a Facebook page to appeal for information about Stephen's killer. It is a permanent and publicly accessible tribute to a young life taken in the most brutal of circumstances. The family urge people to please take the time to log on to www.facebook.com and go to the page link for the Support-the-justice-4-stephen-campaign.

―――

To mark the tenth anniversary of Stephen's death, Gardaí in Tallaght issued a fresh appeal on 1 September 2011. The appeal reminded people that the unsolved killing had featured on a

Crimeline programme and had been re-examined by cold-case detectives who had made an arrest in 2006. The appeal stated that a suspect, who is now in his fifties, was not prosecuted after a file was sent to the Director of Public Prosecutions. "I am confident that there are people out there who know what happened that night, or who may have been confided in afterwards," said Superintendent Eamon Dolan. Liz Hughes also took part in the appeal, and pleaded with anyone who knows what happened that night to contact Gardaí. "It would be a comfort to know what happened to Stephen, even after all these years," she said. Anyone with information was urged to contact Tallaght Garda station, or the Garda Confidential Line at 1800 666 111, or any Garda station.

In February 2012, Gardaí from Tallaght station arrested a 52-year-old man for questioning in connection with the case. The man was arrested on the northside of Dublin and held for a number of hours under Section 4 of the Criminal Justice Act before being released. The arrest came as a result of the ongoing investigation carried out by Tallaght-based detectives since the appeal for information was made on the tenth anniversary of Stephen's killing.

The reward for information to help solve this killing is also still available. Contact Crimestoppers on 1800 25 00 25. Callers can keep their anonymity and still claim the reward if their information leads to the killer being brought to justice.

Liz tells me she thinks it is fear which has stopped people coming forward with information. She is urging people to find the courage to do the right thing. "Don't be afraid anymore. It's gone on too long."

07 | IRISH COLD CASES

The establishment of the Garda Cold Case Unit came far too late for the case of Tommy Powell. The five-and-a-half-year-old boy was found beaten to death in a disused graveyard in Dublin's south inner city on 21 June 1961. Tommy's killer or killers were never identified and never brought to justice. Tommy met his death just a short walk from where the Cold Case Unit is based. At the back of Harcourt Street Garda complex lies Camden Street, and one of the side streets off this is Camden Row, which runs at the back of what is now Kevin Street DIT, close to the old Meath Hospital. Nestled off Camden Row is an old church ruin and graveyard. The last burial here was around the time of the Easter Rising in 1916. In June 1961 it was overgrown with grass and weeds, and a place where children from the local area would often play. Tommy Powell didn't play there though, he had never been in the graveyard before he met his death there.

Tommy lived with his family in a flat at Cuffe Street just around the corner. He was a pupil at the national school on Clarendon Street and was a well-liked young boy. On the afternoon of Tuesday 20 June 1961 Tommy finished school as normal and was collected by his mother. They headed home and Tommy played outside with other children at Mercer House flats. But when his mother went to call him for tea he wasn't there. She began looking around everywhere but there was no sign.

An 11-year-old girl later told Gardaí that she saw Tommy walking along Wexford Street towards Camden Street between 4.15 p.m. and 4.30 p.m. The girl knew Tommy and saw that he was walking alone near the De Luxe Cinema. The girl continued walking on and when she came to the junction of Kevin Street and Cuffe Street she looked back up the street but couldn't see Tommy.

All that Tuesday night Tommy's mother and father and neighbours searched for him. His father called into the Gardaí and reported Tommy missing. All Garda stations and the Central Detective Unit at Dublin Castle were alerted. At the time of Tommy's disappearance Ireland was basking in positive international headlines. Prince Rainier and Princess Grace of Monaco were on a four-day official state visit, and Dublin was hosting the Congress of the Patrician Year, a Catholic event celebrating the fifteenth centenary of the death of St Patrick. Tens of thousands of people were on the streets of Dublin to greet the Papal Legate, Cardinal Agagianian.

Tommy's body was found by two young men just before 1 p.m. the following day. The two had got over the wall of the disused graveyard and had walked into the church ruin, which was situated in a corner of the old cemetery. The two were looking at headstones in this area when they suddenly saw Tommy's body at one end of the church ruin. Tommy lay partly covered with long grass. He had suffered a number of visible injuries to his head consistent with a sustained attack. The two men ran to Kevin Street Garda station where Garda Francis Mulderrig was on duty. He raced back with the youths to the cemetery and when he saw Tommy's body he immediately sealed off the scene.

State Pathologist Dr Maurice Hickey found that Tommy died as a result of gross brain damage resulting from head injuries. A jury later certified that Tommy was murdered by a person or persons unknown on the night of 20 June 1961. A major criminal investigation was carried out at the time headed by detectives from Kevin Street. No clear motive was ever established for Tommy's shocking death. He was fully clothed when his body was found.

Detectives searched the full cemetery, which measured almost 200 square feet. They found blood on the church wall close to where Tommy's body was found, and they also found blood on surrounding grass. Gardaí quickly came to the conclusion that Tommy had been killed where his body was found. But they never found the person or persons responsible for the murder of this five-and-a-half-year-old boy. A number of children who would play in the old cemetery spoke with Gardaí but none had ever seen Tommy Powell playing there. Detectives considered the theory that Tommy had been enticed to the cemetery, perhaps by older children, and that a row had simply gone too far. A brick was found embedded in the ground under where Tommy's body had been discovered. Perhaps he had struck his head on this stone while being attacked by someone or some people and those responsible had panicked and fled the scene. Officers considered how Tommy had actually got into the cemetery. The large iron gates were locked, but children often got over a six-foot-high wall at Liberty Lane. Tommy might well have willingly got over the cemetery wall, perhaps with other children. But no-one ever came forward to say they had been in Tommy's company or had even seen him after he was sighted by the 11-year-old girl walking on nearby Wexford Street on the afternoon that he vanished.

Tommy's murder caused huge concern not only in Dublin but right across the country. There was a real fear that the uncaptured child-killer would strike again. But no similar murder would ever occur. Whoever murdered Tommy Powell did not strike again, or certainly not in the same way. As neighbours continued to comfort Tommy's family and do everything they could for them, the Garda investigation eventually ground to a halt and the case would never be solved.

Two months before Tommy Powell was murdered, another killing occurred in Dublin where the killer or killers would never be brought to justice. Sixty-eight-year-old bachelor Harry Cahill was working alone at the Iona Garage in Glasnevin in the early hours of Friday 7 April 1961 when he was struck on the head by someone in what was most likely an attempted robbery. The alarm was raised when someone called to the garage shortly before 3 a.m. and found Harry Cahill stumbling towards him, covered in blood. Mr Cahill was rushed to the Mater Hospital and Gardaí were first alerted when a reporter from the overnight desk at the *Irish Press* newspaper rang Mountjoy station looking for information about the incident. When Gardaí went to the Mater Hospital they were told that when Harry Cahill had arrived by ambulance he had been conscious, but he was now semi-conscious and as well as being treated for his head injuries he was suffering from severe shock. Gardaí asked if they could speak with him but medical staff said they simply couldn't allow it at that time. Harry Cahill soon fell unconscious and was moved to St Laurence's Hospital for specialist treatment and an operation, but he never regained consciousness and he died on the Saturday night.

State Pathologist Dr Maurice Hickey found that Harry Cahill's brain substance had been extensively torn and bruised on his left side, and the main brain was also extensively torn. Death was due to brain damage resulting from multiple blunt force injuries to the head. The pathologist declared that the injuries were not caused by a fall.

Gardaí examined the garage and found pools of blood. Sergeant Edward Geraghty and Garda Thomas Fahy were the first officers to enter the premises, which was sited close to the Royal Canal. They saw three pools of blood on the garage floor at the entrance to the office. There was blood on the woodwork surrounding the office door and it seemed that this general area was where Harry Cahill had been attacked. Although he had been conscious when he was first found, he had been unable to say what had happened to him. He did tell one of the medical staff that he had fallen, but it seems that this was an effect of the gross head injuries he had received in the course of an attack.

A large murder investigation was begun with detectives from right across Dublin drafted in to catch Harry Cahill's killer or killers. One line of enquiry was that he might have fallen victim to a group of criminals from the Finglas area. It was suspected that particular criminals had been in the area in the early hours of that morning. Detectives had established that the garage takings had been removed by the person who had been on the shift before Harry Cahill and left at the home of the garage owner. This would have meant there was very little except the float left in the garage during the early hours. Was it possible that a thief or thieves had set upon Harry Cahill when they realised that there was very little money to be found on the premises? Ultimately that question would remain unanswered and Harry Cahill's murderer would never be brought to justice. The Iona Garage is no longer there. A popular pub is now sited at the location where Harry Cahill began a fateful overnight workshift on 7 April 1961.

Twenty-one-year-old Cecilia McEvoy was on her way to the pictures when somebody strangled her to death in Co. Laois on the evening of Monday 5 November 1962. Cecilia had left her home at Grange, near Stradbally, to head to Port Laoise. She never made it to the cinema. It was the following morning that two men found Cecilia's body while they were driving through an open expanse of land known as The Heath, three miles north of Port Laoise. It was clear from the marks on Cecilia's neck that she had been strangled. She was still wearing her red-and-white dress and fawn cardigan. Her green overcoat was covering most of her body—it had apparently been draped sideways over Cecilia by her killer. Cecilia's brown shoes were missing as was her brown handbag and her scarf. Those items would never be found and Cecilia's murderer would never be identified.

While the murders of Tommy Powell, Harry Cahill and Cecilia McEvoy were three crimes from the early 1960s which would never be solved, in subsequent decades there would be hundreds more cases of innocent people murdered and their killers never brought to justice. Less than ten years after Tommy Powell was beaten to death in Dublin, another child was murdered and the killer was never caught. Ten-year-old Bernadette Connolly had gone cycling on a quick errand for her mother when she was abducted and murdered in Co. Sligo on 17 April 1970. It was the middle of a Friday afternoon when a killer abducted Bernadette from a country road and put her bike up on an embankment above the road. The bike was found later that evening during a search for Bernadette, but there was no sign of the little girl.

The investigation into Bernadette's disappearance took place as a major investigation was continuing in Dublin after Garda Dick Fallon was shot dead on 3 April. The unarmed Garda was murdered by bank raiders at Arran Quay. His murder would also not be solved and in recent years his family has been in contact with the Cold Case Unit as part of efforts to seek justice for a man who gave his life for the State.

On Thursday 6 August, three and a half months after Bernadette Connolly disappeared, her body was found by a woman loading turf at Limnagh on the Roscommon/Sligo border. Where Bernadette's body was found was fifteen miles from the quiet lane where she had been abducted. She was still wearing her white vest with three religious medals pinned to it. She was also wearing her brown anorak, blue blouse and pinafore dress.

In recent years Bernadette's family has repeatedly asked Gardaí to do everything they can to try and solve this most distressing case. A fresh investigation has now been undertaken under the direction of an Assistant Commissioner. The family has asked Gardaí to locate the three medals which Bernadette was wearing when her body was found. Those medals were taken by Gardaí for forensic examination in 1970. Some years ago the family was told that the medals could not be found, nor could Bernadette's bike, which Gardaí had also taken to Dublin for forensic examination over forty years ago.

——

In the early hours of 12 March 1972 the body of 52-year-old cinema cashier Kathleen Farrell was found at Blackmillershill at Little Curragh in Co. Kildare. Ms Farrell was single and had worked as a cashier at the Tower Cinema in Kildare town. Her body was found lying in furze and she was fully dressed. Pathologist Dr Francis Martin later carried out a post-mortem examination at Naas Hospital and found that Kathleen Farrell had died as a result of asphyxia. There was also evidence to suggest she had been manually strangled. Gardaí began a major murder investigation but eventually no-one would be brought to justice.

Indeed in many of the unsolved murders dating back over many decades, it is clear that Gardaí conducted very thorough investigations. Officers did their absolute best with the resources they had, but still killers evaded justice. In January 1974 a 72-year-old widow was strangled to death in an horrific attack at her home at Killincarrig Road in Greystones, Co. Wicklow. Before being strangled Ann Meldon had also been hit a number of times on the head with a steel-tipped walking stick. There was a steel circular disc attached towards one end of the stick and this had left a number of visible injuries to Ann's head. Ann's body was found in her home by friends and neighbours who were concerned that they hadn't seen her. She was found lying on her back in the bedroom of her ground-floor flat. A highly regarded lady, Ann and her husband had previously run The Southern Lake Hotel in Waterville in Co. Kerry before retiring to Greystones.

Local Garda Sergeant Matt Shanley was on duty at Greystones station when the emergency call was received early in the afternoon of 24 January 1974. Sergeant Shanley raced to Killincarrig Road, close to Greystones train station, arriving at 1.20 p.m. He saw Ann Meldon's body lying in her bedroom and immediately sealed off the area. He saw a walking stick lying across Ann's body and it was clear she had been the victim of a sustained attack.

When detectives studied the crime scene they saw there was no sign of forced entry. Based on a last known sighting of Mrs Meldon it would later be determined that she had been murdered sometime between 9.30 p.m. on Wednesday 23 January and 12.30 p.m.the following day. Detectives would later form a view that the murder most likely happened on the Thursday morning rather than the previous night. One very good clue to the killer's identity emerged when two small triangular cast iron segments were found underneath Ann's body. The iron pieces did not belong in Ann's flat. Ann's own steel-tipped walking stick, which had been used to beat her, was lying across her body. As well as being subjected to a severe beating with implements, Ann Meldon had been strangled.

The crime scene was suggestive of a woman being the culprit. The use of a walking stick to commit an attack showed a sustained amount of violence. The two-foot-long steel-tipped walking stick could in itself have caused fatal injuries if considerable force had been used. Ann had suffered 24 injuries including 17 wounds to her head from the 2-inch steel circular disc which was at one end of the walking stick, but none of those injuries had been fatal. The crime scene bore the appearance of someone who had tried to use the stick to murder Ann in a frenzy, but when they didn't have the apparent physical strength to commit murder that way, they had then strangled Ann to death.

But there was also another weapon used to attack Mrs Meldon. The two iron pieces which were alien to her apartment were the clue to the other implement used in the murder. Gardaí studied the pieces closely; they didn't match anything in Ann Meldon's apartment, yet had been found under her body. It seemed like they were part of a bigger implement, but that object wasn't in Ann's apartment. As investigations continued detectives discovered that the pieces were part of a fireside companion set.

It was on 6 February, two weeks after the murder, that Gardaí, led by Detective Inspector Hubert Reynolds, found more pieces of the companion set. Using a magnet attached to a rope Detective Garda Michael Keating retrieved other metal pieces from a shore in the back garden of the building where Ann had lived. These metal pieces were then given to Sergeant Matt Shanley and it was found that all the pieces matched together to fit a fireside companion set. Ann didn't own such a set, and Gardaí formed the view that the murderer had brought such an object with them to Ann's home to use as a murder weapon. It is believed that Ann was struck on the head with a cast-iron balancer which is found in the bottom of fireside sets. During the attack pieces of the set broke away and the killer had later picked up all the pieces they could see and had dumped them in a shore out the back. But the killer didn't realise that two of the metal pieces were lying under Ann's body and they had left the crime scene leaving a strong lead for detectives to follow.

A pair of small-sized yellow gloves which may have been used by the killer were later found in another part of Greystones and these gloves were sent for analysis. This was an era before the establishment of Ireland's own Forensic State Laboratory, and a number of items from the Ann Meldon murder investigation were sent to England to be analysed by Scotland Yard. Detectives came to the view that Ann's killer had called to her door and had overcome the 72-year-old before she had time to react. They had struck her with the base of a fireside set which they had brought with them. When this didn't kill Ann, the attacker had grabbed a steel-tipped walking stick which they saw in the apartment. Despite being beaten a number of times with this implement, the victim was still alive, and it was then that the killer strangled Ann to death. They then fled the scene, dumping metal pieces from the now broken fireside set in the shore in the back garden.

Less than a month after the murder of Ann Meldon a woman in her twenties was arrested on suspicion of murder. The woman was later released and ultimately no-one was ever brought to justice for the murder. The investigation had moved from an initial flurry of activity and excellent police work to eventually hitting a brick wall. Ann Meldon's murder would ultimately become a cold case and four decades later her killer has never been caught and convicted.

———

When the Garda Cold Case Unit was set up in 2007 it announced that it was examining 207 unsolved murders, the earliest of which had occurred in 1980. The team chose the year 1980 simply because they had to start somewhere. That particular year bore witness to the murder of a man who was shot dead while watching a football match in a pub in Dublin's south inner city. In more recent decades there have been many gun murders which have occurred in pubs, but in 1980 the murder of John 'Jackie' Kelly was the only such killing that year. A suspect was identified and arrested but was never charged with the murder.

It was on the evening of Wednesday 17 September 1980 that Jackie Kelly went to Grace's Pub on Townsend Street to watch Manchester United contest a UEFA Cup match. Jackie had earlier gone with two friends to Lansdowne Road to watch Limerick FC narrowly lose 1-2 to Real Madrid in another European game. Jackie was from St Andrew's Court near Macken Street and had previously worked as a postal worker and in a taxi firm. When the match at Lansdowne Road was over, Jackie and his friends decided to walk back to Grace's Pub to catch the Manchester United game on television. It was also a chance to properly toast Jackie becoming the newest member of a local football team.

Jackie Kelly was sitting in the pub watching the television when a dark figure came in the door. The gunman was wearing a balaclava and a helmet and jacket. Everyone's first reaction was to think it was a joke, but then the shots rang out. The killer pointed the revolver at Jackie Kelly and fired three times. The gunman then turned as if to leave the pub but paused and turned back to Jackie and fired three more times before calmly walking out the door. Jackie Kelly slumped to the floor and all of a sudden everyone realised what they had just witnessed was all too real. Jackie was rushed to St Vincent's Hospital in a critical condition. Doctors did all they could but ultimately his wounds proved fatal and Jackie died ten days after being shot.

A team of Gardaí led by Detective Inspector Con Hearty investigated the fatal pub shooting. They got a very good lead within hours when a helmet, balaclava and jacket were found dumped in a rubbish chute at nearby flats at Countess Markievicz House. They also found a sawn-off shotgun and shotgun cartridges. The finds at Markievicz House led detectives to a dump in south Co. Dublin. Some waste had already been collected by the council in the south inner city and taken to the dump before the alarm was raised. Detectives got to the dump in time and they supervised the unloading of waste into the dump. Detectives soon found a revolver; it was later confirmed as the murder weapon.

Jackie Kelly's murder occurred at a time that Gardaí were investigating the murder of a young Belfast woman, Deborah Robinson, who was killed while on a day trip to Dublin in early September. Deborah's body was found hidden in a ditch in Clane in Co. Kildare and detectives had been working flat out to try and catch the killer. Eventually the murderer would be caught through the emerging forensic science of fibre analysis. While Deborah's killer was later given a life sentence for murder, the other murder to occur in Ireland that September would not be solved and Jackie Kelly's killer would remain free.

Just over two weeks after Jackie was shot, two men were arrested and questioned at Pearse Street Garda station about the shooting. Detectives had the murder weapon, they had clothing possibly worn by the killer. The two men who were arrested were later released without charge. No clear motive was ever established for the murder of a popular young man. Although this murder is over thirty years old, there is a feeling that people may still talk and give information that they didn't give in 1980. It is possible that someone who was instilling fear in the area is no longer in a position to do so. A lot can happen in thirty years and perhaps Jackie Kelly may one day get justice.

———

At the offices of the Serious Crime Review Team, or the Cold Case Unit as it is known, Detective Superintendent Christy Mangan leads a team of a dozen detectives. What he and his colleagues have done since they were established in 2007 is immerse themselves in the hundreds of unsolved murder files from 1980.

Each case is subject to a preliminary assessment, and if there is anything to merit a case being given a full review we will conduct it. That can involve a forensic review of all materials from a case, we look at what witnesses may now be available and we look at any other fresh investigative options. We use forensic profilers and crime scene interpreters. We are looking at what might have happened at a particular crime scene and why a suspect may have behaved in a particular fashion.

While the Cold Case Unit has caught the interest of the general public, it has more importantly seen a number of families of murder victims making direct contact with officers.

People have called directly here to the front gate at Harcourt Square looking to speak with us about the murder of a loved one which happened ten, twenty, thirty years ago. We often find that families are aggrieved about the lack of interaction with the Gardaí down the years. A case may have been unresolved and no-one brought to justice and then contact was minimal between Gardaí and a victim's family. In the Serious Crime Review Team we offer to establish ongoing contact through family liaison officers. Families obviously want answers and want somebody brought to justice. Sometimes you mighn't have the evidence to bring someone to court but you might still be able to fill in the story for a family, to tell them things about what happened at a particular time which led to an unsolved murder. We can clear up a huge amount of matters for families, but naturally what families ultimately want is their loved one's killer or killers brought to justice.

One thing which the Cold Case Unit quickly found was that not all evidence from decades-old murder investigations had been kept. As murder files have gathered dust over twenty, thirty, forty years, items are now unavailable due to the passage of time. "It can happen that evidence is not available, it has happened in many jurisdictions," agrees Christy Mangan. "But not having certain exhibits will not stop us going forward with a case, it's the result of the original forensic examination that is important."

Long before the Cold Case Unit was set up, the possibility of solving many historic murders was well known. Some excellent police work and a healthy dose of good luck had united when married father-of-five John Crerar was finally arrested in July 1999 for the abduction and murder of Phyllis Murphy in Co. Kildare twenty years previously. The good police work was shown in the intelligence of Gardaí Finbarr McPaul and Christy Sheridan who for two decades kept safe the blood samples given voluntarily by men in 1980. Similar good work was shown in the tenacity of Detective Inspector Brendan McArdle from the Garda Technical Bureau who re-investigated the unsolved murder and brought those bloodstain cards to a laboratory in England. The good luck which emerged in the case was shown in the fact that John Crerar was one of those people who had been asked to give his blood sample back in 1980, and there was also good luck in that he was still alive when Gardaí came looking for him in 1999 once the laboratory identified his DNA as being a match for the semen found on Phyllis's body. Crerar was finally unmasked as a predatory abductor and killer who had lived a lie for twenty years. He is now serving a life sentence and Phyllis's family, who still feel her loss, have some measure of comfort.

———

There have been a number of criminal trials down the years which have occurred decades after the crimes were actually committed. In the year 2000 a Belfast man stood trial at the Special Criminal Court in Dublin for the murder of Garda Patrick Reynolds, who was shot dead at a flats complex in Tallaght in February 1982. The accused's fingerprints and his glasses were found in the flat where the proceeds of an earlier bank robbery carried out by the INLA were being divided when Gardaí arrived to investigate reports of suspicious activity. The court also heard identification evidence, where a Garda identified the accused as having been at the scene in Tallaght eighteen years before. For almost two decades the man had been wanted by Gardaí; it was known he had moved to France but he eventually surfaced back in Ireland when he was arrested following an armed bank robbery. However, the three judges of the non-jury court acquitted the accused, saying it was possible the glasses and their owner had been in the flat some time prior to the killing rather than on that night, and the court said it couldn't then rely solely on identification evidence from so long ago. The accused returned to prison to serve out the remainder of a sentence for an armed robbery committed in Co. Mayo.

Another cold-case trial linked to the Troubles took place in 2008 when a former IRA leader stood trial for kidnapping supermarket boss Don Tidey a quarter of a century before. Mr Tidey had been abducted on 24 November 1983 by an armed IRA gang in Dublin and held hostage at Derrada Wood in Co. Leitrim for 23 days. An Irish soldier, Private Patrick Kelly, and a recruit Garda, Gary Sheehan, were shot dead during the operation which led to Don Tidey's release. A fingerprint was discovered on a milk carton found at the scene and it was later alleged at the 2008 trial that the fingerprint was that of the accused. The milk carton itself had since been lost but the court ruled that it was entitled to consider the fingerprint evidence. However, the three judges of the Special Criminal Court ruled that evidence of an incriminating statement alleged to have been made by the accused was inadmissible, and on the tenth day of the trial, when the State said it had no further evidence to offer, the man was acquitted. No-one has ever been charged specifically in relation to the murders of Private Patrick Kelly and Recruit Garda Gary Sheehan.

Over 120 people lost their lives in the Republic of Ireland as a result of the Troubles and most of those cases remain unsolved. A small number of those deaths did not involve a third party—the first death of the Troubles in the Republic, for example, was in October 1969 when a loyalist was blown up by his own bomb near Ballyshannon in Co. Donegal. However, the vast majority of the deaths were of innocent people who were blown up or shot dead as the violence in Northern Ireland spread south of the border. While the figure of 120 or so deaths pales in comparison to the more than 3,400 lives lost in Northern Ireland during the same period, there is one major difference between how Troubles-related killings are being dealt with on either side of the border. In Northern Ireland there is a specific team of investigators—the Historical Inquiries Team—whose one and only purpose is to investigate all the unsolved Troubles-related deaths which occurred in Cos. Derry, Tyrone, Armagh, Antrim, Down and Fermanagh. In the Republic there has been no such initiative. In the wake of the Good Friday Agreement in 1998, there was no special team set up in the Republic to match the work of the Historical Inquiries Team. The task of investigating all such murders has now fallen to the Garda Cold Case Unit.

Of the 120 or so deaths in the Republic, over 80 of them occurred in the 1970s. The unsolved deaths from the 70s included the murders of three Gardaí and two members of the RUC. In April 1970 Garda Dick Fallon became the first member of An Garda Síochána to lose his life as a result of the Troubles. Garda Fallon was unarmed when he was shot dead in Dublin by a group of bank robbers who were members of the Republican group Saor Éire. Just over two years later Garda Inspector Sam Donegan became the second Garda to lose his life in the Troubles. He was fatally injured by a bomb which had been left on the Cavan-Fermanagh border. Inspector Donegan was one of a team of Gardaí carrying out searches on roads near Newtownbutler when the device exploded. The IRA was blamed for the murder and was also believed responsible for the murder of the third Garda to die in the Troubles. In October 1976 Garda Michael Clerkin was one of a number of officers to respond to an anonymous phone call reporting suspicious activity at a deserted cottage near Port Laoise. As officers examined the cottage a booby-trap bomb exploded and Michael Clerkin was killed and a number of other Gardaí were

seriously injured. Similar to the deaths of Garda Dick Fallon
and Inspector Sam Donegan, the authorities vowed to bring
the killers to justice, but no-one was ever convicted in any of
these murders.

Two RUC officers were also killed in the Republic in the
1970s. Detective-Constable John Doherty, who was attached to
Omagh station, was shot dead by IRA gunmen as he was visiting
his mother near Lifford in Co. Donegal in October 1973. The
detective was turning his car in a narrow laneway near the
house when the ambush occurred. And in December 1979, RUC
reservist Stanley Hazelton was shot dead by the IRA near the
village of Glaslough in Co. Monaghan. He was ambushed and
murdered as he crossed the border two days before Christmas
to collect the family's turkey. Just like the murders of three
Gardaí killed in the line of duty in the 1970s, these two murders
of off-duty RUC officers would never be solved.

On Friday 17 May 1974, loyalist car-bombs exploded in
Dublin and Monaghan claiming 34 lives. Among those
murdered were a young couple and their two girls, aged 17
months and 5 months. A young woman and her unborn baby
were also among the victims. Most of the 34 people died
instantly, but one man lived for two months in hospital before
dying from his injuries. As with so many other atrocities, the
Irish Government promised that the killers would be pursued,
but within three months the Garda investigation had effectively
wound down and no-one was ever brought to justice. It seems
there was a feeling that the killers were back over the border
and could not be apprehended. Co-operation between Gardaí
and the RUC at the time would seem to have been minimal. A
recent Government-initiated report found that some Garda
documentation from the original investigation had gone
missing, and it was impossible to tell what other documentation
there might have been because of the antiquated Garda filing

systems in place in the 1970s. The Justice for the Forgotten group, which represents a number of the bereaved families, continues to seek answers from the British authorities about what they know of those responsible for the atrocities.

And there are so many other unsolved murders from the early years of the Troubles where the killers may still be alive, or where answers might still be obtained if the cases were actively pursued. In December 1972, bus driver George Bradshaw and bus conductor Thomas Duffy were killed when a loyalist bomb exploded just off Dublin's O'Connell Street. The following February another bus driver, Thomas Douglas, was also killed by a loyalist car-bomb, which was again left very close to O'Connell Street. The vehicle had earlier been stolen in Belfast. A loyalist bomb also claimed the lives of two young teenagers in December 1972. Fourteen-year-old Geraldine O'Reilly and 16-year-old Patrick Stanley were killed when a car-bomb exploded outside the post office in Belturbet, Co. Cavan. The early hours of 1973 also brought more random violence and death to the Republic, when Briege Porter and her fiancé Oliver Boyce were murdered by loyalists in Co. Donegal. Briege and Oliver were returning home from a New Year's Eve party when they were attacked near Burnfoot, about four miles from the border.

The random murders continued throughout the 1970s and a common theme would be that most of the deaths would remain unsolved. In June 1975 Christopher Phelan was found stabbed to death close to the railway line in his hometown of Sallins in Co. Kildare. It appeared that the 48-year-old had struggled with his attackers before he was murdered. Gardaí believe that Christopher may have disturbed loyalist terrorists, who were attempting to blow up a train carrying members of the Republican movement who were travelling to Bodenstown Cemetery. And in November of that same year, 38-year-old

John Hayes was working a shift at Dublin Airport when a loyalist bomb exploded in the arrivals terminal. John was killed instantly and nine others were injured. The murder of John Hayes is the only murder to have occurred within Dublin Airport and to this day it remains unsolved.

The IRA were also killing people with explosives and bullets in the Republic during the 1970s. In July 1976 the newly arrived British Ambassador Christopher Ewart-Biggs, and a civil servant, Judith Cook, were both killed in an IRA ambush in Sandyford in south Dublin. The two victims died when a landmine exploded underneath the Ambassador's armour-plated car. The car had just left the Ambassador's residence 200 yards away. The bomb had been triggered by a command wire and three men were seen driving away from the scene, but no-one was ever brought to justice. Just over three years later, in Co. Sligo, the IRA planted a bomb on a boat owned by Lord Louis Mountbatten, who was a cousin of Britain's Queen Elizabeth. The craft was off the coast of Mullaghmore when the 50lbs of explosives detonated. Seventy-nine-year-old Lord Mountbatten was one of four people killed. His 14-year-old grandson Nicholas Knatchbull died too, as did 83-year-old Lady Doreen Brabourne, who was the mother-in-law of Lord Mountbatten's daughter. Fifteen-year-old Paul Maxwell was also killed in the explosion. Paul was from Co. Fermanagh and had taken a summer job as a boatman for Lord Mountbatten in Sligo. One IRA man was later jailed for life for the murders. The other members of the gang were never brought to justice.

The full extent of the killings carried out in the Republic of Ireland by the IRA has only become apparent in recent years. It is only in the wake of the Good Friday Agreement, signed in 1998, that we now know that the IRA abducted a number of people in Northern Ireland and in Dublin, killed them and then secretly buried their bodies. Mother-of-ten Jean McConville disappeared in Belfast in 1972—her body was found by chance buried at a beach in Co. Louth in 2003. She had been shot in the head by the IRA and then her body was hidden. Nineteen-seventy-two was also the year that Kevin McKee, Seamus Wright and Joe Lynskey all vanished from Belfast. Their bodies have not yet been found but it's believed Kevin McKee and Seamus Wright are buried in Co. Meath. Columba McVeigh was abducted in Dublin and killed in 1975 and his body is believed to be buried in Co. Monaghan. Brian McKinney and John McClory were taken from Belfast in 1978 and shot dead. Their bodies were found in Co. Monaghan in 1999. Brendan Megraw was also taken by the IRA in Belfast in 1978; his body has still not been found but it's believed he was secretly buried in Co. Meath. Danny McIlhone was abducted from Dublin in 1981 and shot dead in Co. Wicklow. His body was found in 2008 after fresh information was given to the Independent Commission for the Location of Victims' Remains. The Commission has also recently found the bodies of Peter Wilson, Gerard Evans and Charlie Armstrong. Peter's body was found buried in Co. Antrim—he was last seen in Belfast in 1973. Gerard Evans's body was found in Co. Louth in 2010—he was last seen in Castleblayney in 1979. Charlie Armstrong's body was found buried in 2010 in Co. Monaghan—he was last seen in Co. Armagh in 1981. The IRA returned the body of Éamon Molloy in 1999 when it came clean about some of the abductions and murders it had committed. Éamon Molloy had last been seen in Belfast in 1975. And it has long been known that the IRA hid the body of SAS Captain Robert Nairac after he was shot dead in Co. Louth in 1977. His is one of six bodies which the IRA have so far failed to give back to families.

What is particularly striking about the number of cases of people abducted, murdered and secretly buried by the IRA in the 1970s and early 80s is that most of the bodies are believed to be buried in the Republic of Ireland. These secret burials were going on under the noses of Irish authorities in the period from 1972 until 1981. One ray of hope that has emerged in recent years is that members of the IRA will return the bodies of their other victims. It is clear that former members of the IRA have been speaking directly with the Independent Commission for the Location of Victims' Remains, pointing out areas of land which should be searched. The attraction in speaking with the Commission is that there is no question of any information ever being used for prosecuting anyone—the information is only used for prioritising search areas.

——

Back at the offices of the Serious Crime Review Team, Detective Superintendent Christy Mangan says that he and his team are reviewing all unsolved murders which have occurred since 1980 and that includes murders linked to the Troubles.

Those cases are factored into our work, and we have had contact with families who have lost someone as a result of terrorist-related activity. We are carrying out preliminary reviews of some of those cases. If there is someone coming forward with new information, or if there are new forensic opportunities we will certainly look at cases. We are looking primarily at all murders which have occurred since 1980, that year was chosen because you have to start somewhere, but if there is any reason, we will look at cases further back and we have been looking at some cases from the 1970s.

The Cold Case Unit is made up of a dozen detectives who all have experience in major criminal investigations. Mangan himself was a Detective Inspector on the northside of Dublin and was one of the Gardaí to lead the investigation into the discovery of a dismembered body which was found in Dublin's Royal Canal in 2005. The body was later identified as that of a Kenyan man, Farah Swaleh Noor. Two Dublin sisters were later convicted of the killing and their mother also served a sentence for helping to conceal the crime. Prior to being one of the senior detectives in Dublin, Mangan served with the Garda National Drugs Unit and the Central Detective Unit.

The structure of the Cold Case Unit saw Christy Mangan as the Detective Superintendent, with one Detective Inspector, two Detective Sergeants and four Detective Gardaí. When the Unit was launched Brendan Burke was appointed as the Detective Inspector. He had previously served in the National Surveillance Unit, the Drug Unit, and the Central Detective Unit. Alan Bailey and Michael Buckley were appointed as the two Sergeants. Bailey had been an Incident Room Co-ordinator in the investigation of serious crime since the mid-80s. He had previously worked at Dublin's Bridewell station, and he had also been one of the detectives on Operation Trace, which had investigated the disappearances of women in Leinster in the 1990s. Michael Buckley had also been involved in a number of serious crime investigations and had served in Drogheda, Ballymun and Santry. The four Detective Gardaí assigned to the newly formed Unit were David O'Brien, Annelisa Hannigan, Maurice Downey and Padraig Hanly. O'Brien had been an Incident Room Co-ordinator in the investigation of serious crime in the North Central Dublin area and had been in the Special Detective Unit; Hannigan had worked with the Paedophile Investigation Unit at the National Bureau of Criminal Investigation and had been involved in a number of major investigations; Downey had been an Incident Room Co-ordinator in west Dublin and had also worked in the Central Detective Unit and with the Investigation Unit of the Immigration Bureau; and Hanly had been an Incident Room Co-ordinator in the Dublin Metropolitan Region Northern Division and again had been involved in many serious crime investigations. When Detective Inspector Burke retired from the force, Detective Inspector Eamonn Henry became the latest addition to the Cold Case Unit.

"Before the Unit was set up we studied Cold Case Units in other jurisdictions," says Christy Mangan.

We looked at the Scottish model, the Welsh, the English and also Cold Case Units in the USA and we spoke with the PSNI. We learned a great deal from those links. Reviews of unsolved murders are labour-intensive, resource-intensive. You don't want to generate unrealistic expectations for families. You have to be very down-to-earth and tell people that your intention is to progress a case, but that this will not always be the result. You have to manage the expectations. When we were set up we began looking at all the unsolved cases since 1980. During each preliminary review we were asking if there was fingerprint evidence, if there was DNA evidence, if there was witness identification evidence, if all the case papers had been preserved, if the case exhibits had been preserved, if there were new forensic opportunities or new witnesses available. Sometimes when a murder occurs, people leave the country. We would always consider if those people might be available now. We are always considering if there might be a change in someone's mindset all these years later, a change in allegiances, someone who might be able to speak with us now who didn't back then.

It was soon after the Cold Case Unit was set up in October 2007 that it began looking at the unsolved murder of Brian McGrath. It would be July 2009 before the work of the Unit came to a climax and a jury returned verdicts at the Central Criminal Court, finding Brian's wife Vera guilty of murder and Englishman Colin Pinder guilty of manslaughter. At the time of the killing Pinder had been the fiancé of Brian's daughter Veronica. It was Veronica whose bravery in giving evidence in court had helped finally solve the murder. The case was the first murder to be officially marked as 'solved' due to the work of the Cold Case Unit.

———

The Cold Case Unit also took on a number of other cases immediately after it was set up. That's the way the Unit works, examining a number of murder files at any one time. Some cases move quicker than others, some see breakthroughs, some hit brick walls. The Unit learned a valuable lesson with one of the first cases it reviewed. A prime suspect in the murder of a woman in Limerick in the 1980s had left Ireland even before the murder was discovered. The Cold Case Unit had taken on the international hunt for this man, who after fleeing Ireland had moved through North and South America, mainland Europe and then to England. The cold-case detectives obtained an address for the man, and arrangements were being made for his arrest when word came through that he had in fact died just a few weeks before. The disappointment felt by the Unit was almost palpable but they picked themselves up and started investigating other cases.

This particular case gives an insight into the life of a suspected killer 'on the run'. The man had fled Ireland within a short time of the woman's murder, flying from Shannon

Airport to Heathrow. Gardaí established that he cashed traveller's cheques in London and Peterborough within a short time of arriving in England. He then flew to Miami where he was found unconscious by members of the Florida Highway Patrol after attempting to take his own life. He was later discharged from hospital and returned to England, where he then withdrew money from a bank account in Torquay. During all this time, the murdered woman's body had still not been found. It was two and a half months after the murder that the alarm was raised when concerned neighbours and extended family of the woman asked Gardaí to force entry to her home. The victim was found in an upstairs rear bedroom, covered by a quilt. She had been strangled with a man's necktie.

As detectives began a murder investigation, the man who would become the prime suspect was continuing to travel around England. His car had been located at Shannon Airport and Gardaí liaised with other police forces to alert them that the man was wanted for questioning about a murder in Ireland. However, it would appear that there was no real active international pursuit of this man back in the 1980s. Gardaí carried out a full enquiry, forensically examining the scene and speaking with neighbours of the murdered woman, but with the prime suspect now gone from Ireland, it would seem the investigation hit a wall, and eventually wound down. Over the following years word came back to Gardaí that the suspect had been in Portimao in Portugal and back in the United States, but on each occasion he was long gone by the time Irish detectives were alerted. On one occasion in the early 1990s he actually contacted the British Consulate in the American state of Georgia and said he wanted to return to Ireland and turn himself in, and he even collected a new passport and got a taxi to the airport. However, he never boarded the flight to Ireland and the following year he surfaced in Mexico. He later called to the British Embassy in Spain to renew his passport. When Gardaí sought further details from Madrid they were told that none could be given as the man was 'sought for interview' as opposed to there being a warrant for his arrest. Again by the time Gardaí learned the man had been in Spain, he had vanished again.

It was only when the Cold Case Unit was established in 2007 that a full and vigorous international pursuit of this suspected murderer was undertaken. Utilising the latest investigative techniques and capitalising on enhanced international police co-operation through Interpol, Gardaí put out a worldwide search strategy. Perhaps because the man had evaded justice for three decades, it turned out that he was still using his real name. He was tracked down to an address in England and arrangements were made for Gardaí to finally go and knock on his door. However, just before they travelled, word came back from British police that the man had died on 16 September 2007. He had visited his doctor a week beforehand complaining of breathing difficulties. At the time of his death, the man had fallen on hard times and had been homeless. He had no criminal convictions in any country, and it would appear that his conscience was plagued by events which had occurred in Ireland in the 1980s. Cold-case detectives often speak of how somebody's circumstances can change dramatically following a murder. It might be the killer, or it might be a witness, but invariably people with something weighing heavily on their mind are more often than not affected greatly by what they know. In this particular case, the prime suspect for the murder of a 51-year-old woman spent a lifetime 'on the run' before dying penniless in a hostel at the age of 64. His only remaining possession was a harmonica, which was forensically examined to get DNA and absolutely confirmed the man's identity.

This particular murder can never be classified as 'solved'.
No-one has been brought to justice, but it would appear that
if the suspect was still alive he would have faced a criminal trial.
The murder is still unsolved, but no-one else is being sought
in connection with the killing. The Cold Case Unit learned a
valuable lesson in this case; sometimes time catches up with a
killer before they do. However, the Unit are convinced that
most of the hundreds of killers responsible for murders in the
1980s and 90s are still out there somewhere.

———

When detectives went to the Garda archives to begin looking at
unsolved murder files, one of the first cases they came across
was the killing of 54-year-old Nora Sheehan, who had been
suffocated to death during an attack in Co. Cork in June 1981.
Nora was murdered sometime between 6 June and 12 June. She
had left her home at Ballyphehane on the southside of Cork city
on the evening of Saturday 6 June 1981 and travelled to the South
Infirmary Hospital where she was treated for a dog bite to her
arm. After leaving the Accident and Emergency Department
Nora had never made it home. Somewhere along her journey
she was abducted. Six days later her body was found at Shippool
Wood near Innishannon, seventeen miles west of Cork city. Two
forestry workers found Nora's body hidden down a steep incline
behind a two-foot wall which divided the roadside and the
wood. Pathologist Dr Robert Coakley would later conclude that
Mrs Sheehan had been choked to death during a struggle
sometime between four and seven days before his examination,
and this indicated that Nora was quite possibly murdered on
the night she had vanished in Cork city. Local Superintendent
Edward Hogan and Detective Superintendent John Butler of
the Garda Technical Bureau made an appeal at the time for help

in catching the killer. The Gardaí had released photos of a fawn-coloured shoe, similar to the shoes Nora had been wearing on the night she disappeared. The shoe for the right foot had been found near Nora's body, but the left one was missing. The shoes were under the brand 'Model Girl' by Tylers and had a brass type buckle.

The initial murder investigation had identified a man in his thirties as being a suspect in the murder. However, that investigation hit a major difficulty when both the Pathologist, Dr Coakley, and Detective Superintendent John Butler died unexpectedly. As cold-case detectives read through the full murder file, they saw that there were a number of lines of enquiry that they could now pursue three decades on. The murder of this woman who had been randomly abducted while walking home from hospital had long troubled the people of Cork city and the original investigating Gardaí, who never forgot the case. The Cold Case Unit decided that the unsolved murder was one which they would fully review, and they publicly confirmed they were re-investigating the case.

Another of the earliest unsolved murder files from the 1980s is the murder of Charles Self, who was found stabbed to death in his home in Monkstown in south Dublin in January 1982. Charles was originally from England and had worked as a set-designer with RTÉ since the early 70s. An analysis of the case indicated that Charles had somehow known his attacker. The murder weapon was a knife which had been taken from the kitchen and later discarded by the killer in the sitting room. Charles's body was found in the hallway of his home close to the living room. A major investigation was undertaken at the time but the killer was never brought to justice.

Another case where a man was attacked in his home was that of Christopher Payne, who suffered horrific injuries in an assault on 13 May 1988. The 38-year-old died at Beaumont Hospital on 28 November of that year—over six months after he had been attacked by a gang in his home at Rutland Grove in Crumlin. At the time of the attack Christopher was undergoing dialysis treatment for a kidney disorder and had just returned from a hospital visit when he was set upon by a number of individuals. The victim was struck on the head with a number of implements and was left in a vegetative state before he died. As part of a cold-case review, detectives have studied the full original murder file and have also enlisted the assistance of the State Pathologist to review the medical evidence.

On the afternoon of 7 July 1989 the body of 32-year-old Limerick taxi-driver Henry Hurley was found at Reascamogue, Sixmilebridge, in Co. Clare. He had been beaten and strangled. Mr Hurley's 1989 registered Nissan Sunny was found a short distance away. The victim was last seen alive at around 3 a.m. in Co. Clare and it's believed two men had got into his taxi in Limerick city a short time earlier. The Garda Cold Case Unit are actively investigating this case, and part of their enquiries have focused on two Englishmen who had arrived in Ireland and had been travelling around the country at the time of the murder. It's believed the motive for Mr Hurley's murder was robbery. Similar to many other cold-case investigations, the Crimestoppers Trust has offered a reward for information leading to the conviction of Henry Hurley's killers.

When the Cold Case Unit was set up, one of the first cases to come its way was the murder of Brian Stack, who was the Chief Prison Officer at the high-security Portlaoise Prison. Brian was off duty and had just left the National Boxing Stadium on Dublin's South Circular Road, when a gunman walked up behind him on the night of Friday 25 March 1983. The gunman pointed a gun at the back of Brian's neck and fired once. Brian's injury was fatal, but he did not die immediately: he would suffer for eighteen months, paralysed and brain-damaged before his body could no longer cope with the internal injuries caused by the bullet. Brian died on 29 September 1984. The father of three boys had dedicated his working life to serving the Irish State and, along with so many other murders, it is galling that Brian Stack's killers have never been brought to justice. The gunman escaped on a stolen motorbike driven by an accomplice. What is without doubt is that Brian was shot because of his job at Portlaoise Prison. There are a number of lines of enquiry which are being actively pursued by Gardaí. Detectives have considered that the murder may have been carried out by paramilitaries, or by members of a criminal gang. The Cold Case Unit carried out a full review of the case and have made a number of recommendations in terms of a fresh investigation. Brian's wife Sheila and his sons Austin, Kieran and Oliver have met with detectives on a number of occasions recently and have also visited Dáil Éireann as part of their efforts to see the case solved. The family know that if Brian was shot dead by paramilitaries, it is possible that because of the Good Friday Agreement the killers might not serve any great length of time in prison if they were to be convicted. But the Stack family want answers, they want someone to be held accountable, they want the killers to be identified.

When the Cold Case Unit completed its review of the Brian Stack case they gave their recommendations to another team of detectives from the National Bureau of Criminal Investigation, who are now pursuing the case. That's the way the Cold Case Unit operates: there are so many cold cases where if a fresh investigation will be particularly time-consuming (the Brian Stack case, for example, should see every prisoner who ever came in contact with the victim being

interviewed), a team of other detectives is assigned to the case
to work full-time on it.

_____

At the Garda archive of unsolved murders in Santry in north
Dublin, there are many other files from the 1980s. They include
a 34-year-old man shot dead in Dublin on St Stephen's Day in
1983. The victim was shot in the head with a shotgun at a flats
complex at Dunne Street, off Portland Row on Dublin's
northside. Two men were arrested the following day and held
under Section 30 of the Offences Against the State Act on
suspicion of the murder. However, both men were later
released and the murder would eventually become a cold case.
This was the last murder of 1983, but there had been a number
of others. For example, in April of that year a man was
murdered in Ballymun in north Dublin. There was no link
between the St Stephen's Day murder and the April murder,
but the one similarity is that no-one would ever be brought to
justice for either killing.

Indeed the year 1983 bore witness to a number of murders
in Ireland which would never be solved. On 16 December 1983
recruit Garda Gary Sheehan and Army Private Patrick Kelly
lost their lives as they assisted in the rescue in Co. Leitrim of
IRA kidnap victim Don Tidey. The IRA killed a number of
other people in the 1980s in crimes for which no-one would
be brought to justice. John Corcoran was shot dead in
Ballincollig in Co. Cork in March 1985 and the IRA killed two
off-duty RUC officers in separate attacks in Co. Donegal.
Samuel McClean was shot dead at Ballybofey on 2 June 1987,
and fellow off-duty officer Harold Keys was killed in an IRA
ambush at Ballintra in Co. Donegal on 15 January 1989. In
August 1985 a Northern Ireland businessman was shot dead

by the IRA at his family's second home, a bungalow in Donnybrook in south Dublin. Forty-six-year-old Seamus McAvoy was a well-respected business figure who normally resided at the family's estate at Coalisland in Co. Tyrone. At the funeral mass Cardinal Tomás Ó Fiaich described the killing as an attack on the very fabric of Irish Catholic people. The murder was never solved.

In June 1980 a former member of the UDR was shot dead by the IRA while he was visiting a cattle-market in Ballybay, Co. Monaghan. One man was later jailed for life for the killing, but more than one person must have been involved. Two months later, another UDR member was shot dead by the IRA in the Republic of Ireland. The 59-year-old victim was ambushed 400 yards inside Co. Donegal near the border village of Pettigo. Gardaí made some progress in their investigations, but not everyone involved in the killing was brought to justice.

Another murder which is blamed on the IRA is the shooting dead of Eugene Simons, whose body was found buried near Knockbridge in Co. Louth in May 1984. The victim was from Co. Down and had last been seen on 1 January 1981. His body was only discovered because soil had shifted at bogland and a man out walking his dog made the shocking discovery. A forensic examination showed the 26-year-old had been shot in the head. The Gardaí who carried out the investigation suspected Eugene had been killed by the IRA, who then buried his body in bogland just off the Dundalk to Carrickmacross road. The IRA never admitted responsibility for the killing. However, unbeknownst to everyone but themselves, the organisation had at that stage killed and secretly buried a number of other people in the 1970s and early 80s.

The 1980s also saw a number of murders linked to an INLA feud. In January 1987 Mary McGlinchey, who was the wife of INLA leader Dominic McGlinchey, was shot dead as she bathed

her sons in the family home in Dundalk. In February 1994 the
McGlinchey children also lost their father, when he was shot
dead at a phone-box in Drogheda. Neither the murder of
Mary McGlinchey nor Dominic McGlinchey has ever been
solved. Similarly no-one has been brought to justice for the
double-murder of two INLA members shot dead at a hotel in
Drogheda in January 1987, nor for the shooting dead in Dublin
in 1991 of a hairdresser who was a former prominent INLA
member. In 1982 a 37-year-old man from Co. Armagh was shot
dead outside a pub at Dublin's North Strand. The attack was
blamed on the INLA. In October 1983 a Belfast man was shot
dead and his body was left by a roadside near Redhills in
Co. Cavan. Again the INLA were linked to the killing, and again
no-one was ever brought to justice for the murder. In 1985, a
28-year-old man's body was found just north of the border in
Co. Armagh. It's believed he was killed by the INLA at
Ravensdale in Co. Louth. The murder was never solved, and if
it ever is it will involve ongoing close co-operation between
both police forces on the island.

The concept of the work of the Cold Case Unit is that every
unresolved murder is considered on its merits. If there is
evidence to be pursued it will be pursued without fear or favour.
The Unit recognises that every homicide victim has left grieving
relatives and friends, all of whom deserve the very best from the
State. No matter whether a murder victim was themselves
involved in criminality or subversive activity, if their killer or
killers can still be caught at this stage, they will be pursued.

Elsewhere in the archives there are files on a number of
innocent women who were murdered in the 1980s and whose
killings were never solved. A 38-year-old woman was found

murdered in her home in south Dublin in 1985, and another woman, aged 35, was found dead on open ground in the south of the country in 1984. There is no link between these crimes. The woman found dead on open ground had been missing for two months, and State Pathologist Dr John Harbison came to the conclusion that the woman had been strangled and her body then hidden in a ditch. And there were other murders of women which would never be solved. In 1987, 76-year-old Lilly Carrick was murdered as she walked home in Dublin city, and in September of that year 79-year-old Nancy Smyth (see Chapter 2) was murdered in her Kilkenny home by an attacker who then set a fire in an unsuccessful attempt to hide his crime.

In January 1985, an elderly woman was murdered at her home in Mallow in Co. Cork. The victim sustained broken ribs and injuries to her face and throat during the murderous attack. A suspect was identified and later stood trial at the Central Criminal Court, which heard that his fingerprint was found on a broken glass in the victim's home and a bloodstain matching his blood group was discovered on a chair. The suspect's wallet was also found at the scene. After an eight-day trial a jury found the accused not guilty. Having been found innocent the man left Ireland to live in England, but five years later he was jailed for life for killing a man in London. The prisoner was later repatriated to Ireland and died in an Irish prison. The circumstances of this entire case clearly show that behind every 'unsolved' murder there is a story, a bigger picture. The case of the woman murdered in Mallow is still officially unsolved, but no other suspects have emerged since her body was discovered over a quarter of a century ago.

On 11 July 1987 29-year-old mother of two Antoinette Smith disappeared in Dublin city. She and a friend had earlier been to the David Bowie concert at Slane Castle. The two women had later gone into Dublin city and Antoinette's friend had last seen her in the city centre. Almost nine months later, on 3 April 1988, a man out walking in the Dublin-Wicklow Mountains spotted a body. The weather over previous weeks had caused the soil at bogland to shift and Antoinette Smith was finally found. Her killer or killers had placed two plastic bags over her head and had buried her body in bogland at Glendoo Mountain near Glencree. Antoinette was still wearing her t-shirt from the David Bowie concert which read 'David Bowie, Slane 87, Big Country, Groovy.'

The failure to catch the killer of Antoinette Smith is very worrying, not just in terms of getting justice for Antoinette, but also given the fact that a number of women disappeared in Leinster in the 1990s. Gardaí often speak about the need to establish a crime scene to gather any traces which a killer may have left behind. Detectives often say if they could find the bodies of missing people who have been murdered, not only would they bring some solace to grieving families, but they would also have much more evidential material to work with. The detectives who investigated Antoinette Smith's murder carried out extensive enquiries but ultimately failed to catch the killer. So, someone who was adept at abducting a woman, murdering her and burying her body in the mountains continued to walk free, and many people have wondered if he, or they, have struck again since.

––––

The 1980s saw a number of other unsolved murders. In 1986 a man was strangled to death in his home in Kells in Co. Meath. The 46-year-old victim lived alone and his body was found in the kitchen. Elsewhere, a 39-year-old man from Bray suffered fatal head injuries in an attack on Dublin's northside in 1987. Later that year the body of a missing Dublin man was found in the Dublin Mountains. The discovery was made by a Garda search party, which was actually searching the mountainous terrain for the Beit paintings which had been stolen from Russborough House in Co. Wicklow. The man had been shot dead, and it's believed his body lay undiscovered since early 1986. The decade ended as it had begun, with an innocent publican dying following an attack. In October 1981 Lorcan O'Byrne was murdered when armed gunmen burst into the living quarters above his family's pub, The Anglers Rest near Dublin's Chapelizod (see Chapter 1). In 1989, a publican was beaten during a robbery elsewhere in Leinster. He was treated in hospital but died some days later. His attacker was never brought to justice.

———

At the Forensic Science Laboratory, in Dublin's Phoenix Park, Dr Martina McBride is the official liaison with the Cold Case Unit, and it is through her that many items have been submitted for forensic re-examination. As well as investigating all unsolved murders since 1980, the Cold Case Unit has also decided to re-examine many unsolved sexual assault and rape cases. Detectives have found that there is a possibility that semen or blood which an attacker left at a crime scene in the 1970s or 80s may still be available to be retested. At the time of these attacks, all that could be identified was a person's blood group, but with advances in forensic science those same samples may now unmask the DNA of each attacker. A special Cold Case investigation, known as Operation Fiach, has been established to see if any long-term unsolved rape cases may finally be solved.

The possibilities that forensic science now provides for catching killers is immense. Every contact leaves a trace, everything from sweat, dandruff, saliva, nasal discharge, ear wax, hair, skin, blood, semen. It is a certainty that, in the future, more criminals will be caught as a result of their DNA. The work of the Cold Case Unit, and that of detectives around the country, could only be made easier by the establishment of a DNA database of all known criminal offenders. Such a database has long been promised by successive governments.

As well as liaising with the Forensic Science Laboratory, the Cold Case Unit also works closely with State Pathlogist Dr Marie Cassidy and with Clinical Anthropologist Laureen Buckley. The Unit has asked Dr Cassidy to review medical notes and crime scene photographs on a number of unsolved cases, and on two occasions has asked her to carry out post-mortem examinations on bodies which have been exhumed. The Unit also works with a forensic psychologist. Unlike fictional television programmes, real-life cold cases are never solved in a day, or even a week. But real-life cold-case investigations do avail of all the latest investigative methods, including profilers.

There are dozens upon dozens of unsolved murders from the 1990s which the Cold Case Unit is tasked with reviewing. Among those cases are a number of murders of men who lived alone and who were killed during robberies. Late on the night of 31 December 1990 66-year-old John Kennedy was stabbed to death during an apparent robbery at his home at Pearse Park in Drogheda. It's believed that after killing his victim the culprit stole John's bike to make his getaway. There was widespread revulsion in Drogheda at the murder of a quiet and well-regarded man. The possibility that the murderer was local to Drogheda has always been a strong possibility. The Cold Case Unit is currently reviewing this case.

In June 1995 a man who lived alone was murdered at his home at Stapleton Place in Dundalk and the following September a Co. Limerick farmer was shot dead outside his home. In May 1998 83-year-old Eddie Fitzmaurice was beaten, tied up, gagged and left to die in his home by a gang who broke into his home at Bellaghy, Charlestown, on the Sligo-Mayo border. Eddie lived alone above his drapery shop. He was attacked sometime on Friday evening 1 May 1998 or early on Saturday morning 2 May. The investigation by Gardaí in Mayo was massive, with 59 people being arrested and questioned in connection with the case. It's believed Eddie was targeted by a gang of travelling criminals.

One of the most shocking aspects of the murder is the suffering which Eddie Fitzmaurice was subjected to. His attackers had tied his wrists together and his ankles were also bound so tightly that his circulation was severely restricted. Over a number of hours if not days Mr Fitzmaurice used his elbows, knees, buttocks and shoulders to slowly move himself along the ground towards a window in an attempt to summon help. By the time his body was found, five days after the attack, he had managed to move from one bedroom, across a hall and into another front-facing bedroom close to a window looking out on the street below. However, having made it that far, Eddie simply had no more strength. Because his killers had dragged him from his bed, Eddie was dressed only in his pyjamas and at some stage during those five days and nights, as he lay on his back with his hands tied behind him, Eddie Fitzmaurice froze to death.

Another attack on a man who lived alone was the murder of 70-year-old Tommy Casey, who died after suffering an horrific beating at his home at Oranmore, Co. Galway, in January 1996.

The bachelor and retired farmer had been targeted for robbery by a four-person gang of travelling criminals made up of two men and two women. The women's role was to distract the victim at the front of his house while the men entered through the back. A mother and daughter from Co. Tipperary were later jailed after admitting burglary charges relating to the incident and one man, also from Co. Tipperary, was given a six-year sentence after pleading guilty to the manslaughter of Tommy Casey. The court heard how Tommy had been found dead on the floor of his kitchen eight days after he had been attacked. The four members of the gang had actually been arrested by Gardaí in Galway city some hours after the attack on Tommy Casey when officers found housebreaking implements, a dagger and a balaclava in their car. However, Gardaí were unaware of the attack on Tommy Casey and none of the occupants of the car raised the alarm, and it was eight days later before Tommy's body was found. If the gang had owned up to what they had done, Tommy's life might have been saved.

In terms of discussing crime statistics and whether a case is solved or unsolved, the Tommy Casey murder is an important one to consider. It's believed that four people were involved in the gang which targeted Tommy Casey. The two female members who never entered Tommy's home were jailed for burglary, and one man was jailed for manslaughter. However, the other man left Ireland and his whereabouts are not known. He is still wanted for questioning about the murder of Tommy Casey. So is the Tommy Casey murder solved or unsolved? Three out of four members of a gang were brought to justice for their roles. To say it is totally unsolved is not doing justice to the good detective work that went into the case, but similarly to say it is totally solved ignores the fact that a very dangerous individual skipped the country and could now pose a danger elsewhere in the world.

A similar situation exists in the murder of 68-year-old bachelor farmer Paud Skehan who lived alone and who was attacked by at least two people who broke into his home at O'Briensbridge in Co. Clare in April 1998. Paud was dragged from his bed, and was punched in the face and kicked. He was then bound and gagged and doused in lighter fluid as his attackers screamed at him to tell them where he kept his cash. Finally his attackers fled, leaving Paud lying on his concrete sitting room floor with a blood-soaked blindfold on his face, his hands bound, and his feet tied to the bannisters. Paud suffered fatal brain damage, but his suffering was not over. For hours he lay shivering in sub-zero temperatures and he developed bronchial pneumonia.

For almost eight weeks Paud Skehan fought for his life. For those 54 days he was in a coma as his family kept a bedside vigil at the Mid Western Regional Hospital in Limerick, but Paud never recovered. His only recognition of sounds or voices was on the day he was rushed to hospital, but that was it. Paud's injuries were fatal, and in early June 1998 his life-support machine was turned off.

One of Paud's murderers is now serving a life sentence for the crime. Career criminal William Campion from Limerick specialised in 'tie-up' jobs where he and accomplices would break into people's homes and tie up the terror-stricken occupants while stealing their cash. He was caught and convicted for Paud Skehan's murder because when arrested he was still wearing the FILA runners he was wearing when he stepped in Paud's blood while attacking him. The good work of Gardaí and the Forensic Science Laboratory led to the identification of Campion's runners as being the very pair which had been present at the murder. Campion was given a life sentence for murder and a concurrent nine-year sentence for burglary at Paud's home.

So is the murder of Paud Skehan solved? Certainly, the capture of one of Paud Skehan's attackers was Garda work at its very finest. Utilising good detective work and capitalising on some good luck, an extremely dangerous random attacker was put behind bars. But what about his accomplice, the one who got away? From an analysis of the crime scene, Gardaí believe there were two people involved in the attack on Paud Skehan and that second person is still out there somewhere and has never been identified. To say the murder of Paud Skehan is unsolved does not do justice to the successful prosecution of one of his killers, but to say it is solved ignores the fact that only one of his killers was taken off the streets. Like so many crimes, the murder of Paud Skehan might be better described as both partially solved and partially unsolved.

A similar situation could be applied to the murder of publican Tom Nevin at his Co. Wicklow pub—Jack Whites —in March 1996. His wife Catherine is currently serving a life sentence for Tom's murder. The jury also found her guilty of asking three men on three separate occasions to murder her husband. But while Catherine Nevin was caught and convicted and jailed for life, she did not pull the trigger. The hitman who murdered Tom Nevin and then tied up Catherine Nevin, so as to make the killing look like a robbery and attack on both husband and wife, has never been identified and never been brought to justice. The conviction of Catherine Nevin represented policing at its finest, but even still, the gunman got away.

———

Throughout the 1990s there were a number of murders of women which would eventually become cold cases. In June 1992, headlines had been dominated by the discovery in the Dublin

Mountains of the body of Patricia Doherty. A native of Annascaul, Co. Kerry, Patricia Doherty was last seen alive on 23 December 1991. She lived with her family at Allenton Lawns in Tallaght, and had travelled to The Square to get Santa hats for her children. Patricia's disappearance was totally out of character and her family reported her missing, but it was only in June 1992 that a man out cutting turf at Killakee in the Dublin Mountains found Patricia's body. She had been strangled, and her body had been left in a bog drain. No-one has ever been arrested in connection with this unsolved murder.

On 16 December 1993, mother-of-one Marie Kilmartin vanished from Port Laoise. It was from a phone box across the road from her flat that an as yet unidentified man made a call which led Marie to her death. Gardaí have established that a two-and-a-half minute call was made at 4.25 p.m. to Marie from that phone box. She left her flat soon afterwards and was never seen alive again. For 176 days her body lay hidden beneath water in a bog drain on the Laois-Offaly border. A large concrete block was on top of her chest. She was fully clothed, dressed in her matching jacket and skirt, double-breasted herringbone overcoat and lace-up boots. Whoever had killed her had used their bare hands to strangle her before throwing her body into the bog drain and putting debris on top of Marie. In September 2008, detectives arrested a man and questioned him about the murder. Another man and a woman were questioned on suspicion of withholding information. The three were later released.

The 1990s witnessed a number of baffling disappearances of women. In March 1993 American woman Annie McCarrick disappeared after going for a walk in the Dublin-Wicklow Mountains. In July of that same year Eva Brennan disappeared in south Dublin. Imelda Keenan vanished in Waterford in January 1994. Jo Jo Dullard vanished in Co. Kildare in

November 1995 and Fiona Pender, who was six months pregnant, disappeared in Tullamore in October 1996. Seventeen-year-old Ciara Breen is missing from Dundalk since February 1997 and mother-of-one Fiona Sinnott was last seen in Co. Wexford in February 1998. In July 1998, a teenage woman vanished from Droichead Nua in Co. Kildare. Despite significant Garda efforts to try and solve these cases, no trace of any of these missing women has yet been found.

The Cold Case Unit utilises the Violent Crimes Linkage Analysis System (VICLAS), a computer system operated by the Garda Behavioural Analysis Unit. Information from every violent crime, including murders and sexual assaults, is loaded into its database. The system is continuously searching for possible links between crimes and is of particular benefit in Operation Trace, which is investigating the spate of unsolved disappearances of women in Leinster in the 1990s. VICLAS compiles thousands of pieces of information on every single violent incident and highlights possible links between crimes. It might be something as seemingly innocuous as the same make of car seen at two crime scenes, or something more definitive such as the same description of an attacker involved, the same modus operandi; everything from speech pattern, facial tics, clothing worn, weapons used, is all input into VICLAS. The system assesses all information about the time, date and location of crimes, allowing for any similarities to show up. Such an analysis might red-flag a particular person who works in a particular location, or who lives in a particular place, or who drives a particular route at a particular time every day or week or month.

One major attraction of the VICLAS system is the very fact that, because all significant details of violent crimes are preserved forever more on computer, it ensures that there is a 'corporate memory' within An Garda Síochána of historic unsolved crimes. The three-member team which operates the system has assisted Gardaí right around the country, but their work was particularly beneficial to the Cold Case Unit and in late 2009 a decision was taken to amalgamate VICLAS into the Unit. The three Gardaí who worked with the system all transferred into the Cold Case Unit. Detective Sergeant Noel Mooney had been part of the Serious Crime Squad since 1985 and was also a psychologist. Detective Garda Mary Fallon and Detective Garda Tony Keane had also many decades of experience in investigating serious crimes. As the newest members of the Cold Case Unit they helped to enhance Garda links with both the FBI and Canadian police, including profilers. "VICLAS and behavioural analysis are employed by many law enforcement agencies around the world," says Detective Sergeant Noel Mooney.

> There are fewer borders around the world than in years gone by, the world is a smaller place. Police forces share information about both solved and unsolved crimes. VICLAS looks for patterns, it looks for the minority of people who commit the majority of crime. We are looking to identify both local and cross-border criminals. We look at victimology, offender-victim interaction, assessing everything we know about the victim of a crime and how they might have become a target for a violent person. We study crime scene dynamics, geographic profiling and forensic and autopsy reports. VICLAS was initially spearheaded by the Royal Canadian Mounted Police and the system is similar to the FBI's Violent Criminal Apprehension Program.

In an article for the *Garda Review* magazine published in 2009, one of Noel Mooney's colleagues in the Cold Case Unit, Detective Sergeant Alan Bailey, described the many different areas considered by detectives during the course of a cold-case review. "A review examines and considers all facets of an investigation," he wrote.

> Details surrounding the reporting of the crime; the initial response of Gardaí; crime scene identification and preservation; fast track actions; forensic, arrest and search strategies; house to house and other main lines of enquiry; interview strategy; exhibit handling and storage; witness support; liaison; interview and protection. A weighting matrix is applied to assist in determining prioritisation of cases for root and branch review. The matrix ranges on a table of high to low. The highest case prioritisation will have the complete original case papers, significant original exhibits with potential for DNA and other forensic and technical evidence. The cases at the lower end of the matrix will have no case papers, no exhibits and no new forensic opportunities.

———

One unsolved case at the higher end of the weighting matrix is the murder in December 1992 of 56-year-old Grace Livingstone. Grace was shot dead in her home in Malahide in north Co. Dublin (see Chapter 5) and among a number of areas which may be advanced in the case is the possibility that Grace's killer left his DNA on the tape used to bind and gag her. Grace's was one of a number of murders of women who were attacked in their homes in the 1990s. In December 1996 French film-maker Sophie Toscan Du Plantier was beaten to death during a sustained attack outside her holiday home at Schull in west Cork. In June 1997 28-year-old Mandy Fong was strangled to death in her home in Crumlin in south Dublin. Just three months before that murder, two women were stabbed to death after someone broke into their sheltered accommodation at

Grangegorman on Dublin's northside. Fifty-nine-year-old Sylvia Shields and 61-year-old Mary Callinan suffered multiple injuries when they were attacked as they slept in their beds in early March 1997. Even before the setting up of the Cold Case Unit, this double-murder has been the subject of a cold-case review in recent years.

The failure by Gardaí to solve the murders of Grace Livingstone and Sophie Toscan Du Plantier led to the families of both victims separately taking matters into their own hands. Grace's husband Jimmy and her children Tara and Conor brought a case to the High Court on the basis that Gardaí had failed in their 'duty of care' to the family. The case was settled to the family's satisfaction after four days, and Jimmy then contacted the Garda Cold Case Unit and asked them to fully re-investigate the case. A team led by a senior investigating officer is currently working on the unsolved murder. Meanwhile in France, Sophie Toscan Du Plantier's family and friends have been behind recent efforts by authorities there to mount an investigation into her murder. Although the brutal killing took place in Ireland, French officials agreed to the family's request that, in the absence of any current action by Irish authorities, a French judge should investigate the case. As part of subsequent enquiries Sophie's body was exhumed in 2008 and French investigators have met with senior Gardaí to study the unsolved murder file.

In every county in Ireland there are long-term unsolved murders. Co. Donegal, for example, has a number of unsolved killings. On 25 May 1991, Sinn Féin councillor Eddie Fullerton was shot dead by the UFF at his home in Buncrana. The killers had crossed the border late at night and hijacked a car near

Mr Fullerton's home, before using a sledgehammer to break open his front door and shooting him dead. The killers then drove to Co. Derry and set fire to their hijacked vehicle. A forensic examination later linked the murder weapon to other killings in Northern Ireland. In 2009 two men were questioned in the North about the killing. The Fullerton family and Sinn Féin have consistently called for a cross-jurisdictional investigation to establish the truth surrounding the murder.

Co. Donegal has also witnessed other murders linked to the Troubles. In March 1996 John Fennell from Belfast was beaten to death at a caravan park in Bundoran. It's believed he was killed as part of an INLA feud. A man was arrested and questioned about the killing within hours of the crime, but he was released without charge and to this day the murder remains unsolved.

Just over a decade later, the north of the county was the scene of another Troubles-related murder when former Sinn Féin official Denis Donaldson was shot dead at a remote cottage at Doochary near Glenties. Mr Donaldson had been Sinn Féin's head of administration in the power-sharing executive at Stormont, but in December 2005 he appeared at a press conference in Dublin to state that he had been a Special Branch agent for more than two decades. His killer or killers fired a shotgun to gain entry to his cottage, injuring their victim in the process. Denis Donaldson was then killed by shotgun blasts fired inside the cottage. The IRA immediately denied it was involved and Sinn Féin condemned the killing. One line of enquiry is that the 56-year-old was killed by another paramilitary group or a number of individuals with a personal animosity based on Denis Donaldson's admission that he had been secretly working for police.

The county has also witnessed non-Troubles-related unsolved murders. In January 2005 Shaun Duffy was murdered at his home just outside Dungloe in the west of the county. Mr Duffy, who worked as an undertaker and horse dealer and part-time doorman, was found lying face-down on a sofa in his living room. He had been shot in the arm with a crossbow, stabbed four times and had suffered nine blows with a blunt object. Deputy State Pathologist Dr Michael Curtis came to the view that the most likely cause of Mr Duffy's death were the stab wounds he had suffered to his chest, neck and abdomen. The shocking brutality of the crime stunned this normally peaceful part of the country. It seemed that robbery might have been a motive, and it was quite possible that more than one person was involved. Gardaí mounted a major criminal investigation with up to 50 detectives working on the case. Around 800 statements were taken in this rural area. There was a hope that the killer might be caught quickly, but that did not happen and the crime remains unsolved.

County Donegal is also home to one of the oldest missing persons cases, which is still being actively investigated. Mary Boyle was six years old when she vanished at Cashelard, near Ballyshannon in the south of the county in March 1977. Mary was last seen at 3.30 p.m. on Friday 18 March. She was wearing a lilac-coloured hand-knitted cardigan, and her brown jeans were tucked into her wellington boots. There are only two possible explanations for Mary's disappearance. Did a desolate patch of marshy ground swallow up the little girl? Or is there a sinister explanation? Was she abducted from the quiet Donegal countryside that afternoon? Is there someone in this part of the country or beyond who still holds the secret to Mary's disappearance?

———

Mary Boyle is one of two children who are long-term missing in the Republic of Ireland. Philip Cairns was 13 years old when he vanished while walking back to school in south Dublin on 23 October 1986. It was just after lunchtime and Philip was making his way back to Coláiste Éanna in Rathfarnham. Philip left his home at Ballyroan Road to make the fifteen-minute journey back to school, but somewhere along the journey he was abducted. One week later Philip's schoolbag was found by two teenage girls at a dark curving laneway a few hundred yards from Philip's home. The canvas bag was found at a shortcut between Anne Devlin Road and Anne Devlin Drive.

The discovery of Philip's schoolbag is unique in a missing person enquiry, in that a trace of a missing person was found one week after his disappearance. There are only two real possibilities—either the schoolbag was left in the laneway by Philip's abductor, or it was left by an innocent person, perhaps someone who found the bag elsewhere and panicked when they realised it was the schoolbag of missing Philip Cairns. The bag has been safely maintained by Gardaí in the hope that advances in forensic science may unlock the identity of people who handled the bag.

The disappearance of Philip Cairns is still actively investigated by detectives at Rathfarnham Garda station. In recent years a number of excavations were undertaken on foot of new information received by Gardaí, but no trace of Philip has been found in the more than a quarter century since he vanished.

North of the border, the Police Service of Northern Ireland is still investigating the disappearance in 1974 of two schoolboys in Belfast. Thomas Spence was just 11 years old, his friend John Rodgers was 13. They were both due to get a bus from the Falls Road to their special needs school on the morning of

Tuesday 26 November 1974. Both boys left their houses to walk the short journey to the bus-stop as normal. One woman saw Thomas Spence at the bus-stop waiting as normal. But when the bus pulled up shortly after 9 a.m. neither boy was at the stop. It was broad daylight on one of the busiest roads in west Belfast and two young boys had vanished without trace.

The disappearance of Thomas and John has been the subject of cold-case reviews in recent decades but no trace of either boy has been found. There is a hope that people from the nationalist community who might not have given information to the RUC at the time of the disappearances might now feel confident to speak to the PSNI, given the cross-party support for the new police service.

The PSNI is also tasked with searching for missing Tyrone teenager Arlene Arkinson, who it is feared was murdered in August 1994 and her body hidden. Arlene was just fifteen years old when she vanished after a night out. Down the years a number of extensive searches have been undertaken both in Co. Tyrone and Co. Donegal but no trace of Arlene was found. In late August 2011 the PSNI began a series of fresh searches in the Co. Tyrone area using the most up-to-date specialist equipment and sniffer dogs. Up to forty areas were to be searched.

Northern Ireland has more than 3,200 unsolved murders which are directly attributable to the Troubles. The Historical Inquiries Team is currently reviewing all of those cases. The disappearance of Thomas Spence and John Rodgers in 1974 and the disappearance of Arlene in 1994 have absolutely nothing to do with the Troubles. Another very troubling case which is non-Troubles-related is the murder of 18-year-old German backpacker Inga-Maria Hauser, who had hardly set foot on the island of Ireland when she was murdered and her body hidden at Ballypatrick Forest in Co. Antrim in April 1988 (see

Chapter 3). The ongoing pursuit of her killer by the PSNI is heartening for her family.

———

Official figures for unsolved murders can never be the absolute precise number. There are dozens of missing persons cases, for example, which are officially classified as 'missing persons', but which may well be cases of murder where a victim's body has been hidden by the killer or killers. In my research on missing persons I have come across up to thirty such cases in Ireland. These cases extend from those people abducted, shot dead and secretly buried by the IRA in the 1970s and early 80s, to women who have been killed and secretly buried by either serial killers, or by someone they knew. Organised criminal gangs have also increased their practice of hiding the bodies of some of the people they kill. It's not a totally new phenomenon for such gangs to go to these lengths. One Dublin man is missing since the late 1980s and it is now feared he was shot dead and buried somewhere in north Co. Dublin. Gardaí only became aware of the case in 2009 when a prominent criminal walked into Store Street Garda station and said he wished to confess to his role in the murder and secret burial. He brought detectives to a location at Oldtown in the north of the county and pointed out a location where he said the body had been hidden. The man who contacted Gardaí took his own life a short time later. An extensive excavation was conducted at the field near an old graveyard where the man said the body had been buried, but no trace of the missing man was found.

The abduction and suspected murder of Brooke Pickard (see Chapter 4) is one of a number of unsolved crimes to occur in the 1990s where the victim is still missing. In March 2010 a jury at the Dublin County Coroners Court reached a verdict that a man who vanished on 28 February 1996 had been unlawfully killed. William 'Jock' Corbally was driven from Chapelizod to a field in Baldonnel in west Dublin where he was ambushed by a gang and beaten with a pickaxe handle, a lead pipe and a baseball bat. Jock had most likely been taken from Baldonnel to a location near Straffan in Co. Kildare where his body was then hidden. Despite extensive searches in a number of locations in Kildare and Dublin no trace of Jock has ever been found. The car which is believed to have been used to transport Jock's body was later found burned out at Knocksedan in north Co. Dublin.

In January 1999, 17-year-old father-of-one Patrick Lawlor vanished from Dublin's Ballyfermot. His loved ones knew immediately that his disappearance was out of character, and Garda investigations established that he had last been seen on 6 January. Detectives believed that the answer to Patrick's disappearance was local and over the following years they conducted many searches and made many appeals for information. It was three years after Patrick vanished that a young man who was in custody about another matter suddenly broke down and said he had witnessed the killing of Patrick Lawlor. The relentless pressure of poster campaigns, public appeals, and Garda enquiries had finally yielded a result.

The young man described seeing Patrick being hit with a stone and falling down. He said Patrick had then been secretly buried at a narrow strip of land along the Grand Canal. It had taken a number of hours for two people to dig the hole using a plank of wood and after putting Patrick's body into the hole and filling it in again, the two had washed their hands and feet in the nearby canal water.

A short time after telling Gardaí this story, the young man was brought by Detective Inspector Pádraig Kennedy, Sergeant

Ray Murphy and Garda Declan Walsh to the scene. It was late at night and the Gardaí shone their torches at a point which the man nominated between the seventh and eighth locks of the canal. Detective Inspector Kennedy gave the witness a ruler and asked him to put it into the ground where Patrick's body lay, and sure enough that was exactly where the teenager's body was recovered the next day.

No-one was ever brought to justice for the actual killing of Patrick Lawlor. The man who helped recover Patrick's body was later given a five-year sentence for acting to impede the arrest of a person responsible for the manslaughter of Patrick Lawlor. Patrick is now laid to rest in Palmerstown Cemetery.

In November 1999 34-year-old Martin Nolan from Tramore vanished from Co. Waterford. Serious concern was raised for his safety when blood was discovered at Ballygarron Wood near Waterford Regional Airport soon after his disappearance. Eight months later his body was found in the Comeragh Mountains at Clondonnell close to the Waterford-Tipperary border. Local Gardaí have continued to vigorously investigate this murder.

The practice by some violent criminals of hiding the bodies of their victims was to continue in the following decade. Just like the cases in the 1990s, no-one was ever brought to justice for the killing of father-of-one Neil Hanlon, who vanished from Crumlin on 29 September 2001 and whose body was found buried in a local field on 9 February of the following year. For four months Neil was classified as a missing person and for all that time his body lay hidden just a few minutes' walk from his home. Following extensive investigations detectives focused their attention on a section of land at the back of St Kevin's VEC. Detective Inspector Tom Mulligan organised search parties to carry out a minute examination of the area close to a boundary wall which consisted of grass and weeds. Gardaí Michael Houlihan and William Ryan moved a discarded fridge and found recently dug soil. Under the direction of Sergeant John Walsh they slowly began to unearth the site and they soon found Neil's body.

Gardaí carried out a full murder enquiry and built up a wealth of information about the movement of individuals suspected of having knowledge of what had happened to Neil. The 22-year-old was subjected to a ferocious attack and died after being stabbed. When his body was found buried in the field he was still wearing three distinctive rings, including a gold ring with the word 'Dad'. Neil had previously battled drug addiction and had spent time in the Cuan Mhuire centre in Athy, which was set up by Sr Concilio to assist people battling alcohol and drug dependencies. While at the centre Neil gave an interview to RTÉ's *Would You Believe* programme and in light of what later happened to this kind-hearted, softly spoken young man, the footage is particularly poignant. "When I get up in the morning I get down on my hands and knees and ask for help from God," he told the interviewer. "That's my higher power today." The recovery of Neil's body allowed his family to lay him to rest at Mount Jerome Cemetery in Harold's Cross, but the failure to catch his killers has left both his family and Gardaí very frustrated.

———

The 1990s witnessed the proliferation of gun murders, most of which would never be solved. The IRA and INLA continued killing people with firearms, and criminal gangs, who were mostly based in Dublin, also began to kill more people by shooting them dead. The IRA shot dead gang leader Martin Cahill in Ranelagh in August 1994. Two months after that killing, a colleague of Cahill's was shot dead in Drimnagh. Earlier that year, loyalist gunmen were responsible for the shooting dead of a doorman at a Dublin pub. A republican function was being held at the pub and the killers had intended to kill more people but had been challenged by their victim. Dublin had by now become used to gun murders. In March 1993 a man was shot dead on North King Street on the city's northside and in October a man was shot dead on the southside as he watched a Halloween bonfire. In July 1992 a man was shot dead at a shop in Darndale, and a hairdresser was killed in an INLA shooting at Marino the previous year. The decade had begun with the shooting dead of a man in west Dublin. None of these crimes has ever been solved.

The mid to latter part of the 1990s saw the situation deteriorate even further. In 1995 men were murdered in Baldoyle, Ballyfermot, Finglas and Tallaght. In June Francis Preston was shot dead as he reversed his car out of his driveway in Baldoyle by a gunman who made his escape on a bicycle. In August Gerard Connolly was killed when he went to answer the doorbell at his house in Ballyfermot. He was shot twice when a gunman fired through a glass-panelled door. The month of November 1995 saw four gun murders in three separate incidents. Eric Shorthall was walking in Ballyfermot when he was shot dead by the pillion passenger on a motorbike. Christopher Delaney was shot at the back door of his home in Finglas. And in the early hours of 24 November 1995 29-year-old Catherine Brennan and 35-year-old Eddie McCabe were shot dead at Cookstown Road in Tallaght.

The double-murder of Catherine Brennan and Eddie McCabe shocked the Irish public and left two families devastated by the loss of a loved one. Catherine was an innocent mother of two who had taken a lift from Eddie McCabe to the Primo garage near The Square Shopping Centre to get cigarettes. She had only met Eddie just over an hour earlier after she and a friend accepted a lift home from a nightclub. At 4.08 a.m. Catherine was seen on the garage CCTV buying cigarettes. Around twelve minutes later she and Eddie McCabe were shot dead over a mile away at Cookstown Road.

From an analysis of the crime scene, Gardaí know that Eddie had pulled his car into the side of the road and had got out and walked to the back of the vehicle. Perhaps he had been flagged down by someone, perhaps he knew who the person was. Given the fact that Eddie got out of his vehicle, it seems that he didn't sense any danger. Or perhaps he was having an argument with someone and didn't realise the imminent danger he was in. Whatever transpired, Eddie was shot twice in quick succession. Firstly, the gunman pointed the gun at Eddie's chest and fired at point-blank range. And as Eddie fell backwards onto the side of the road the killer pointed the gun at his head and fired again.

As these events were happening behind the car, Catherine Brennan struggled to open the passenger door of the car. In the previous few seconds she may have looked behind her and seen Eddie being shot, or she may have been looking ahead but then heard the two gunshots coming from the back of the car. Whatever way it happened, the fear that engulfed Catherine must have been incredible. She managed to get the car door open but before she could get out of the car and make it to safety the gunman shot her once in the head and she died instantly.

Catherine Brennan was a hard-working single mother who was saving hard to help Santa surprise her children with bikes for Christmas. She worked as a cleaner in Killinarden Community School and her life revolved around her son and daughter. Her life was as far removed from violence as you could imagine, and her family were left devastated by her savage and unexplained loss.

Eddie McCabe was a married father of four young boys. In an interview on RTÉ News in the aftermath of the murder,

Eddie's wife Linda held her children closely as she described how her husband was a good father. With tears streaming down her face she said there was no reason why anyone could have had a grudge against him, and she urged anyone with information to speak with Gardaí. As is the case with so many unsolved murders, over the following years few reporters contacted the McCabe family to see how they were coping.

On Friday 1 December 2006, Eddie McCabe's eldest son, Eddie Junior, was found critically injured in a laneway at Tyrconnell Road in Inchicore. He had been severely beaten, suffering horrific injuries to his face, in particular to his eyes. He was rushed to hospital and survived for a week before he died on 8 December. Eddie Junior was just ten years old when his father was murdered in Tallaght in November 1995. He had sat with his heartbroken mother as she gave that interview to RTÉ News back then. And just eleven years later he too became a murder victim, and although Gardaí at Kevin Street continue to pursue his case, Eddie Junior's killers have not been brought to justice, just like his father's killer or killers.

As Gardaí began to investigate the double murder of Catherine Brennan and Eddie McCabe, the following months saw more unsolved gun murders. By the end of 1996 two men had been shot dead in Dublin city (two separate murders—one at Parnell Street and the other at Ellis Street), and there were also fatal shootings in Finglas and Coolock. Nineteen-ninety-seven saw a lull in such murders, due in no small part to the Garda response to the murder of journalist Veronica Guerin, which saw considerable resources deployed to upset the workings of criminal gangs. However, by 1998 gangs were murdering at will once again. One man was shot dead in Drumcondra and another man was murdered in Stepaside in south Co. Dublin. The murder rate increased even further in 1999 and so too did the rate of such crimes which would never be solved. There were a number of gun murders in Dublin and one in Dundalk. Indeed Co. Louth had also borne witness to a number of other gun murders in the 1990s, including the murder of a man who was found shot dead in his car at Collon in 1992. Both Limerick and Cork were also the scenes of gun murders in the 1990s which would never be solved, and as a new millennium dawned, over time it would become apparent that the rate of such killings would only increase.

Every case is different, and behind every unsolved murder there is a bigger picture and often a story of major efforts to catch the killer. In May 1994 a man from Co. Louth was shot dead at a biker's event in Co. Wicklow. The victim was a hard-working, innocent man who was attacked by criminals who were also at the event. The victim died after being shot once in the head. No-one was ever convicted of the murder. However, substantial work by detectives led to one Dublin man pleading guilty to a charge of possessing the firearm in Co. Wicklow sometime before it was used. Certainly it can be said that Gardaí 'failed' to fully solve the case, but they did unmask one person who was later jailed for handling the murder weapon, and that is a lot more than often happens in cases of gun murder.

———

In July 1996 the body of missing man Patrick O'Driscoll was found buried in a shallow grave in woodland at Lotabeg, near Mayfield in Cork. Patrick's dismembered body was buried near the base of a sycamore tree. His skull and torso were found in a sports bag and other parts of his body were found nearby. His body was found three weeks after a man who had been on trial for Patrick's murder walked free from the Central Criminal Court at the direction of the trial judge. The accused had faced trial for murder even though Patrick's body had, at that time, not been found. The accused was also suspected of involvement in the disappearance of two other men—Cathal O'Brien and Kevin Ball—who have not been seen since April 1994. Cathal O'Brien from Co. Wexford was a 22-year-old socially conscious young man who had befriended a homeless man, Kevin Ball, while working as a volunteer with the Simon Community. Cathal lived in a flat at Wellington Terrace on the north side of Cork city. Despite extensive searches by Cathal's family over many years, no trace of either man has been found.

There are a number of other cases of people who vanished in Cork in the 1990s. One of those is 23-year-old Michelle McCormick, who disappeared from Owenahincha Holiday Park in west Cork in July 1993. When last seen she was wearing black cycling shorts, a black top and flip-flop shoes. Investigations have led Gardaí to fear that Michelle was killed and her body thrown into the sea at Kinsale Harbour in a bag weighed down with stones. Almost ten years after her disappearance a man was charged with the manslaughter of Michelle McCormick, but the case was later withdrawn and the man walked free from court.

———

In many unsolved killings, the belief of Gardaí is that the answer to unlocking the mystery may lie within the local community. In April 2011 the family of Padraic O'Cofaigh made an appeal on RTÉ's *Crimecall* programme for help to find the person responsible for killing the 18-year-old in an apparent hit-and-run incident in Co. Meath on 9 June 1996. Padraic had been walking home from a disco which he had attended in the nearby village of Athboy close to the Rathcairn Gaeltacht, when he was hit by a car on the Dunderry Road. Padraic was found lying on the road at 3.15 a.m. by a couple driving home. As part of the appeal Detective Inspector Alf Martin said there were people who were out that night who were now fifteen years older and he urged people with information to come forward. He said the case had been reviewed on an ongoing basis and that the Cold Case Unit had given advice to local detectives. The Garda said that he believed the answer was quite possibly in the local community, and his colleague Garda Aoife King made an appeal in Irish. The focus of the appeal was very much directed at local people in this part of Co. Meath.

———

In Galway, detectives continue to investigate the shocking murder of taxi-driver Eileen Costello O'Shaughnessy, who was beaten to death on the night of Sunday 30 November 1997. Eileen was coming towards the end of her shift when her killer struck. It was at 8.15 p.m. that Eileen last checked in with the dispatcher at Galway Taxis. Eileen said she was going to Claregalway, a town six miles north of Galway on the N17 road to Tuam. The dispatcher assumed Eileen had a fare in the taxi. About twenty minutes later the dispatcher tried to contact Eileen by radio to pick up another fare in Claregalway, but Eileen didn't answer her radio.

At 11.44 p.m. three men found Eileen's bloodstained taxi. The silver Toyota Carina was parked oddly in the middle of a car park off the N17 road. The car lights were off and there was no-one inside but the driver's window was open and the keys were in the ignition. It was soon established that the vehicle had been driven by Eileen Costello O'Shaughnessy, who was unaccounted for. A major search was immediately undertaken, but it was the next morning before Eileen was found at a muddy boreen near Claregalway. It was clear that Eileen had been beaten to death in her taxi and her body then left in the laneway before her killer drove the taxi back towards Galway city. Eileen's murder has been the subject of a number of cold-case reviews, but her killer has not been brought to justice.

____

There were many other murders in the 1990s which would not be solved. A 27-year-old woman was beaten to death in an apartment in Dublin city in December 1996. A 21-year-old woman was stabbed to death at the Grand Canal near Baggot Street in June 1998. Two months previously the body of a man was found in Co. Louth, just a few yards from the Armagh border. The victim, who was from Belfast, had been stabbed to death. As the new millennium approached, the violence continued when a man was beaten to death in Greystones, Co. Wicklow, in December 1999. The year 2000 would prove that unsolved murders were only going to increase in number as time went on. The body of Kieran Smyth was found in a field near Ashbourne, Co. Meath, in February. His hands and legs had been tied, his head was covered with heavy tape and he had been shot. Gardaí built up an amount of intelligence about people suspected of involvement in the paramilitary-style murder, but no-one was charged. In July 2000 Dundalk publican Stephen Connolly was shot dead by a lone gunman. It's believed Mr Connolly was murdered by renegade members of the INLA because he refused to pay them money as part of a protection racket. In August INLA member Nicky O'Hare was shot dead in Dundalk. As the year continued there were also more non-paramilitary related murders. In November 2000 Francis Fitzgerald was shot dead in his flat at Annamoe Terrace, Cabra, in north Dublin. The following month Eddie Ryan was shot dead at a pub in Limerick city. That murder was one of the first in a feud which would claim many more lives in

Limerick throughout the decade. Some of those murders would be solved and some would not. Indeed, the rest of the decade would see shocking levels of violence.

———

In December 2000 Sandra Collins disappeared from the village of Killala in Co. Mayo. The 28-year-old had gone to the shop for sausages at 7.45 p.m. but never came home. The last sighting of Sandra was in a chip-shop later that night, at around 11.15 p.m. Detectives have been trying to establish where Sandra was in the three and a half hours between leaving the shop and entering the chipper, and it's believed the answer may be crucial to finding out what happened to her thereafter. Sandra never made it home from the chip-shop and her family and Gardaí both fear she was murdered and her body hidden. Sandra's fleece was later found on the ground at the old pier in Killala and the sausages she had bought on the evening she disappeared were still in her pocket. The water around Killala was thoroughly searched but no trace of Sandra was found, and a working theory is that the fleece may have been planted at the pier by someone who had attacked Sandra. In 2011 Sandra's family said they now believed that she had been pregnant at the time of her disappearance.

Also in 2011 Gardaí based at Ballina carried out a number of arrests as part of their ongoing efforts to locate Sandra Collins. A man in his forties was arrested on suspicion of murder and later released. Another man and a woman were arrested separately and held on suspicion of withholding information and both were also subsequently released.

———

Recent decades have seen the proliferation of CCTV play an important part in assisting Garda investigations. It is only because someone set a video camera recording in the Rossfield Estate in Tallaght in September 2001 that we know that 12-year-old Stephen Hughes Connors died as a result of an arson attack on the makeshift hut he was sleeping in (see Chapter 6). The person who set the camera recording was trying to catch whoever was causing criminal damage to vehicles nearby, but by sheer chance it captured on film the man who walked up to the hut and set it on fire. Unfortunately, the footage was not of sufficient quality to clearly identify the facial features of the arsonist. But the very fact that the footage was recorded is to be welcomed. If that footage had not existed, it is quite possible that it would never have been established that Stephen had been violently killed and the fire might have mistakenly been put down to a tragic accident. It might never have been known that a man had deliberately set fire to the hut shortly after 5.10 a.m. that Friday morning. It begs the question—how many violent acts have been committed which have actually never been detected as being violent? How many murders have been committed, where the cause of death has mistakenly been put down as accidental?

In July 2002 a fight between two groups of Chinese men on Dublin's O'Connell Street was captured by the myriad of CCTV cameras which are positioned on the city's main thoroughfare. The footage, recorded at 1.30 a.m., showed a number of the men were armed with knives, and the knife-fight ensued at the north end of O'Connell Street, close to the Parnell monument. A 22-year-old man, Qui Hong Xiang, was fatally stabbed. After suffering his injury, he ran towards Parnell Square before collapsing on the pavement. He was rushed to the Mater Hospital but pronounced dead a short time later. There was nowhere else in Ireland with more CCTV cameras than O'Connell Street, but still the killer got away. The footage helped Gardaí to prosecute four other men who were involved in the same fight, but the DPP took the view that the footage did not clearly show the person who had inflicted the fatal wound on the victim. No murder or manslaughter charge was ever brought, and this killing which was captured on camera remains unsolved. The case gives a valuable lesson in that CCTV is an essential part of crime-fighting, but it is not foolproof.

———

In recent years a number of shocking murders have occurred for which no-one has been brought to justice. On 19 November 2006 mother-of-two Baiba Saulite was shot dead on the doorstep of her home in the Holywell estate in Swords, Co. Dublin. An inquest into her death which was held in 2011 heard that Gardaí had evidence to suggest her murder had been a contract killing. A file recommending charges had been sent to the Director of Public Prosecutions, but the DPP decided not to bring anyone before the courts. The inquest heard that the murder investigation could not now be progressed without new evidence.

Less than a month after Baiba Saulite was murdered in cold blood, another innocent person was murdered by criminals. Apprentice plumber Anthony Campbell was working at a house at Scribblestown Park in west Dublin when gunmen burst in. In an upstairs bedroom the intended target of the gunmen, Martin Hyland, was shot six times as he slept. Anthony Campbell was held at gunpoint where he was working downstairs. He raised his arms in defence but he was shot once in the head by callous killers who took his life so their identity would not be revealed. Anthony was a decent young man who travelled from his home in Dublin city that morning to do a plumbing job in Scribblestown Park. He was in the wrong place at the wrong time. Just like the murder of Baiba Saulite, authorities said no stone would be left unturned, and all necessary resources would be deployed to catch Anthony's killers. But despite the best Garda efforts, no-one was ever brought to justice for this double-murder. An inquest into both deaths, which was held in 2011, heard that 14 people had been arrested by detectives, but without any new information the investigation had now stalled.

The year 2006 witnessed many other murders in Dublin which would also remain unsolved. Mother-of-one Donna Cleary was at a house party when she was shot dead in March, after shots were fired indiscriminately into the house because a group of people were refused entry. That same month a 27-year-old man, Shay Bradley, was shot dead in Cabra. Gerard Goulding was shot dead on open ground in Donaghmede in April 2006 and the following month 42-year-old Patrick Harte was murdered outside his home at Edenmore. The father of two was shot dead as he returned home from a school run. In June Keith Fitzsimons was shot dead as he spoke with two other men at Millwood Road in Kilbarrack. Gardaí do not believe Keith was the intended target of the attack. Later that same month 22-year-old James Perdue was shot dead outside an apartment complex in Donaghmede. Wayne Zambra was shot dead while leaving a pub in Dublin's south inner city in August 2006 and in September Gary Bryan was shot dead in Walkinstown. In November Raymond Collins from Summerhill was shot dead near Croke Park and on 14 December Gerard Byrne was shot dead outside a supermarket in the Irish Financial Services Centre. On 27 December Stephen Ledden was shot in the head as he slept in a house at Upper Oriel Street in Dublin's north inner city.

The year 2006 also witnessed gun murders in other parts of the country. Thomas Moran was 27 years old when he was found shot dead at Carew Park in Limerick city in November. Thomas had left his house at O'Malley Park saying he was meeting some people and would be back in five minutes. His family never saw him alive again, and a murder investigation is continuing. Also in November 2006 26-year-old Paul Reay was shot dead in Drogheda, Co. Louth. His killer posed as a road worker to flag down the victim's car before firing through the window of the vehicle.

And there are dozens of other murders in the earlier part of that decade and the latter part which are among the unsolved files. A woman originally from Malawi, Paiche Onyemaechi, was found murdered at Piltown, Co. Kilkenny, in July 2004. She had been missing from her Waterford home for a number of weeks. It's believed she was murdered at another location before her body was left at Piltown. On 16 December of that year 23-year-old Patrick Lawlor from Darndale in north Dublin vanished without trace, and his family fear that he was murdered and his body hidden. Patrick's car was later found abandoned at a lay-by near Dublin Airport, but it is suspected that the vehicle may have been put there after Patrick was possibly abducted. The last trace of Patrick was when his mobile phone showed activity at the Baskin Cottages area near Kinsealy on the morning he disappeared.

A number of innocent men have been victims of gun murders in Ireland in recent years. In April 2005 29-year-old Joseph Rafferty was shot dead by a lone gunman at the Ongar estate in west Dublin. Joseph was a decent, hard-working family man who it's believed was targeted for assassination by criminals from Dublin's south inner city. On New Year's Eve 2002 39-year-old car dealer Sean Poland was shot dead during a robbery at his home at Blackwater, Ardnacrusha, in Co. Clare. Sean's partner was tied up by the gang during the attack. It's believed a gang of Limerick city criminals was responsible for the murder. Over 20 people were subsequently arrested, but just like Joseph Rafferty's murder in 2005, Sean Poland's murder on the last day of 2002 would eventually become a cold case.

The year 2003 was a particularly violent one, especially in terms of gun murders which would become cold cases. In January 2003 Niall Mulvihill was shot in his taxi at Spencer Dock Bridge. He drove towards the Mater Hospital but passed out near Dorset Street and died a short time later. Also that month Raymond Sallinger was shot dead in a pub in Dublin's south inner city. In March Charles Merriman was found shot dead at St Margaret's Road in Ballymun. In April 2003 27-year-old Paul Ryan from Raheny was shot dead on the side of the road near the village of Coolderry near Birr, Co. Offaly. In May Robert Fitzgerald was shot dead in Moyross in Limerick. In June Ronald Draper was shot dead while working as a doorman at a pub on Dublin's Eden Quay. John Ryan was gunned down at a house in Thomondgate, Limerick, in July and David McGuinness was shot dead at Balrothery in Tallaght the following day. In August Thomas Canavan was shot dead in a pub in Inchicore and Bernard Sugg was shot dead in a pub in Blanchardstown. In October Peter Sheridan was found shot dead at Scribblestown Lane in Finglas and Michael Campbell-McNamara was found shot and stabbed to death near Southill in Limerick. For every year in recent Irish history there are many unsolved murders.

———

At the offices of the Cold Case Unit at Harcourt Square, Detective Superintendent Christy Mangan says the detectives in his unit make hundreds of recommendations in every case they review. "If we then give a case back to local detectives for those recommendations to be followed, resources from the National Bureau of Criminal Investigation can be deployed to assist with that. There is no point in making a large number of recommendations if they are not going to be acted upon, you have to act upon them and act quickly. When we provide a report on a case, that doesn't mean our input is finished; we are there to assist to ensure the recommendations are brought to a finality." Those recommendations might be that a witness be re-interviewed, or a fresh search be undertaken for a murder weapon, or fresh forensic tests be carried out.

Christy Mangan stresses that reviewing an unsolved murder enquiry can often take longer than the original enquiry lasted.

It can be a slow process, it depends on the particular case. You are endeavouring to locate witnesses, to locate exhibits, to re-interview the original Garda teams. You can find that some of the people involved are deceased and that can cause problems in that part of the picture is not there for you, and that can be difficult. And sometimes suspects may have passed away, but in the majority of cases we are looking at, we believe the suspects are alive. They are out there and we are going to be knocking on their doors. We have got a massive response from the general public and we are very thankful for that. We rely very much on the public to assist us. And the families of victims have been very receptive to us. They have given us a huge amount of assistance.

While there are some cases which the Cold Case Unit are investigating away from the media glare, there are others which they have publicly confirmed they are actively re-investigating. These are cases where members of the Unit have carried out a preliminary review and found that there is merit to going further and committing to carrying out a full review of all case material in an effort to see if a killer or killers can finally be brought to justice. On the Serious Crime Review Team page on the Garda website there are a number of cases in which the Cold Case Unit are appealing to the public to give assistance. Two of the most recent such cases are the separate murders of Irene White and Emer O'Loughlin, which both occurred in 2005.

Forty-three-year-old mother-of-three Irene White was washing dishes in her home when she was attacked by an intruder and stabbed to death in Dundalk on 6 April 2005. She suffered multiple injuries to her chest and back. Irene's body was found by her 79-year-old mother at 12.30 p.m. when she made her daily walk from her mobile home in the back garden into her daughter's house to share a meal with her. Irene's mother died six months later, on what would have been Irene's 44th birthday.

Detectives have been seeking to identify a man seen running from the vicinity of Irene's house at 10.15 a.m. on the day of the murder. He was described as being aged between 30 and 40, and he was wearing jeans, a dark jacket and a peaked cap. He ran through Ice House Hill Park, adjoining Irene's house, into O'Hanlon Park and left the area in a dark-coloured car which had been parked nearby. A number of arrests were made by detectives investigating Irene's murder but the crime remains unsolved.

Two days after Irene White was murdered another shocking murder occurred, this time in the west of the country. There is no link between the two cases. It was on the morning of 8 April 2005 that the body of 23-year-old Emer O'Loughlin was found in a burnt-out caravan at Ballybornagh, Tubber, in

Co. Clare. The Garda Cold Case Unit have been examining this case and as part of their enquiries Emer's body was exhumed in 2010. Detectives believe Emer suffered a violent attack which caused her death and that her killer then set fire to the caravan in an attempt to make the death look like an accident. Gardaí wish to speak with a man who it's thought may have faked his own death and may in fact have fled the country. The man's clothing and personal belongings were found abandoned on one of the Aran Islands, and it was initially thought he might have jumped into the sea, but it's now believed the clothing may have been deliberately placed there as part of an elaborate scheme to attempt to throw detectives off the scent. Gardaí are liaising closely with other police forces through Interpol in an effort to track this man.

While the work of the Cold Case Unit is by its nature quite slow, results are beginning to show. The successful prosecution of the two killers of Brian McGrath (murdered at his Westmeath home in 1987) was the first major achievement of the Serious Crime Review Team. The Unit is working on a number of other cases where it is felt criminal charges may be brought. More and more families of murder victims are making contact, asking for their loved one's unsolved murder to be reviewed. In 2011 the Unit lost two of its most experienced detectives when Alan Bailey and Noel Mooney both retired after more than 30 years' service each. As the work of the Cold Case Unit evolves, perhaps not only will two new Gardaí come into the Unit to fill those shoes, but the Unit's manpower may also increase. "In relation to what we do in the Serious Crime Review Team, we do bring some sense of justice to families of victims," reflects Christy Mangan.

That may be with the successful resolution of a case, or even that a family know we are looking at a case and they know that we haven't forgotten their loved one. And the whole concept of cold-case investigation is that it transfers the fear of a crime, which originally existed with the victim, it transfers it back to a suspect a long, long number of years later. In particular a person who feels they got away with a particular crime, now we are coming after them yet again. We are not going to cease in our efforts to solve the unsolved. We owe it to the victims and the victims' families and we owe it to the public. We are bringing accountability to those who have murdered, they are not going to get away with murdering another human being.

———

St Kevin's Park is a well-maintained, small park a short distance from the Garda offices at Harcourt Square. It's nestled behind DIT Kevin Street, close to Wexford Street and Camden Street. The old church ruin where Tommy Powell's body was found on 20 June 1961 is still there within the park. It was the year after the five-year-old boy was found murdered here that Dublin Corporation took control of the church ruins and graveyard. The Corporation, and more recently Dublin City Council, have done a fine job in making this a peaceful and welcoming park. At the time of Tommy Powell's murder, the old graveyard was overgrown and almost beyond repair. Today, mature trees and closely cropped grass, park benches and hedges provide a space to reflect. Some of the original headstones remain undisturbed while others have been placed along the outer walls of the church ruin and perimeter walls of the park.

There is nothing here to mark it as the location where Tommy Powell was found murdered. The file on his case has been kept safe all this time at the National Archives on Bishop Street, less than a five-minute walk away. In one sense Tommy's murder was so long ago, yet in another it was only a half century ago. The Minister for Justice at the time was Charles Haughey. In a parliamentary question at the time about the number of unsolved murder cases, the Minister listed six unsolved murders as having occurred between 1952 and 1961. In his reply the Minister stated that "Garda investigations still continue in relation to all of them."

It's natural to speculate, it's human nature. Was Tommy Powell killed by an older child or children? If so, they might only be in their sixties or seventies now. Even if he was killed by someone in their twenties or thirties they could quite possibly still be alive. There is nothing in the case file to suggest any particular line of enquiry. There was simply no motive for killing a little boy who was last seen walking alone on nearby Camden Street. His killer may have died long ago, but might they just possibly still be alive?

EPILOGUE

Brian McGrath was finally laid to rest on Saturday 18 September 2010. It was less than two months since his wife had been found guilty of his murder, a murder which had occurred more than 23 years previously. Vera McGrath was now serving a life sentence, while Colin Pinder, who had been found guilty of manslaughter, was still awaiting sentence. He would later be jailed for nine years.

Local funeral director Michael Cassidy met Gardaí at Mullingar Hospital and received the body of Brian McGrath. Back in 1993, when forensic science of the time had failed to establish Brian's identity to a mathematical certainty, it was Michael Cassidy who had taken care of the burial of the 'unidentified' man, who everyone believed was indeed Brian McGrath. Michael had been present at the exhumation of the body in May 2008, pointing out to detectives the precise plot where he had buried Brian fifteen years previously. Now he was helping to bring Brian on his final journey.

Michael brought Brian's coffin to the Church of the Immaculate Conception in Coole, where Brian's daughter Veronica and sons Andrew, Brian Jnr and Edward and other members of the family said a final farewell. Local people came to the church to pay their respects, people who had known Brian back in the 1980s and who knew his children. Also present were many of the Gardaí who had worked on the successful cold-case investigation. Detective Inspector Martin Cadden from Athlone was there, as were many of the cold-case detectives who had travelled from Dublin. The head of the Unit, Christy Mangan, was present, as was Detective Garda

David O'Brien and Detective Garda Annelisa Hannigan. The new Detective Inspector in the Unit, Eamonn Henry, also attended the funeral, as did Detective Garda Maurice Downey, the man who had initiated the first enquiries when he received that phone call in 2007 from retired detective John Maunsell, who was urging the newly formed Unit to review the unsolved case.

Now the murder was indeed solved, and Brian McGrath's killers were behind bars. In death Brian's name had become well known throughout the country and indeed overseas as word had spread about the solving of a 23-year-old murder case in which the victim's body had been secretly buried, dug up and burned, reburied, found and later buried in a cemetery, exhumed and analysed forensically, and was now being laid to rest for the final time. Brian McGrath had a life which was a mixture of happiness and pride in his four children, but he had faced much tragedy not only in death but in his early years. Brian had been abandoned as a baby when he was born in Monaghan in August 1944 and when he was found by a Garda he was brought to local nuns. He never discovered who his birth mother was and when he was ten years old Brian was placed in Artane Industrial School. When he became an adult he joined the Irish Army, but left soon afterwards. In the 1960s he met his future wife Vera, who was from Dublin. They lived in London for a time and Southampton and also in Dublin. In 1979 they bought a cottage near Coole in Westmeath and the family moved to the country. It was eight years later that Brian McGrath vanished.

Brian and Vera's daughter Veronica McGrath bravely told the truth at the Central Criminal Court trial. She told of witnessing Colin Pinder and her own mother Vera beating her father to death and then secretly burying him in the field next to the family home. She outlined the extreme lengths to which the killers had then gone to try and hide evidence of the murder, by digging up and burning Brian's body and then burying it again. Veronica had first come forward in 1993, meeting with detective John Maunsell and making a full statement about the crime she had witnessed. The failure to get justice back then had left Veronica and the Gardaí very frustrated. When the Cold Case Unit had first contacted Veronica all those years later she did not hesitate to say she was still prepared to give evidence. It was through her determination and strength that she and the Gardaí finally got justice for her father.

Parish priest Fr Michael Walsh celebrated the funeral mass at the church in Coole. Afterwards, members of the community who had come to pay their respects shook hands with the McGrath family and offered their condolences. Gardaí also extended their sympathies to Veronica, Andrew, Brian Jnr, and Edward. After the funeral mass Brian's body was slowly driven from Coole through the town of Castlepollard and on to Whitehall Cemetery. There Brian's coffin was placed back in the same plot from where he had been exhumed over two years beforehand. During that period Brian's body had been cared for at the Dublin City Mortuary in Marino. It was only at the conclusion of the trial of his killers that Brian's body could be reburied.

By the time Brian was laid to rest for the final time in September 2010 the Garda Cold Case Unit had assessed the files relating to hundreds of unsolved murders, and the Unit had selected dozens of those files to be actively reviewed. There was much work ahead, many families seeking answers and seeking justice.

Ultimately Brian McGrath got justice, ultimately the full story of his violent death was revealed. His murder was solved through a combination of brave witnesses, advances in forensic science and pathology, the good fortune that suspects were still alive, and a determination by detectives to pursue justice for a man who suffered a horrific death. As Brian McGrath was reburied at Whitehall Cemetery his family now had closure, and Brian could finally and forever more rest in peace.